MARIE ANTOINETTE'S DAUGHTER

Books by Alice Curtis Desmond

FAR HORIZONS

SOUTH AMERICAN ADVENTURES

LUCKY LLAMA

FEATHERS

JORGE'S JOURNEY

SOLDIER OF THE SUN

FOR CROSS AND KING

MARTHA WASHINGTON—OUR FIRST LADY

THE SEA CATS

GLAMOROUS DOLLY MADISON

THE TALKING TREE

ALEXANDER HAMILTON'S WIFE

BARNUM PRESENTS: GENERAL TOM THUMB

BEWITCHING BETSY BONAPARTE

YOUR FLAG AND MINE

GEORGE WASHINGTON'S MOTHER

TEDDY KOALA: MASCOT OF THE MARINES

SWORD AND PEN FOR GEORGE WASHINGTON

MARIE ANTOINETTE'S DAUGHTER

Marie Antoinette's DAUGHTER

ALICE CURTIS DESMOND

ILLUSTRATED WITH PHOTOGRAPHS, MAPS, AND DIAGRAMS

[redacted]

DODD, MEAD & COMPANY
NEW YORK

Library of Congress Catalog Card Number: 67-26151
Printed in the United States of America
by The Cornwall Press, Inc., Cornwall, N. Y.

With love and gratitude
to
THOMAS C. DESMOND
the most understanding
and best of husbands

ACKNOWLEDGMENTS

In 1778, when little John Quincy went to Europe with his father, John Adams, he saw the streets of Paris lighted by thousands of candles in honor of the birth of a princess, Marie Thérèse Charlotte, to Queen Marie Antoinette of France. The descendant of a long line of kings, in Madame Royale's veins mingled the blood of two of the great reigning families of Europe, the house of Bourbon and the house of Hapsburg.

The story of Marie Antoinette has always fascinated American readers. But, strangely enough, the world has almost forgotten that she had a daughter. The greatest portion of material available on her exists only in the French language, which accounts for the lack of linguistic balance in the sources listed in the Bibliography. This book was written mostly from original sources, collected on three trips to Europe that my husband and I made to get the necessary research material and photographs. I consider it advisable to quote the words of eyewitnesses as often as possible, to give authenticity to a work, and I wish to thank especially Messrs. E. Franco of London and Raymond Clavreuil of Paris, both of them experts on the

French Revolution, who helped me to collect the contemporary memoirs listed in the Bibliography.

I also did research at the National Archives in Paris, and I am most grateful to Mesdames Agnes Renand and Marie Dodash, who made available to me their files on Madame Royale; to Julian G. Hannay of London and Miss Dorothy Rae-Jones of Aylesbury, Buckinghamshire, England, who allowed us to visit Hartwell House; to Mrs. Ulla Elsin of Stockholm, who showed us in Sweden the places associated with Fersen; and to Mrs. Kathleen Glucksberg of Trieste, Italy, with whom we visited the Bourbon tombs in Yugoslavia.

To Thomas C. Desmond this book, like all of my others, is lovingly dedicated, for it was my husband who took me to Europe; it was his personal office staff, Mrs. Alice Mason and Miss Marjorie Burnett, who typed the manuscript. And, as usual, I owe a debt of gratitude I can never repay to my dear friend and the editor of ten of my books, Miss Dorothy M. Bryan of Dodd, Mead & Company, who patiently nursed *Marie Antoinette's Daughter* along to completion. Without her, an unwieldy mass of typewritten pages might never have evolved into a readable book.

CONTENTS

ILLUSTRATIONS

PHOTOGRAPHS

Following page 72

Maps and Diagrams

CHRONOLOGICAL TABLE

1770.	May 16.	Louis XVI and Marie Antoinette married
1778.	December 19.	Birth of Marie Thérèse Charlotte
1781.	October 22.	Birth of Louis Joseph, the first Dauphin
1785.	March 27.	Birth of Louis Charles
1786.	July 9.	Birth of Sophie Béatrix
1789.	May 5.	Opening of the States General
	June 3.	Death of the first Dauphin
	July 14.	Capture of the Bastille
	October 1.	Banquet for the Flemish regiments
	October 5.	People of Paris march on Versailles
1791.	June 20.	Flight to Varennes
1792.	February 13.	Fersen sees Marie Antoinette for the last time
	April 20.	France declares war on Austria
	June 20.	First storming of the Tuileries
	August 10.	Second assault on the palace
	August 13.	Royal family taken to the Temple
	September 3.	Murder of the Princesse de Lamballe
	September 21.	France becomes a republic
	December 11.	Trial of Louis XVI
1793.	January 21.	Execution of the King

	July 3.	Dauphin taken from his mother
	August 2.	Marie Antoinette goes to the Conciergerie
	October 16.	Execution of the Queen
1794.	January 19.	Antoine Simon and his wife leave the Tower
	March	Jardin couple take a boy to America
	April 6.	Simon carries a boy to Vitry
	May 1.	Bellanger sketches the boy prisoner
	May 9.	Aunt Babet taken to the Conciergerie
	June 13.	Commune makes deal with Charette
	July	Simon executed
	July 28.	Robespierre beheaded; Laurent appointed head jailer at the Tower
	November 8.	Gomin comes
1795.	April 1.	Lasne replaces Laurent
	May 5.	Dr. Desault called in
	June 8.	Boy prisoner in Tower dies: Provence takes the title of Louis XVIII
	June 20.	Thérèse gets a woman companion
	December 19.	Madame Royale set free and leaves for Vienna
1799.	May 3.	Thérèse goes to Russia to join her uncle
	June 10.	Marries the Duc d'Angoulême
1801.	January 21.	Louis XVIII forced to leave Russia
	June	Skeleton of a boy dug up at the Tower
1808.	August	Louis XVIII, his wife, and the Angoulêmes seek refuge in England
1810.	June 20.	Fersen murdered
1814.	May 3.	Louis XVIII becomes king of France
1815.	March 20.	Bourbons flee on Napoleon's return from Elba
	July 8.	Second Restoration
1816.	June 16.	Duc de Berry marries Princess Marie Caroline of Naples
1819.	September 21.	Louise d'Artois born
1820.	February 13.	Ferdinand assassinated
	September 29.	Henri, Duc de Bordeaux, born

1824.	September 16.	Louis XVIII dies; Artois becomes Charles X, king of France
1830.	July 31.	Charles X abdicates
1832.	April	The Duchesse de Berry tries to regain the throne of France for her son
1836.	November 6.	Charles X dies
1844.	June 3.	Duc d'Angoulême dies
	August	Thérèse buys Frohsdorf
1845.	November 10.	Louise d'Artois marries the Duc de Lucca
1846.	November 16.	Henri, Comte de Chambord, marries the Archduchesse Marie Thérèse of Modena
1851.	October 19.	Death of Queen Marie Thérèse of France
1864.	February 1.	Louise, Duchess of Parma, dies
1873.	October	Comte de Chambord refuses to become king of France under the tricolor
1883.	August 24.	Death of Henri V of France

The Bourbon Line

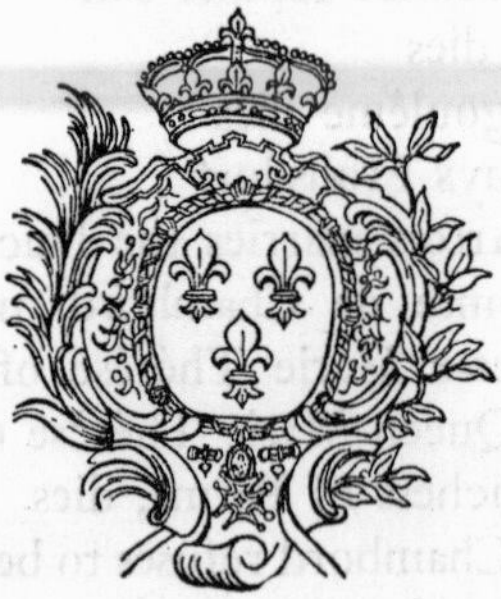

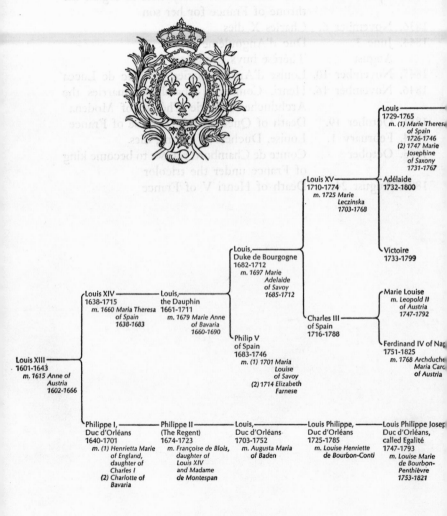

- **Louis XIII** 1601-1643 *m. 1615 Anne of Austria 1602-1666*
  - **Louis XIV** 1638-1715 *m. 1660 Maria Theresa of Spain 1638-1683*
    - **Louis, the Dauphin** 1661-1711 *m. 1679 Marie Anne of Bavaria 1660-1690*
      - **Louis, Duke de Bourgogne** 1682-1712 *m. 1697 Marie Adelaide of Savoy 1685-1712*
        - **Louis XV** 1710-1774 *m. 1725 Marie Leczinska 1703-1768*
          - **Louis** 1729-1765 *m. (1) Marie Theresa of Spain 1726-1746 (2) 1747 Marie Josephine of Saxony 1731-1767*
          - **Adélaide** 1732-1800
          - **Victoire** 1733-1799
        - **Charles III of Spain** 1716-1788
          - **Marie Louise** *m. Leopold II of Austria 1747-1792*
          - **Ferdinand IV of Nap** 1751-1825 *m. 1768 Archduche Maria Carc of Austria*
      - **Philip V of Spain** 1683-1746 *m. (1) 1701 Maria Louise of Savoy (2) 1714 Elizabeth Farnese*
  - **Philippe I, Duc d'Orléans** 1640-1701 *m. (1) Henrietta Marie of England, daughter of Charles I (2) Charlotte of Bavaria*
    - **Philippe II (The Regent)** 1674-1723 *m. Françoise de Blois, daughter of Louis XIV and Madame de Montespan*
      - **Louis, Duc d'Orléans** 1703-1752 *m. Augusta Maria of Baden*
        - **Louis Philippe, Duc d'Orléans** 1725-1785 *m. Louise Henriette de Bourbon-Conti*
          - **Louis Philippe Josep Duc d'Orléans, called Egalité** 1747-1793 *m. Louise Marie de Bourbon-Penthièvre 1753-1821*

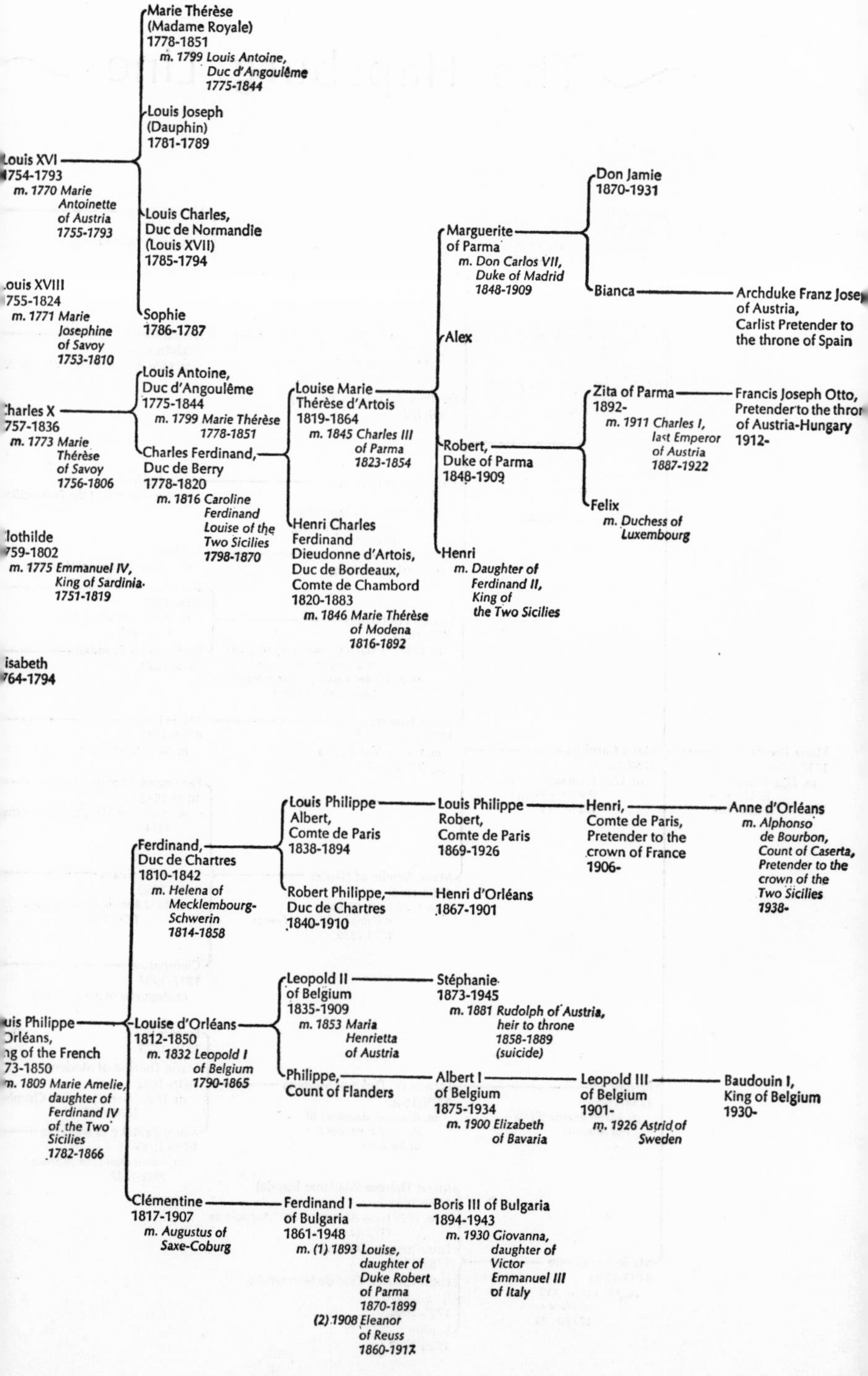

Marie Thérèse (Madame Royale) 1778-1851
m. 1799 Louis Antoine, Duc d'Angoulême 1775-1844
Louis Joseph (Dauphin) 1781-1789
Louis XVI 1754-1793
m. 1770 Marie Antoinette of Austria 1755-1793
Louis Charles, Duc de Normandie (Louis XVII) 1785-1794
Sophie 1786-1787
ouis XVIII 755-1824
m. 1771 Marie Josephine of Savoy 1753-1810
Louis Antoine, Duc d'Angoulême 1775-1844
m. 1799 Marie Thérèse 1778-1851
harles X 757-1836
m. 1773 Marie Thérèse of Savoy 1756-1806
Charles Ferdinand, Duc de Berry 1778-1820
m. 1816 Caroline Ferdinand Louise of the Two Sicilies 1798-1870
lothilde 759-1802
m. 1775 Emmanuel IV, King of Sardinia 1751-1819
isabeth 764-1794
Louise Marie Thérèse d'Artois 1819-1864
m. 1845 Charles III of Parma 1823-1854
Henri Charles Ferdinand Dieudonne d'Artois, Duc de Bordeaux, Comte de Chambord 1820-1883
m. 1846 Marie Thérèse of Modena 1816-1892
Marguerite of Parma
m. Don Carlos VII, Duke of Madrid 1848-1909
Alex
Robert, Duke of Parma 1848-1909
Henri
m. Daughter of Ferdinand II, King of the Two Sicilies
Don Jamie 1870-1931
Bianca
Archduke Franz Jose of Austria, Carlist Pretender to the throne of Spain
Zita of Parma 1892-
m. 1911 Charles I, last Emperor of Austria 1887-1922
Francis Joseph Otto, Pretender to the thro of Austria-Hungary 1912-
Felix
m. Duchess of Luxembourg
Louis Philippe Albert, Comte de Paris 1838-1894
Louis Philippe Robert, Comte de Paris 1869-1926
Henri, Comte de Paris, Pretender to the crown of France 1906-
Anne d'Orléans
m. Alphonso de Bourbon, Count of Caserta, Pretender to the crown of the Two Sicilies 1938-
Ferdinand, Duc de Chartres 1810-1842
m. Helena of Mecklembourg-Schwerin 1814-1858
Robert Philippe, Duc de Chartres 1840-1910
Henri d'Orléans 1867-1901
Leopold II of Belgium 1835-1909
m. 1853 Maria Henrietta of Austria
Stéphanie 1873-1945
m. 1881 Rudolph of Austria, heir to throne 1858-1889 (suicide)
uis Philippe Orléans, ng of the French 73-1850
m. 1809 Marie Amelie, daughter of Ferdinand IV of the Two Sicilies 1782-1866
Louise d'Orléans 1812-1850
m. 1832 Leopold I of Belgium 1790-1865
Philippe, Count of Flanders
Albert I of Belgium 1875-1934
m. 1900 Elizabeth of Bavaria
Leopold III of Belgium 1901-
m. 1926 Astrid of Sweden
Baudouin I, King of Belgium 1930-
Clémentine 1817-1907
m. Augustus of Saxe-Coburg
Ferdinand I of Bulgaria 1861-1948
m. (1) 1893 Louise, daughter of Duke Robert of Parma 1870-1899
(2) 1908 Eleanor of Reuss 1860-1917
Boris III of Bulgaria 1894-1943
m. 1930 Giovanna, daughter of Victor Emmanuel III of Italy

The Hapsburg Line

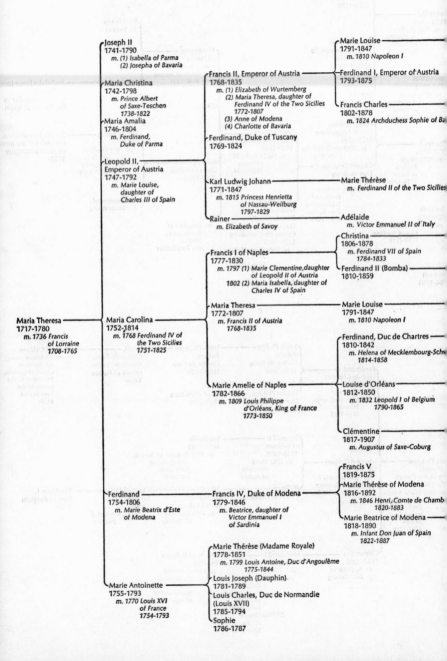

- **Maria Theresa** 1717-1780
  m. 1736 Francis of Lorraine 1708-1765
  - Joseph II 1741-1790
    m. (1) Isabella of Parma
    (2) Josepha of Bavaria
  - Maria Christina 1742-1798
    m. Prince Albert of Saxe-Teschen 1738-1822
  - Maria Amalia 1746-1804
    m. Ferdinand, Duke of Parma
  - Leopold II, Emperor of Austria 1747-1792
    m. Marie Louise, daughter of Charles III of Spain
    - Francis II, Emperor of Austria 1768-1835
      m. (1) Elizabeth of Wurtemberg
      (2) Maria Theresa, daughter of Ferdinand IV of the Two Sicilies 1772-1807
      (3) Anne of Modena
      (4) Charlotte of Bavaria
      - Marie Louise 1791-1847
        m. 1810 Napoleon I
      - Ferdinand I, Emperor of Austria 1793-1875
      - Francis Charles 1802-1878
        m. 1824 Archduchess Sophie of Ba
    - Ferdinand, Duke of Tuscany 1769-1824
    - Karl Ludwig Johann 1771-1847
      m. 1815 Princess Henrietta of Nassau-Weilburg 1797-1829
      - Marie Thérèse
        m. Ferdinand II of the Two Sicilies
    - Rainer
      m. Elizabeth of Savoy
      - Adélaide
        m. Victor Emmanuel II of Italy
  - Maria Carolina 1752-1814
    m. 1768 Ferdinand IV of the Two Sicilies 1751-1825
    - Francis I of Naples 1777-1830
      m. 1797 (1) Marie Clementine, daughter of Leopold II of Austria
      1802 (2) Maria Isabella, daughter of Charles IV of Spain
      - Christina 1806-1878
        m. Ferdinand VII of Spain 1784-1833
      - Ferdinand II (Bomba) 1810-1859
    - Maria Theresa 1772-1807
      m. Francis II of Austria 1768-1835
      - Marie Louise 1791-1847
        m. 1810 Napoleon I
    - Marie Amelie of Naples 1782-1866
      m. 1809 Louis Philippe d'Orléans, King of France 1773-1850
      - Ferdinand, Duc de Chartres 1810-1842
        m. Helena of Mecklembourg-Schw 1814-1858
      - Louise d'Orléans 1812-1850
        m. 1832 Leopold I of Belgium 1790-1865
      - Clémentine 1817-1907
        m. Augustus of Saxe-Coburg
  - Ferdinand 1754-1806
    m. Marie Beatrix d'Este of Modena
    - Francis IV, Duke of Modena 1779-1846
      m. Beatrice, daughter of Victor Emmanuel I of Sardinia
      - Francis V 1819-1875
      - Marie Thérèse of Modena 1816-1892
        m. 1846 Henri, Comte de Chamb 1820-1883
      - Marie Beatrice of Modena 1818-1890
        m. Infant Don Juan of Spain 1822-1887
  - Marie Antoinette 1755-1793
    m. 1770 Louis XVI of France 1754-1793
    - Marie Thérèse (Madame Royale) 1778-1851
      m. 1799 Louis Antoine, Duc d'Angoulême 1775-1844
    - Louis Joseph (Dauphin) 1781-1789
    - Louis Charles, Duc de Normandie (Louis XVII) 1785-1794
    - Sophie 1786-1787

uke of Reichstadt (Napoleon II)
811-1832

rancis Joseph, Emperor of Austria — Gisela, 1856-1921; Rudolph, 1858-1889; Valérie, 1868-1924
330-1916
m. 1854 Elizabeth of Bavaria 1837-1898

aximilian, Emperor of Mexico
332-1867
m. 1857 Carlota, daughter of Leopold I of Belgium 1840-1927

harles Louis — Francis Ferdinand, 1863-1914 (murdered); Otto Francis
333-1896
m. Maria Annunziata of Sicily

Otto Francis — Charles I, — Francis Joseph Otto,
1865-1906
m. 1886 Maria Josepha of Saxony

Charles I, last Emperor of Austria
1887-1922
m. 1911 Zita of Parma 1892-

Francis Joseph Otto, heir to Hapsburg throne
1912-

abella II of Spain — Alphonso XII of Spain — Alphonso XIII of Spain,
30-1904
n. 1846 Don Francisco de Asís 1822-1902

Alphonso XII of Spain
1857-1885
m. Maria Christina of Austria 1858-1929

Alphonso XIII of Spain, last King of Spain
1886-1941
m. 1906 Victoria of Battenberg

ancis II
36-1894
'deposed 1860 on unification of Italy)

uke of Reichstadt (Napoleon II)
11-1832

uis Philippe Albert, mte de Paris — Louis Philippe Robert, — Henri, Comte de Paris, — Anne d'Orléans
38-1894

Louis Philippe Robert, Comte de Paris
1869-1926

Henri, Comte de Paris, Pretender to the crown of France
1906-

Anne d'Orléans
m. Alphonso de Bourbon, Count of Caserta, Pretender to the crown of the Two Sicilies 1938-

bert Philippe, Duc de Chartres — Henri d'Orléans
40-1910

Henri d'Orléans
1867-1901

opold II of Belgium — Stéphanie
35-1909
n. 1853 Maria Henrietta of Austria

Stéphanie
1873-1945
m. 1881 Rudolph of Austria, heir to throne 1858-1889 (suicide)

ilippe, unt of Flanders — Albert I of Belgium — Leopold III of Belgium — Baudouin I,

Albert I of Belgium
1875-1934
m. 1900 Elizabeth of Bavaria

Leopold III of Belgium
1901-
m. 1926 Astrid of Sweden

Baudouin I, King of Belgium
1930-

rdinand I of Bulgaria — Boris III of Bulgaria
51-1948
n. (1) 1893 Louise, daughter of Duke Robert of Parma 1870-1899
(2) 1908 Eleanor of Reuss 1860-1917

Boris III of Bulgaria
1894-1943
m. 1930 Giovanna, daughter of Victor Emmanuel III of Italy

n Carlos VII, Duke of Madrid — Don Jamie, 1870-1931; Bianca
48-1909
n. Marguerite of Parma

onso

Bianca — Archduke Franz Joseph of Austria, Carlist Pretender to the throne of Spain

MARIE ANTOINETTE'S DAUGHTER

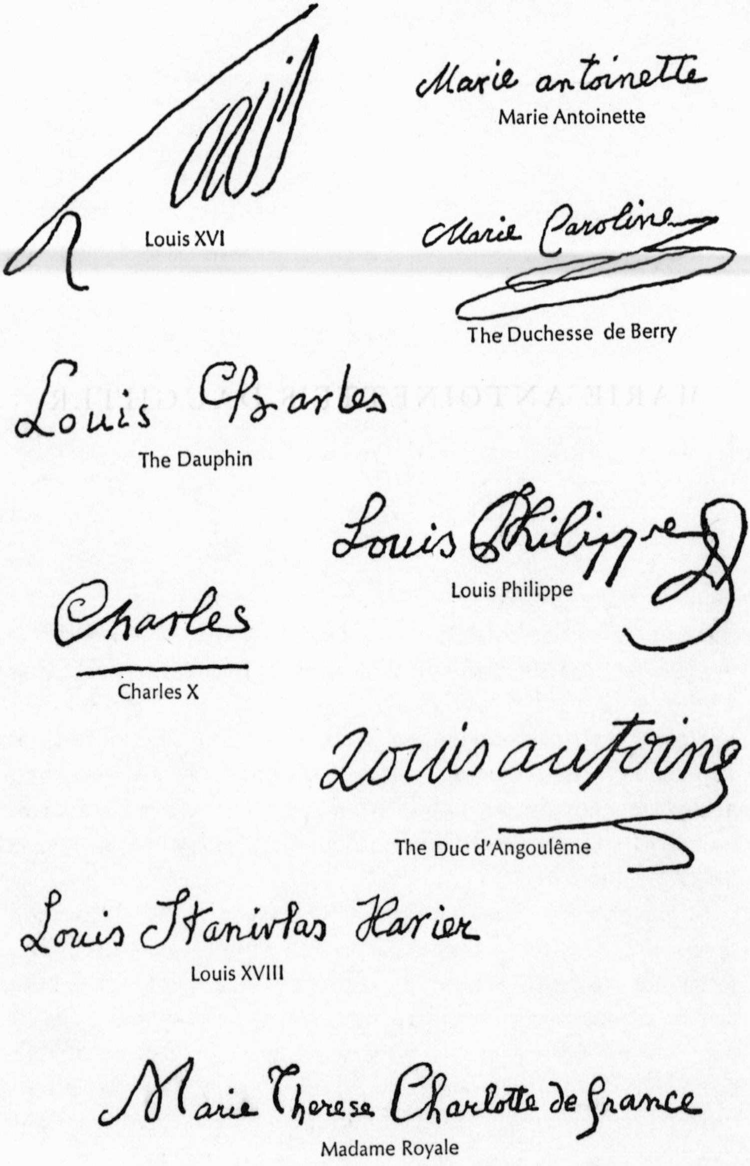

SIGNATURES OF SOME OF THE OUTSTANDING PERSONALITIES IN THIS BOOK

1

A NATION IS BORN— AND A CHILD

THE ROAD OUT from Paris was crowded with carriages, for it was April 19, 1778, and everyone who had the honor of being admitted to the *levée du Roi* (the King's getting up) was hurrying out that morning to Versailles. The Duc d'Orléans and the Prince de Condé, cousins of Louis XVI, were in their gilded coaches drawn by six horses. Lesser nobility and ambassadors rode in velvet-lined *calèches;* judges and lawyers, in plainer cabriolets.

In contrast to these elegant vehicles was a slow-plodding fiacre such as the bourgeoisie were obliged to hire. Yet, strangely enough, when this humble carriage reached the palace, it passed without challenge through the gilded gates of the Cour des Ministres into which all might go, and stopped in the Cour de Marbre where only the coaches of the King, those of the princes of the royal blood, and ambassadors might enter.

A man in a plain brown coat, with gray hair hanging loose, and wearing spectacles, stepped out. He was followed by a young naval officer. Entering the palace, the pair walked up the marble staircase into the Oeil de Boeuf, the anteroom to the King's apartment (so named because it had an oval window in the wall shaped like a bull's-eye), where the nobles in their velvet suits, with jeweled swords and powdered wigs, stood waiting to be admitted to the royal presence.

When the clock in the Oeil de Boeuf struck eleven, the door of the monarch's state bedroom was opened to admit those entitled to the *petite entrée*, namely the members of the royal family, the four Gentlemen of the Bedchamber, and his Grand Master of the Wardrobe. Louis XVI of France rose from his vast curtained bed. He put on his slippers and was helped by François Hue, head usher of His Majesty's chamber, into a sumptuous dressing gown. The King's nightcap was removed, his white wig put on. His valets, Hue and Cléry, would dress him. But if either of his brothers, the Comte de Provence or the Comte d'Artois, was present, they had the right to hand Louis his coat, his decorations, and his sword.

Meanwhile, the two men who had arrived in the shabby fiacre waited in the Oeil de Boeuf with the less important personages, who would be received when His Majesty was dressed and gave the order for the *grande entrée* to begin. When the door opened, those who had been granted the honor of a morning audience filed in. But seeing that the old gentleman simply clad in brown, without a wig or sword, was not in court dress, the Grand Chamberlain refused to allow him to enter.

"Let him by!" ordered a handsome, portly man standing by the door. The Grand Chamberlain instantly obeyed, for the nobleman who had rebuked him was Louis Xavier Stanislas, Comte de Provence or Monsieur, the elder of the King's two younger brothers.

Provence turned to the plainly-dressed old man. "Dr. Franklin," he said, "it is a pleasure to welcome you to Versailles." For the elderly statesman was America's envoy to France, Benjamin Franklin, who had come to present John Paul Jones of the new United States Navy to the King.

People were still talking about how, in February, Captain Jones, on his little ship the *Ranger*, had sailed into Quiberon Bay with the flag of a new nation and demanded that the French fleet recognize the Stars and Stripes. When Jones received a return salute, gun for gun, it was France's first acknowledgment of the colonies' independence.

America had been fighting England for three years, but Washington's small army had suffered defeat after defeat, and, although the French helped Britain's rebellious colonies secretly by sending them arms, Louis XVI's ministers hesitated to come out openly on the Americans' side. It would mean war with England, and France, hard up because of the extravagant reign of Louis XV, could not afford a war.

Then the Americans won a great victory in October, 1777, defeating Burgoyne's army coming down from Canada. Six months later, Benjamin Franklin was in Paris, as the head of an alliance of commerce and defense between the two countries, for, now that it looked as though America might win, France, about to declare war on her old enemy England, had signed a secret treaty with the British colonies in America, and Louis XVI was receiving Franklin openly at Versailles for the first time.

America's envoy stood before His Majesty more at ease than half of the courtiers about him, for Franklin and Louis had met informally before and discovered that they were congenial. The King was in his late twenties, a big, well-meaning, not-too-bright fat man, who liked to hunt and tinker with machinery. He found a kindred soul in the American scientist. Franklin had brought Jones to Versailles today to have him tell His Majesty about his successful raids on British shipping off the Scottish coast. But Franklin also took the occasion to remind the King that General Washington was desperately in need of men, supplies, and ships, if he was to continue the war against England.

Anxious to end the *levée* and ride off to hunt, Louis XVI interrupted him, "So you've told me before, Dr. Franklin, and now that we're beginning open hostilities against England, France will be giving America more substantial aid. I've sent the fleet an order that will please you." A wave of His Majesty's pudgy hand indicated that the audience was over. The two Americans, with profound bows, left the room.

Out in the Oeil de Boeuf, where the Comte de Provence stood chatting with friends, Benjamin Franklin was soon recognized. Courtiers crowded about the aged diplomat, asking him questions about the war overseas.

"My dear sister-in-law mustn't miss this," Provence said to himself; and, as Franklin and Jones started down the marble staircase to their carriage, he hurried to the Queen's private suite.

A French king and queen spend most of their life in public. That morning, Marie Antoinette, in her state apartments in the south wing of the palace, had gone through the same public *levée* as had her husband. A tub was rolled in, the Queen took her bath, then she was dressed by her ladies in waiting before any of the nobility (male and female) whose birth gave them the right to watch the royal family dress, eat, and go to bed.

That ordeal over, Marie Antoinette had retired to her gold-and-white boudoir overlooking the Cour de Marbre for a half hour to herself before she must join the King and the court in the chapel for the celebration of Mass. The Comte de Provence found his sister-in-law seated at her desk—a tall, slim woman of twenty-two, her beautiful long, oval face marred only by a full Hapsburg lower lip, writing a letter to her mother, the Empress Maria Theresa of Austria. The Queen looked up, and her blue eyes narrowed with dislike when she saw who it was. "Provence, what brings you here?" she asked.

"Quick! Look out of the window! You'll see John Paul Jones, the American about whom all of Paris is raving. He and Franklin have been with Louis. They're just leaving the palace."

With squeals of excitement, her ladies rushed to the window to catch a glimpse of the American naval hero. But Marie Antoinette never moved.

"Why such indifference, Antoinette?" Her brother-in-law smiled mockingly. "I thought you liked good-looking men. You might add Jones to your string of admirers . . . that is, if your devoted Swedish friend, Count Fersen, doesn't object."

Always, these sly references to Axel von Fersen! The Queen's hands clenched on the letter, and when she spoke her voice was like ice. "I'm writing Mama some news that will interest you, Provence. I'm telling her I think that I'm going to have a baby."

The stricken look on his face was sweet revenge. Married for eight years, Marie Antoinette, because of a slight physical infirmity in her husband, had been childless. Then a year ago, her brother Joseph, joint Emperor of Austria with his mother, had come to Paris and persuaded Louis to have an operation.

As long as his elder brother did not have a child, Louis Xavier Stanislas, Comte de Provence, was Dauphin, as the heir to the French throne was called. "Bad news for you, isn't it, dear?" Marie Antoinette reminded her brother-in-law sweetly. "As the next in line of succession, you're naturally the last person to wish me to have children."

Provence managed to recover himself. "Are you sure? One can be mistaken, you know."

"Fairly sure. Dr. Lassone thinks that my baby will be born in December."

"Have you told Louis?"

"Not yet. He'll be overjoyed."

"Then I'm the first to know. What an honor! But you misjudge me, Antoinette. I'm delighted at the news, for, if the baby is a girl, which is likely, she cannot succeed to the throne of France. So how can the child's birth affect me? I shall still be heir apparent."

Marie Antoinette looked him hard in the eyes. "No, Provence, France wants a Dauphin so badly that I'm certain my baby will be a boy." Then, ignoring him, the Queen resumed her writing. "I cannot be entirely certain until the first of next month," Marie Antoinette told her mother in a letter which is now in the Vienna archives. But as to the sex of the child so eagerly desired, there was no doubt in her mind. She always referred to it as "he."

* * * *

That night two horsemen met at an inn outside Paris. The courier who had galloped from Toulon arrived first and said to the tavern keeper, "My horse is exhausted. Give me a fresh mount. I'm on my way to Versailles with a message for the King."

Shortly, the second courier arrived from Versailles, also demanding a fresh horse, for his had gone lame. The innkeeper had only one in his stable.

"Give me the horse; my message is the more important," pleaded the second courier. "The Queen believes that she is going to have a baby. I carry a letter from Her Majesty to her royal mother, the Empress Maria Theresa of Austria, to acquaint her of the fact."

The first courier had merely come from the naval base at Toulon to inform the King that his promise to Benjamin Franklin had been kept. Twenty French warships had sailed for America. Comte d'Etaing's fleet would make it possible for General Washington to win the Revolution. "What is that compared to a royal child, at last!" the innkeeper said to himself. So who do you think got the horse?

2

LITTLE DAUGHTER OF FRANCE

IT WAS FUN telling Louis. On Wednesday, July 31, at ten-thirty in the evening, Marie Antoinette felt the first movements of the child within her. She climbed to her husband's attic workshop, where he was at his favorite pastime, repairing a clock, and told him the wonderful news. The King, proud and happy, took his wife in his arms.

On August 4, Her Majesty's pregnancy was announced to the court and 40,000 livres were set aside to pay Vermond, the accoucheur, for, of course, the baby would be a boy, while the doctor would get only 10,000 livres if he brought a princess into the world.

Marie Antoinette had so often envied her sister-in-law, the Comtesse d'Artois, her two little boys, the Duc d'Angoulême and the Duc de Berry. She knew that, so long as she wasn't a mother, the French would always consider her a foreigner—"that Austrian woman!" So every precaution was taken to prevent a miscarriage. No more dancing, no more late card parties. Marie Antoinette spent the days quietly, entertained with music and needlework. And, daily, she measured her waist.

"I expect pain, Louis," his wife said, as the month of December came and the birth of her child was daily anticipated, "but what I dread is the public ordeal. Why can't I be like other women and have my baby in private?"

"It's because you're the Queen of France that witnesses must be present," her husband explained. "The people must be sure you've actually given birth to a child and that a changeling wasn't slipped into your bed."

Marie Antoinette flushed with anger. "It would be like your brother Provence to make such an accusation, Louis. You'd better see he has a front seat!"

Jeanne Campan, Her Majesty's first lady in waiting, wrote in her memoirs: "At three o'clock on the morning of December 19, 1778, the Queen felt her time had arrived. The King sent for the doctors, but before they could get there, the news had spread through the palace and her state bedroom began to fill up, for by tradition not only was the nobility privileged to be present at a royal birth, but anyone who cared to come. Inquisitive persons surged into the room in such numbers that, by nine o'clock, it was impossible to move."

Marie Antoinette no longer cared. She lay groaning on her bed, and through the pain, stared unseeingly at the crowd of spectators. "The aristocrats were seated in order of their rank," continues Madame Campan. "Behind them, the general public who had come out from Paris jostled and pushed, many of them standing on chairs to get a better view."

The Queen's public torture lasted for seven hours, until, at half-past eleven in the morning, the child was born. The shock of seeing, by a sign arranged with the Princesse de Lamballe, that she had not given birth to a Dauphin, was too much for Marie Antoinette. She fainted.

"The Queen! Give her air!" cried the doctor.

For once in his life Louis acted promptly. Jeanne Campan tells how "the windows had been sealed up tight to keep out the winter draughts, but forcing his way through the crowd, the King broke a windowpane with his fist and let in fresh air. Guards hustled the spectators from the room, dragging inconsiderate persons who refused to leave out by the collar." The Queen recovered consciousness. She found the King by her side. Tenderly, he placed in her arms the baby who had nearly cost her mother's life.

"Poor little thing, she wasn't wished for," Louis said, "but we'll love her nonetheless, won't we, Antoinette?"

Princesse Louise de Lamballe, who was standing by the bed, wrote in her memoirs that the Queen could not reply, her disappointment being almost more than she could bear. "Well, Louis, you've lost your wager," Marie Antoinette finally said, for the King had bet his mother-in-law, the Empress Maria Theresa, that the baby would be a boy.

In Paris, the bells of Notre Dame Cathedral rang out. The people listened eagerly for the salute of a hundred-and-one cannon shots, in honor of the birth of an heir to the throne. Only twenty-one were fired. Then there was silence.

"So it's only a girl!" the crowd muttered. "Just what you'd expect of that Austrian!"

* * * *

Born on December 19, 1778, three days later the infant known as Madame Royale was carried into the chapel at Versailles to be baptized by Cardinal de Rohan. She was held at the font by her uncle, the Comte de Provence, proxy for her godfather, the King of Spain. Beside Provence stood his wife Josephine, representing the baby's illustrious grandmother and other godparent, the Empress of Austria, as the Cardinal sprinkled holy water on the infant's forehead and named her Marie Thérèse Charlotte.

The feelings of Louis Xavier Stanislas, as he held the baby, can be imagined. This one was a girl, but no doubt now there would be other children. He knew himself to be a far abler man than his dull-witted older brother, and better fitted to be king. This brat in his arms put an end to Provence's hopes. Was she really Louis' child? Had the operation on him been a success? Provence didn't actually dare say that the baby was illegitimate, but he hinted as much by rudely interrupting the christening ceremony to insist that the Cardinal ask who was the child's father.

It was an embarrassing moment. Charles Philippe d'Artois, the youngest of the three royal brothers, didn't see how Provence dared do anything so rude. Artois' own chances for the crown were remote. But Monsieur and the Comtesse de Provence had no children. Therefore, one of Artois' boys might someday succeed their uncle. That is, unless Louis had a son, which his brothers hoped would never happen.

So the members of the royal family stood about the font in the chapel at Versailles that day, three of them bitterly resenting the baby's birth—Louis' two brothers and his cousin, the Duc Louis Philippe d'Orléans, whose fingers also itched for the crown. But little Madame Royale slept peacefully through her christening ceremony. Then, while a *Te Deum* was sung in her honor, the baby was carried back to her nursery in the south wing of the palace through corridors filled with bowing courtiers.

Gifts had been pouring in for days, and the gardens of Versailles were illuminated each night. But when the Queen went to Paris to give thanks to God at Notre Dame Cathedral for a safe delivery, there were no shouts of "*Vive la reine!*" The crowds were silent as Marie Antoinette passed by in her gilded coach. The scheming Duc d'Orléans had seen to it that the price of bread had risen again. Bitter at having to queue up for a whole day to buy a high-priced, moldy loaf, Paris was in no mood to cheer "l'Autrichienne," whose extravagances were notorious, just because she had become a mother.

"The Queen will have to do better next year," a lady wrote on the day following the birth of Madame Royale. But it was three years later, on October 22, 1781, before Marie Antoinette had the son she wanted so much. To avoid the shock of disappointment if the child again proved to be a girl, it had been decided that the Queen should not be told its sex until all danger was past. So when the baby was born, it was silently carried away to be washed and dressed.

Marie Antoinette, seeing the solemn faces around her, thought that she had given birth to another daughter. She was in tears when the King came to her bedside. "Monsieur le Dauphin asks if he can come in," he said, smiling happily.

"Louis! A boy?"

"Yes, my dear, a fine, healthy boy!"

At last she had given birth to a king! When the child was brought to her by the Princesse de Guémenée, Marie Antoinette kissed him rapturously; and Louis kept repeating proudly, as though he could hardly believe it, "My son, the Dauphin."

There was wild rejoicing when Madame de Guémenée, governess of the Children of France, came out into the hall with the infant in her arms to show him to the ladies and gentlemen of the court. A nobleman turned to the Comte de Provence, who had just arrived. "A Dauphin, Monsieur!" he blurted out. "We have an heir to the crown at last!"

The Comte turned pale on hearing the news that appeared to remove him forever from the throne. He rushed past without replying. And from the moment when, suave and smiling, Louis Xavier Stanislas went in to kiss his sister-in-law's hand

and congratulate her, he became the most dangerous of Marie Antoinette's enemies.

Princesse Elisabeth, the King's young sister, was wild with joy. Louis' sour old maiden aunts, Mesdames Adélaide and Victoire, actually expressed approval. Only the Comte d'Artois let fall a remark that betrayed his disappointment. Madame Campan tells how she overheard the six-year-old Duc d'Angoulême, taken by his father to see the baby Dauphin lying in his cradle, say to him, "Papa, how little my cousin is!"

"The day will come, Antoine," replied the Count, "when you will find him big enough."

Suddenly, in the midst of his rejoicing, Louis remembered his daughter. "Where is Thérèse?" the King asked. "She must be sent for, to meet her new brother." With all the excitement, everybody had completely forgotten the poor child.

3

THE MOCK WEDDING

On March 27, 1785, the Comte de Provence saw for a second time a male child come between him and the throne, when Louis Charles, Duc de Normandie, was born to the Queen of France. The new baby was not sickly like Louis Joseph Xavier, the four-year-old Dauphin, but "a regular peasant's child, rosy and plump," his mother wrote her brother Joseph.

As soon as Marie Antoinette recovered from her confinement, she went to Paris to give thanks again at Notre Dame. That evening, the Queen dined with the brother-in-law she liked, Comte Charles d'Artois. His young son, the Duc d'Angoulême, being Grand Prior of the French Knights Templar, a secret order of Free Masonry, Artois made their Temple palace his residence when he came to Paris.

After supper, Marie Antoinette stood at a window in the brightly-lighted mansion, gazing out at the garden where the tall outline of the Templars' centuries-old keep loomed up, black and sinister looking in the darkness. The Queen shuddered, her eyes on that square stone tower with a pointed roof, flanked on its four corners by round, peaked turrets. Why? The day had been a happy one. Surely, now that she was three times a mother, the gossip about her and Count Axel von Fersen would stop, along with the circulating of suggestive verses promoted, if not actually written by, her husband's brother Provence and his cousin, Philippe d'Orléans. Marie Antoinette had prevented Orléans from being made Admiral in Chief of the Navy, a position he did not deserve, and the Duke hated her.

"Charles, that horrible tower gives me the creeps," his sister-in-law said to him. "I wish you'd pull it down."

"Oh, I couldn't do that," replied Artois, "Berthélemy, the Templars' archivist, lives there."

And he didn't destroy the tower.

* * * *

Like most royal princesses, Marie Thérèse Charlotte was brought up first by nurses, then, as she grew older, by governesses and tutors. In 1782, the dissolute Duchesse Julus de Polignac, Mama's best friend, replaced the Princesse de Guémenée as governess of the Daughter of France, one of the highest positions at court—and mostly a sinecure. Under Gabrielle de Polignac's rule eighty people served. It was really a modest household for a royal infant, not so large as that of Thérèse's brother Joseph, who lived in the Dauphin's apartment on the ground floor of the central court of Versailles, that the Comte de Provence had been forced to vacate.

Marie Antoinette kept the child's grandmother in Vienna informed of her daughter's rapid growth. "She is so big and strong, Thérèse might be two years old . . . She has been able to say 'Papa' for two days now . . . Her teeth are not through yet, but you can feel them."

At first, Madame Royale's nursery consisted of several ground-floor rooms, at the end of the south wing, where she learned to walk holding onto the railing of the terrace overlooking the Orangery. But when the Petite Madame was five, she was moved up to a suite under the Hall of Mirrors, connected by a stairway with Marie Antoinette's private apartment on the first floor.

Even there, Thérèse seldom saw her mother. The pleasure-loving Queen of France, her mind occupied with clothes, cards, and the theater, took little notice of her daughter. Madame Royale was many months old before she learned to recognize her. Marie Antoinette admits this in a letter to the Empress of Austria:

> She [Thérèse] walks all by herself, and if she falls, gets up again without help. I must tell you, my dear Mama, of such a charming surprise I had a day or so ago. There were several ladies in my daughter's room, and I made one of them ask her which was her mother. Just think! The little darling, without anyone having said a word to her, toddled to me, smiling. It is the first time she has seemed to know me.

From the time she was a little baby, Thérèse preferred her father to her mother. At an early age, she learned to recognize the big, kindly man, who came to play with her each evening on his return from hunting, to hold out her chubby arms to him whenever he appeared and call him "Papa."

The affection between father and daughter was strengthened by her mother's lack of interest in Thérèse as she grew from infancy to childhood. That her first baby was a girl had been a bitter disappointment to the Queen, and when the child was seen to have all of her father's characteristics and almost none of her mother's, the antipathy increased. Marie Antoinette was content to leave Thérèse's upbringing almost wholly to her nurses and to center all of her affection on her two boys, especially on her second son Charles, a handsome, precocious child, so like herself.

Young as she was, Thérèse felt this neglect. She never

forgave Marie Antoinette for having preferred her brothers to herself. The bitterness of being merely tolerated by her mother shaped the little girl's character early. All her life Thérèse yearned to be loved and needed, which was an unconscious search for the mother love she had lacked, and she was profoundly grateful and loyal to anyone who showed her the least affection.

Thérèse hardly knew her sister, Sophie, born in July, 1786, and dead eleven months later, and by the time the little Madame was eight she seldom saw the older of her two brothers. Dying of tuberculosis and rickets, Joseph had been sent to the Château de Meudon, where he could have quiet and perhaps grow stronger. The move did him no good, and as the Dauphin grew increasingly feeble, his younger brother Charles became of great importance at court, for only a sickly life stood between him and the throne. The blond, blue-eyed Duc de Normandie was a true Hapsburg, his mother all over again. Marie Antoinette was passionately fond of him. She called Charles by the pet name, "*mon chou d'amour*," and his grave-faced sister "*mousseline la sérieuse*," because of Thérèse's sad little face.

Charles was too young to be a playmate. It was with her Artois cousins, Louis Antoine, Duc d'Angoulême, eleven, and Charles Ferdinand, Duc de Berry, eight, who lived with their parents in the south wing, that Madame Royale played hide-and-seek in the labyrinth of stairs and passages between the floors of the vast palace. Visitors caught glimpses of her and the Artois boys riding in the park of Versailles, in a cart drawn by two white ponies their Uncle Provence had given them. Otherwise, the Daughter of France was rarely seen. She had her language, literature, and Bible lessons with the Abbé d'Avaux. Baroness de Mackau, her second governess, taught Thérèse sewing, dancing, and deportment. Only twice a week did she appear in public. These occasions were at the ghastly public meals when the royal family must eat with crowds of strangers watching. There was music and cards were given out, admitting the public. Anyone off the street, if he wasn't too dirty or in rags, could attend.

To a fanfare of trumpets, the King's gold dishes were escorted through the palace from distant kitchens by a group of soldiers. Their Majesties had already dined in private, so in public they smiled dutifully at the crowd and only pretended to eat the food that had previously been sampled by the royal taster, to make sure that it contained no poison. But the little Madame hated being stared at by common people. In those days, small boys and girls dressed exactly like miniature adults, and stiff in her panniered gown and powdered hair, she sat in sullen silence, scowling down at her plate.

"Behave yourself, Thérèse!" Marie Antoinette scolded. "A princess must always smile."

"Madame Royale had the haughty manner of her mother," remembered the Baron de Mailly, writing in his *Souvenirs d'Un Page*, the memoirs of his boyhood, when he served as a page at Versailles. "It was so apparent, even as a child, that it was thought best to correct her of it by small punishments." Her daughter was often more of an irritating nuisance to Marie Antoinette than a source of pride, like her son. The Duc de Normandie was only a baby, but he sat on the Queen's lap at public meals, smiling at everybody.

The royal family was so surrounded by etiquette that it was only at the Petit Trianon, a gem of a palace built by Louis XV for Madame de Pompadour, that they could escape from the formal life at Versailles. Thérèse looked forward to these visits. At Trianon, among thatched-roofed cottages around a lake, was a farm where Mama and her ladies played at being dairymaids.

On December 19, 1787, as a special treat for her ninth birthday, Madame Royale was spending the night at Trianon. That morning she had awakened to find the table by her bed covered with presents. There were gifts from Mama and Papa, from the Aunts, from the Provences and the Artois. Even the Orléans family, who had no love for the senior branch of the Bourbons, had sent her a small remembrance. They made Thérèse feel, for once, more important than her brothers. And Mama, because it was her birthday, had asked a few children to supper and to play until bedtime.

That afternoon, the young guests were all assembled in the drawing room at Trianon, when Marie Antoinette called her daughter to her side and fastened a white veil on her head.

Thérèse jerked away resentfully. "What's this for? I don't like it, Mama. The veil is heavy and pulls my hair."

"If you hold your head high, as a princess should, it won't pull on your hair."

"Mama, is the veil for my First Communion?"

"No, we're going to put on a make-believe wedding and you're the bride. Isn't that exciting? See, your cousin Antoine is to be the groom. Now, Thérèse, do as I tell you." Marie Antoinette's coaxing voice grew sharp, as it often did while talking with her daughter. "You wouldn't want to get punished and not be allowed to visit Trianon again, would you?"

So Louis Antoine de Bourbon, Artois' eldest son, a shy, homely boy of twelve, was made to come and stand by Thérèse's side. Before a group of court ladies and their children the first cousins were "married" by the Abbé d'Avaux, Madame Royale's tutor.

Thérèse yanked off her veil the moment the brief ceremony was over. But before she ran off to feast with the other children on ices and cakes and forget all that had happened, she stopped to give dear Papa a hug. The King, who had ridden over from Versailles, had stood frowning behind the Queen during the mock marriage, for he did not approve of what she was doing.

It was not the ceremony Louis objected to, but the choice of a bridegroom. Their daughter was nine years old. At an age when most girls have hardly put away their dolls, a royal princess is already betrothed, usually to a cousin. In Thérèse's case, it was especially important. The Dauphin was sickly and deformed. It was conceivable that Charles, although more robust, might also die. Their sister could not become queen because the Salic law decreed that only a male could reign over France. But if Madame Royale married the young Duc d'Angoulême, she might someday become queen of France. Provence had no children. So Artois and his boys were next in line.

"But we promised our daughter to Orléans' son," Louis reminded his wife. "What will Philippe say when he hears about this?"

Marie Antoinette tossed her head. "I detest him, I don't care what he says."

She would live to regret those words, for the Duc d'Orléans never forgot this fresh snub. He wanted desperately to marry his eldest son, Louis Philippe, a boy of fourteen, to the only daughter of the senior branch of the Bourbon family. The Orléans had come down from a brother of Louis XIV. They were the first princes of the blood royal, but only fifth cousins, fit to hand the King his shirt at the petite levée, but of inferior rank to Louis XVI and his brothers.

Philippe d'Orléans had tried to marry Madame Henriette, second daughter of Louis XV. Her father turned him down. Instead, he had married the daughter of the Duc de Penthièvre, the richest man in France, but who had come down illegitimately from Louis XIV and Madame de Montespan. It put another blotch on the Orléans escutcheon. But now Philippe had the power to avenge himself. He was immensely wealthy, and he knew how to use his money to put evil interpretations on the Queen's mildest indiscretions and bring on her downfall. From his Paris home, the Palais-Royal, Orléans encouraged the French people to commit crimes they dared not undertake by themselves. Of all the tactless things of which Marie Antoinette was guilty, the mock wedding she put on at Trianon did her the most harm and, unfortunately, had the most far-reaching effect upon her daughter's future.

In 1789, partly because of the aid given to America in her War of Independence, France was bankrupt. Needing money, Louis XVI was persuaded by his ministers to summon the States-General to meet at Versailles and, for the first time, along with the nobles and the clergy, include a third group composed of commoners. For one hundred and seventy-five years, the French kings, being absolute rulers, had not let such a legislative body meet. The clergy and the nobles were exempt from taxes. It was the French peasants who bore the heavy tax burden. Their deputies came from all over France to Versailles on May 5, bitter over this injustice, and determined not to go home until they had a say in the government. The Duc d'Orléans first publicly showed his enmity to the reigning Bourbons by deserting the nobility and marching with the commoners in the procession to the cathedral that opened the meetings.

Thérèse watched the parade pass by the palace, seated beside the sick Dauphin. Joseph's frail, twisted body lay on cushions placed on a balcony. It was a colorful sight, with Papa walking behind the Archbishop of Paris, who was bearing the Blessed Sacrament. They were followed by two thousand persons carrying lighted candles. Mama and her ladies came at the end.

Why were her parents so upset, Thérèse wondered, when they returned to the palace? She was too young to understand the significance of what had happened—how the King had been mildly applauded by the crowd. A hostile silence greeted "Madame Deficit," as they had nicknamed the extravagant Queen. Then cheers of "*Vive Orléans!*" rang out as the most liberal-minded member of the royal family came in sight.

It was the last ceremony that the eight-year-old Dauphin would see. A month later, on June 2, 1789, Joseph's condition became so much worse that his parents were summoned to Meudon. They returned to Versailles two days later. Taking Thérèse by the hand, Marie Antoinette led her daughter to a nursery in the south wing, where Charles sat on the floor, playing with his tin soldiers.

"Come, kiss your brother's hand," Mama ordered.

The Duc de Normandie looked up in surprise when his mother and sister knelt before him. "Monsieur le Dauphin!" the Queen informed the four-year-old boy, and Thérèse knew that Joseph had died.

4

MARIE ANTOINETTE'S FRIEND

COUNT AXEL VON FERSEN, the tall, blond son of Field Marshal Frederic von Fersen of Stockholm, had come to Paris in January, 1774, when both he and Marie Antoinette were nineteen. At a masked ball in Paris, he met the young Dauphine whom the death of Louis XV would make queen of France.

Fersen went back to his native country, Sweden. Four years later, in August, 1778, he returned to France. The King hardly remembered him, but the Queen greeted Axel warmly, and soon "her Rignon" never entered a room where she was without causing Her Majesty to flush, her attraction toward the handsome foreigner evident to all. "I see my friend in the strictest privacy. She is an angel," Axel wrote his sister Sophie, the Countess Adolph Piper of Sweden.

Of course, people talked. There was so much gossip about them that in May, 1780, on the advice of the Swedish ambassador, Count Creutz, Fersen put an ocean between himself and Marie Antoinette by going to America, where he fought in the Revolution as an aide to Rochambeau.

In June, 1783, after serving as second-in-command of Lauzen's forces at Yorktown, Count Fersen was back in

France, and the Queen secured an appointment for him as colonel of a Swedish regiment attached to the French Army. His father wanted him to return to Sweden, where, as the heir to an ancient name, almost any position at the court of Gustavus III was open to him. But Axel refused. He was still devoted to Marie Antoinette, and during the next six years managed to be near her by remaining in Paris as Gustavus' secret agent.

By the summer of 1789, France was on the verge of a revolution. The French volunteers, who took part in the American war, had returned home to tell of a country where there was no king nor nobility, but everyone was equal. It put ideas of liberty and equality into French heads. The burden of taxation to support the court had become unbearable. Marie Antoinette was the chief target of discontent. Louis' subjects were aware that their simpleton of a king was modest in his tastes. It was "that foreigner from Vienna" they hated. The poor people of Paris, who must work ten hours a day to earn a few sous, were furious at hearing of the Queen's fabulous gowns and jewels. The public knew that gambling, prohibited by law, was countenanced at court. Faro was played at Versailles every night. Marie Antoinette wagered for high stakes at cards, and lavished pensions on the Polignac clan and other favorites, while the ordinary Frenchman and his family were half-starved.

In Paris, an effigy representing the Queen was publicly burned. That frightened her. At Versailles, futile little economies were ordered. She even tried to disassociate herself from her frivolous playmates. Gabrielle de Polignac, who had made a fortune as nominal governess of the royal children, was shipped off to Italy. But it was too late.

On July 14, 1789, Count Fersen witnessed in horror the capture of the Bastille, the King's prison in Paris, by a rabble urged on by the Duc d'Orléans. It was clear that the newly-formed National Guard could not control the mob, even with the Marquis de Lafayette, who had fought in the American Revolution, in command. Since French troops were no longer to be trusted, the King sent for two Flemish regiments.

Nearly everyone at court felt better when the foreign mercenaries arrived. On October 1, His Majesty's Swiss bodyguard gave a banquet in the theater at Versailles for the officers of the Flanders troops. "The children being eager to see the affair," the Princesse de Lamballe wrote, "the King and Queen decided to attend."

When Louis appeared at the end of the meal, leading Thérèse by the hand, followed by Marie Antoinette with Charles in her arms, they were greeted with cheers of "*Vive le Roi!*" by the Flemish soldiers. The band played, and Madame Royale and the Dauphin were lifted up onto a big horseshoe table around which the officers were seated, so that everyone could see and admire the royal children.

For Thérèse and Charles, who loved soldiers, it was very exciting. They were too young to know that calling in foreign troops to protect him from his own people had been a tactless thing for their papa to do. In Paris, the banquet for the Flanders regiments was said to have been a drunken orgy. When, four days later, on the morning of October 5, one of Orléans' henchmen told a large crowd of women, chiefly from the fish market of Les Halles, gathered in the garden of the Duke's Palais-Royal, that while they were fainting for lack of food the King had been feasting the Flanders mercenaries, there were angry mutterings of resentment.

In the back of the listening crowd stood Axel von Fersen, who often came to hear what these riot makers had to say. This morning, because of a bad harvest, Paris lacked bread. The bakeries were empty, and Orléans' orators kept feeding the anger of the poor and hungry people by telling them that the King, to make bread scarce and high priced, was hoarding flour at Versailles.

"To Versailles!" someone shouted. "We'll bring back the baker and the baker's wife, and make them give us bread!"

A hired thug, a man dressed as a woman, of which there were many in the crowd because Orléans knew that no soldiers would dare to fire at a woman, brandished a piece of moldy black bread in Fersen's face. "We'll make the Austrian woman swallow this," he vowed, "then we'll tie the foreigner to a horse's tail and drag her through Paris."

With that, the march began. This army of women, and men in women's clothes, several thousand of them, armed with pitchforks and old muskets, set out for Versailles, ten miles away, unopposed by Lafayette and his militia, who stood about helpless.

Fersen jumped on his horse and galloped ahead of the rabble. He must reach Versailles before the dregs of Paris arrived, and save Marie Antoinette, if it cost him his life.

* * * *

That morning, Madame Royale had been busy with her usual school routine at Versailles. She had her German, drawing, and dancing lessons with Louise de Croy-Havré, Marquise de Tourzel, a sedate, gray-haired widow whose husband had been killed while hunting with the King. The Marquise had replaced the Duchesse de Polignac as governess to the Children of France.

Marie Antoinette, being musical, was having Madame de Tourzel teach her daughter to play the clavichord. Thérèse disliked music, but she had practiced her scales so well today that, as a reward, the Baroness de Mackau, her second governess, had promised to drive the Petite Madame over to Trianon this afternoon to join her mother there. Happily anticipating watching the farmer while he milked the cows and fed the ducks and chickens, Thérèse was eating lunch when Fersen arrived from Paris on a winded horse to warn the royal family that a mob was marching on Versailles.

There would be no afternoon drive for Madame Royale. The palace was soon in an uproar. Messengers were sent to Trianon to fetch the Queen and to summon the King, who was hunting in the Meudon woods. The royal couple hurried back to Versailles, and Fersen tried to convince Louis that he and his family were in danger. They should escape to their hunting lodge at Rambouillet while they could. At least, the Queen and her children should go. But Marie Antoinette refused to leave her husband—and he saw no reason for going.

"A king in flight from some women coming to ask for bread? Axel, you must be joking," Louis said and, while he hesitated, the mob arrived.

Alarmed at last, the King, never able to make up his slow mind, began to wonder, "Should we go?" But it was too late now. When the royal carriages were ordered to drive up to the door, the coachmen could not get their frightened horses from the stables to the palace, through the surging mob beating against the locked gates of the Place d'Armes and shouting that they were hungry. "Bread, give us bread!" Behind the grille were drawn up the King's Swiss bodyguard, the two Flanders regiments, and Lafayette, who had followed the the King to let them fire at the rioters, but he mildly replied, marchers to Versailles with his soldiers. His defenders begged "You can't fire on women."

It began to rain. Soaked to the skin, the marchers from Paris went off in search of food and shelter. At two o'clock in the morning, since everything seemed quiet, and the royal family had gone to bed, Lafayette left the palace to get some rest at the home of his wife's family in town.

At five o'clock, the residents of Versailles were all asleep, when a locked door was stealthily opened. "*Ou est-elle, la coquine?*" demanded several voices, as armed men in women's clothes poured into the south wing of the palace, where the Duc d'Orléans stood at the foot of the stairs to show them the way up to Marie Antoinette's apartment.

* * * *

There had been plenty of noises to frighten Thérèse already when she went to bed—firing outside in the Cour de Marbre and angry shouting. "But Monsieur de Lafayette had assured the King and Queen that they had nothing more to fear," Louise de Tourzel wrote in her memoirs. So, at midnight, Thérèse and Charles kissed their parents good night, and went off with the Marquise.

Five hours later, the Petite Madame awoke with a start. What had happened? Her governess, a lighted candle in her hand, stood by her bed. "Get up and come quickly, dear," Madame de Tourzel whispered. "I'm going to fetch your brother." She returned in a few minutes with Charles in her arms, wrapped in a quilt, and, taking Madame Royale by the hand, hurried the children up a private stairway to the King's apartment.

When they arrived, Papa was not there. Awakened by the noise made by the mob as they broke into the palace, Louis had rushed in his nightshirt to his wife's room through a passageway under the Oeil de Boeuf. In a short while, he returned, all breathless because he could not find the Queen. He was relieved to find her safe in his room. She had just come in. Her hair hanging loose and wearing only a yellow wrapper over her nightgown, Marie Antoinette was seated on a sofa, telling the King's sister, Princesse Elisabeth, of her narrow escape.

She had been awakened by shouts of "Death to the Aus-

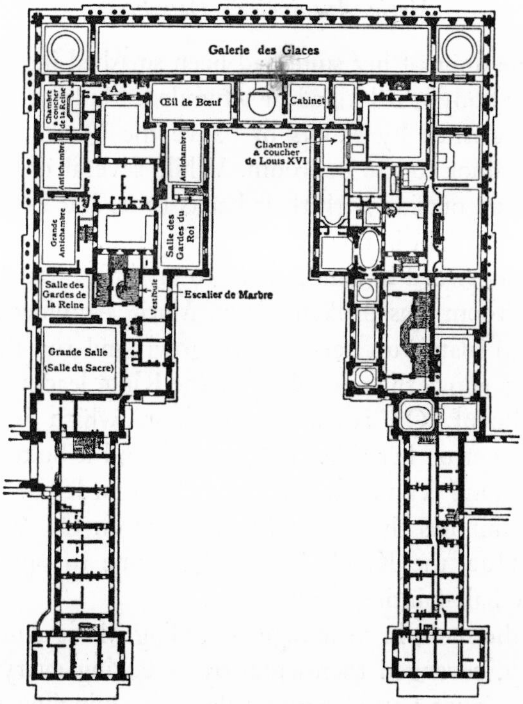

WING OF THE CHATEAU OF VERSAILLES

Chambre à coucher de la Reine: Marie Antoinette's state bedroom, where her daughter was born.

Escalier de Marbre: the stairs by which the mob entered the palace, during the night of October 5, 1789, to murder the Queen.

A; the passage by which Marie Antoinette escaped from her state bedroom into the Oeil de Boeuf, then through the King's Cabinet (Council Chamber), to her husband's bedroom. The Queen's private suite consisted of four small rooms, below the letter A.

Chambre à coucher de Louis XVI: the room where the royal family took refuge, while the mob stormed the palace. Between the Oeil de Boeuf and the King's Cabinet is the balcony, overlooking the Cour de Marbre (Marble Court), on which the Queen appeared with her children.

trian!" The door of her suite had been smashed in; the members of her bodyguard killed or wounded. Madame Thiebaut, her maid, warned by shouts of "Save the Queen!" quickly bolted the door to the bedroom. While several of the Swiss soldiers stood outside with their backs to it, and Fersen, who had spent the night in the Queen's sitting room to protect her, stood inside, sword in hand, ready to give his life if the door to her bedroom was broken down, Marie Antoinette barely had time to snatch up her dressing gown and run through a passageway above the one taken by the King, leading into the Oeil de Boeuf. On reaching the door, which was never locked, except on her side, the Queen found it bolted against her. By whom? Who wanted her to be murdered? For five agonizing minutes she beat with her fists on the door, until François Hue, the King's head valet, came to open it. He found her half-fainting with fright.

While the mob, in their rage at finding Marie Antoinette's bed empty, revenged themselves by wrecking everything in her room, Count Fersen escaped death by mingling with the rioters, unrecognized. Meanwhile, the royal family sat trembling behind locked doors. Later, when the racket somewhat subsided, Hue ventured out and brought them some clothes.

Milling around the palace, the menacing crowd, shouting and cursing, still packed the Cour de Marbre. Standing on a chair before one of the windows, looking out at them, Charles, too young to realize their danger, was amusing himself, teasing his sister by pulling her long blond hair, when the Provences made their tardy appearance. Monsieur was barely able to hide his satisfaction at the turn of events he had helped to bring about. Mesdames Tantes, Adélaide and Victoire, taking fright at reports of earlier riots in Paris, had left Versallies three months ago. So had the Comte and Comtesse d'Artois and their boys. But Elisabeth, the youngest member of the family, a sweet-faced woman of twenty-five, refused to leave her brother Louis, whom she loved dearly.

Lafayette, roused from his slumbers, finally returned to Versailles. He resumed the command of the National Guard, and drove the invaders out of the palace. But they still blocked the courtyards, brandishing the severed heads of the Swiss bodyguards they had murdered.

"The King on the balcony!" the mob shouted.

Writing many years later, François Hue told in his memoirs how he watched in horror Louis "meekly obey." The King appeared on the center balcony of the palace, overlooking the Cour de Marbre, accompanied by Lafayette. It was the Marquis who spoke, assuring the crowd that His Majesty would do as they wished and return with them to Paris. Then the rabble began to howl for the Queen.

"She shrank from the ordeal," Hue wrote. "But thinking that the sight of her innocent children would melt every heart, Her Majesty stepped out onto the balcony, holding by one hand the Dauphin and by the other Madame Royale." Looking down, Thérèse saw a sea of faces hard with hate, raised fists, and brandished muskets. It was the little girl's first sight of a mob. She shrank trembling against her mother.

"No children!" yelled those below.

Gently pushing Thérèse and Charles back into the room, Marie Antoinette remained on the balcony alone, disdainfully facing these hostile people. Were they going to shoot her? She didn't know. Impressed by the Queen's courage, Lafayette stepped through the window to kiss her hand.

But the courtyard still rang with the command, "The King to Paris!" for, shocked by the extravagance at Versailles, Louis' subjects were determined that the royal family should return with them to Paris and live more simply at the Tuileries. The prisoners were given only an hour to pack for the journey. At one o'clock, the helpless group descended the marble staircase, still stained with the blood of their bodyguards, and the procession of carriages set out.

Leading the way, the sham fishwives (men dressed as women) carried on the tips of their pikes the heads of the slaughtered Swiss. Behind, in the first coach, were squeezed the King, the Queen, Princesse Elisabeth, the two royal children and their governess. Beside them walked what remained of the royal bodyguard, disarmed and bloodstained. Then came carriages containing the Provences and the court. Thérèse was never to forget that nightmare ride. It took them more than six hours to drive at a snail's pace the ten miles to Paris. From the houses that lined the way, jeering people leaned out of their windows to watch the show.

In one of the crawling vehicles rode Count Fersen. Now, riding with the Queen to Paris, Axel's feeling for her grew all the stronger because she was helpless and in danger. The drunken crowd surrounded the royal carriages, shouting triumphantly, "We're bringing back the baker, his wife, and the oven boy! We'll no longer be short of bread!"

Marie Antoinette, her son on her lap, stared straight ahead. She seemed not to see or hear. Clinging to his mother, the poor frightened Dauphin whimpered incessantly, "Mama, I'm hungry!" So was Madame Royale. They had been awake since five o'clock that morning. All day they had eaten nothing. But Thérèse, ten now, was too big a girl to weep with terror as Charles was doing. She sat holding Madame Tourzel's hand, biting her lips to keep from crying.

Several times, when Thérèse started to look out of the carriage window, Princesse Elisabeth put her hand over her niece's eyes. Those dead men's heads on pikes were a sight no child should see. Worn out with exhaustion, the little girl finally went to sleep with her head resting on her aunt's shoulder.

An hour later, she woke with a start. The carriage had

stopped. It was seven o'clock and dark and they had reached their first prison, the Tuileries in Paris, a royal palace but uninhabited by the kings of France for fifty years, standing cold, dirty, and almost empty of furniture.

Fersen watched Marie Antoinette and her family enter the dreary place. Then he went off to his house nearby, in the Rue Matignon. On the ninth of October, sick at heart, he wrote his father in Sweden:

> I witnessed everything. I returned to Paris in one of the carriages following the King. We were six and a half hours on the road. God preserve me from ever again beholding so distressing a spectacle as those two days.

5

PUPPET ROYALTY

"MAMA, there are mice in my room!" Thérèse wailed.

"Don't be a baby," replied Marie Antoinette. "A mouse won't hurt you."

There were worse things than mice in that huge, dark, smelly building—rats and cockroaches and bats—for since Louis XV had moved out to Versailles and abandoned the Tuileries fifty years ago, royalty had not used the rambling old palace, begun by Catherine de Médicis. Neglect and an army of Bourbon hangers-on who camped out there had ruined the vast, empty apartments and filled them with rubbish.

That night, the only beds available were cots for the royal family. Their attendants slept on benches or tables. "Madame Royale and the Dauphin passed the night without guards," Louise de Tourzel wrote, "in a room whose doors could not be locked or hardly closed. I barricaded them with the few bits of furniture I could find, and sat up all night by the children's bed."

Next morning, when Charles awoke, he demanded his toys that had been left behind, forgotten at Versailles. Both children were tense and nervous. Hearing shouts and the firing of muskets out in the street, Thérèse ran to be comforted by Aunt Babet, who, unlike Mama, would always listen to her childish fears and troubles. "Today," the little girl sobbed, "isn't going to be another yesterday, is it?" Elisabeth kissed her trembling niece and tried to reassure her. But did she know herself what today would bring?

Most of the long, two-storied Tuileries, which once stood across the Place du Carrousel from the Louvre, was uninhabitable. But the squatters, who had occupied the dingy building for years, were moved out. The royal family took rooms in the Pavillon de Flore, the south wing overlooking the Seine River, and made themselves as comfortable as possible. On the ground floor was the Queen's apartment. A private staircase led to the floor above, where the King's rooms, as well as those of his sister Elisabeth, and the children were located. Furniture and servants finally arrived from Versailles. Even Louis' workshop was installed, which made him happy. But there were significant changes. The fourteenth of July, when the Bastille had been seized, was declared the national holiday; and from the roof of the Tuileries there waved a flag with three wide, vertical stripes, red, white, and blue. It had replaced the white banner of the Bourbons, studded with gold fleurs-de-lis (conventionalized iris, called a lily in France), as the new French national flag.

"Why, red, white, and blue are the Duc d'Orléans' racing colors!" exclaimed the Queen, in horror.

Louis hunted no more. Marie Antoinette seldom left the Tuileries. This was a different life for the former frivolous Queen of France. Evenings, the Provences usually came to dine. They left for the Luxembourg, their Paris home, early. Then Louis went to bed and Marie Antoinette returned to her suite to chat with her lady in waiting, Princesse Louise de Lamballe, the widowed daughter-in-law of the Duc de

Penthièvre, and Count Fersen, who came in every evening for an hour or two.

Since the outbreak of the Revolution there had been a steady exodus of the nobility, who fled from France to save their lives, so there were no balls and card parties now. Marie Antoinette had empty hours to devote to her children. To Gabrielle de Polignac in Italy the Queen wrote, "Everyone is leaving, I am alone in my room the whole day. My children are almost always with me and comfort me a little." Thérèse, for the first time in her life, felt that her mother needed her. When she was sent for, Mama usually looked as if she had been crying.

The royal family were semi-prisoners, but, for the children, life at the Tuileries went on much as it had at Versailles. The Dauphin played with the small son of the Comte de Paroy on the terrace beside the Seine, where he had rabbits, birds, a duck pond, and a garden. There, every morning, Charles picked a bouquet of flowers for his mother's dressing table. The Marquise de Tourzel's fifteen-year-old daughter Pauline came to live at the Tuileries. Thérèse and Pauline became close friends. The girls studied their lessons together, and watched the magic lantern the Comte de Paroy, Madame Royale's tutor, installed to make the study of geography easier. Recalling those days, Pauline, by then the Comtesse de Béarn, wrote in her *Souvenirs de Quarante Ans:* "After the Dauphin was put to bed, I went up every night and had supper with Madame Royale, then we played a game of reversi."

Louis XVI, a devout Catholic, listened mornings to his daughter's lessons in the catechism, for on April 7, 1790, Marie Thérèse of France was to receive her First Communion. But when the religious event took place on Wednesday of Holy Week, at St. Germain l'Auxerrois, the parish church of the Tuileries still standing behind the Louvre, Madame Royale's

First Communion was a far simpler affair than it would have been in the chapel at Versailles. There was no gift of a diamond necklace, as there had always been for the daughter of a king of France on this very special occasion, and only Thérèse's mother and her governesses were present. Standing with the Marquise de Tourzel and the Baronesse de Mackau in the cold, dark nave, Marie Antoinette watched her eleven-year-old daughter, in her white dress and veil, go up to kneel at the altar rail. Thérèse's father had refused to attend, because the priest who officiated was one of the clergy who had sworn allegiance to the state, and not to the Pope, a step Louis thought was blasphemous.

In 1791, when they had been in Paris for two years, the royal family wished to spend Holy Week at their palace of Saint-Cloud, in the suburbs of Paris. The Duc d'Orléans, hoping the people would assassinate the King for him, spread the rumor that the trip was planned merely as an excuse for Louis to escape from France and said he should be prevented from leaving Paris. So on Monday before Easter, April 18, when the King and Queen, with their children and Princesse Elisabeth, got into their carriage to drive to Saint-Cloud, a dense crowd which packed the Place du Carrousel made their departure impossible.

"*Gros cochon* (fat pig)" Louis' subjects shouted at him. "You won't leave Paris until you give us a constitution!"

The Queen put her head through the carriage window and pleaded, "Quiet! You're frightening the children!" For, terrified by the howling mob milling about the vehicle, Thérèse and Charles had burst into hysterical tears. At that, the people turned their fury on her. "You foreign hussy! What right have you to give orders?"

For two terrible hours the ruling family of France sat suffering in their coach while Lafayette and his militia tried to clear a passageway for them through the crowd. Finally they were forced to give up their journey. They went back into the palace, where Marie Antoinette turned furiously on the Marquis, whom she considered to be a traitor to his class. Hadn't Lafayette, an aristocrat, brought back from America these frightful ideas of liberty and democracy that had contaminated the French people?

"You're always talking about the United States and praising the American people," the Queen accused him. "Now you see what a French revolution is like!"

* * * *

A chambermaid reported to the National Assembly, as the States-General had become on leaving Versailles and following the King to Paris, that she had seen the Queen packing her diamonds. "The royal family is preparing to escape," the *femme de chambre* told them.

So Lafayette, on orders from the Assembly, doubled his guards about the Tuileries. But throughout the day of June 20, 1791, things there went on as usual. That Monday morning, the King worked at his forge; the Dauphin played with his pets. After lunch, the Queen took Madame Royale for a walk in the garden. "Whatever happens tonight, you mustn't be frightened," Marie Antoinette told her daughter. But what was going to happen, she wouldn't say.

At eight o'clock that evening, the children were put to bed. Then the King and Queen dined with Monsieur and the Comtesse de Provence, who had come to say good-by. They were leaving that night for Brussels. The old aunts had slipped away to Italy four months ago.

When the Provences left at half-past ten, the King went through his usual couché (going-to-bed) ceremony. While his Gentlemen of the Bedchamber stood about in attendance and his valets, Hue and Cléry, undressed him, the Queen went to her daughter's room. She woke the Petite Madame by gently shaking her. "Get up and dress," Marie Antoinette whispered, and told Thérèse's *femme de chambre*, Antoinette Brunier, wife of Dr. Pierre Brunier, physician to the Children of France, to prepare for a journey.

The Queen then went to wake the Dauphin. "We've going where you'll see plenty of soldiers," she promised him.

Six-year-old Charles was very sleepy, but he loved to dress up in his uniform as honorary colonel of the Guards and wave his little sword, so he climbed out of bed and let Louise de Tourzel get him ready. But instead of his uniform, the boy was given a girl's frock and bonnet, while Thérèse was dressed like a peasant child in brown calico.

"I asked Charles what he thought we were going to do," his sister wrote, many years later. "He replied that we must be going to act in a play, since we were in costume."

In a way, they were. Fersen had coached the older members of the party in the parts they must play. He had secured a passport for the Marquise de Tourzel, who would pretend to be the Baronne de Korff, the widow of a Russian colonel returning to St. Petersburg with her children. Louis was to pass as the Baronne's manservant, Durand; Marie Antoinette, as the children's governess, Madame Rochet; Princesse Elisabeth, as her lady's maid, Rosalie.

By half-past ten, everyone except the King was ready. Six hundred soldiers guarded the Tuileries. In every corridor of the palace there were sentries. But Marie Antoinette led her children and Madame de Tourzel safely by them, down to a livery-stable cab, waiting in the Cour des Princes. On the box sat Count Fersen, disguised as a hack driver.

The Queen saw her children and their governess into the cab, which then drove off, while she slipped back into the palace. So as not to arouse the guards' suspicions, it had been arranged that the rest of the family should come out and find their ways separately to the fiacre, which was to wait for them where the Rue St. Honoré crossed the Rue de l'Echelle, several blocks away.

After an hour's anxious waiting, Thérèse noticed a woman walking around the carriage and peering in. Had they been discovered? The little girl's heart almost stopped beating. Then Fersen opened the door, and, to her joy, Aunt Babet jumped into the hack. In her haste, she stepped on Charles, hidden under Madame de Tourzel's skirts. "*Hss!*" his sister warned him. To Thérèse's relief, her brother kept quiet.

The tense little group waited again, for an hour and a half, in an agony of suspense, wondering what could have happened to Louis and Marie Antoinette. "Monsieur de Fersen played his part well, chatting with the other hack drivers and offering them tobacco from his pouch," wrote Louise de Tourzel. "I was trembling, although I tried to appear calm, assuring the children there was nothing to fear."

The long delay was owing to the fact that the King's couché lasted longer than usual. Because Lafayette was present, any appearance of haste must be avoided. As calmly as if nothing unusual were happening, Louis knelt at his bedside with his chaplain and said his prayers. Tonight, he seemed to need God's help with a great many problems. It was eleven o'clock before Hue and Cléry put His Majesty to bed, his candles were snuffed out, and he was left alone in the darkness.

The instant the door closed behind his two valets, Louis jumped out of bed and fled barefoot, in his nightshirt, into his son's room, where the clothes provided for him by Fersen were hidden.

Fifteen minutes later, disguised as the Baronne de Korff's servant, the King left by the Pavillon de l'Horloge, the main entrance to the Tuileries, mingling, unrecognized, with the courtiers who had attended his couché. But after Louis safely reached the cab in the Rue de l'Echelle, there was another wait of a half hour before Marie Antoinette arrived, for, while crossing the dark Place du Carrousel, she was overtaken by the Marquis de Lafayette, driving home. The Queen, terrified, squeezed herself against a wall. Lafayette's coach passed so close to her she could have reached out and touched its wheels. But thanks to the darkness, the Marquis didn't see Marie Antoinette, and after wasting twenty minutes wandering about confused in the maze of little streets, she finally found the fiacre.

When all the royal family had somehow been stuffed into the cab, Fersen mounted the box, whipped up his hired nags, and they started across Paris. The Queen's elegant Swedish friend was not used to driving a carriage. His coachman always did that, so Axel lost his way several times. It was two o'clock in the morning, not midnight, as they had planned, before they reached the gates of Paris. Two precious hours were gone.

6

FIVE DAYS IN JUNE

THE FIRST PART of the journey, as far as Châlons, had been carefully planned by Marie Antoinette and Count Axel von Fersen. Up to that point, for fear of attracting attention, no military escort was to be provided. After that, at Pont de Somme-Vesle, ten miles beyond Châlons, the King had arranged for a relay of troops, the Marquis François de Bouillé's cavalry, to begin to appear.

The two *femmes de chambre*, Madame Brunier and Madame de Neuville, were to go ahead in a cabriolet and join the royal family at Bondy. Meanwhile, a huge green-and-yellow traveling carriage, called a berlin, had been specially built for their journey, under orders from Fersen. It was upholstered in white velvet and loaded with every comfort imaginable—food, linen, silver, wine, even a toilet. This luxurious vehicle was to be driven by his coachmen to the Saint-Martin gate of Paris. There, the five members of the royal family and the Marquise de Tourzel would change into it from their hired hack.

When the cab reached the Porte-Saint-Martin, Fersen drew up beside the berlin, waiting on the Metz road, and the whole party climbed into it. Abandoning the fiacre, the Swedish count mounted to the driver's seat of the coach and cracked his whip at the horses. In a half hour, the fugitives reached Bondy, where the King's bodyguards, Valory, Moustier, and Malden, already in the saddle, and the Queen's two maids, seated in their yellow cabriolet, were waiting before the posthouse.

Having superintended the changing of the horses, six for the berlin, one for the cabriolet, Fersen turned over their reins to the first relay, hired coachmen and postilions, for here at Bondy he was to leave the others, take the Flanders road, and rejoin them on the Franco-Belgium frontier at Montmédy. He would be seeing Marie Antoinette again in a few days. "*Au revoir*, Madame de Korff!" Alex called out gaily as the two carriages drove off, escorted by their guards on horseback.

Everything was going splendidly. By the time dawn came, the royal refugees were well on their journey. The green-and-yellow berlin, preceded by the light, two-wheeled cabriolet, had reached open country. After their long imprisonment in the Tuileries, spied on every minute, it was heavenly to look out at these peaceful farms they were passing and feel free again.

"Remember, if anyone asks you, you're the Baronne de Korff's little girls," Mama said. "Thérèse, you're her daughter Amelie, and Charles, Amelie's sister Aglae. You're a *girl,* Charles, not a boy. Don't forget!"

"We won't," the children promised.

After driving through Meaux at six o'clock, Louis, who loved his food and his sleep, suggested they unpack the picnic baskets that Fersen had provided. Chicken bones and empty wine bottles were tossed out of the coach window, after which Papa showed Thérèse and Charles their route to the frontier on a map he had brought along.

"Beyond Châlons, we've nothing to fear," Louise de Tourzel, in her memoirs, quotes the King as saying, "for we're to be met at Somme-Vesle by the first detachment of troops."

But, shortly after, the heavy berlin broke down. New though the coach was, it was so overloaded with baggage that the traces gave way. Two hours were spent in repairs. It was four o'clock, Tuesday afternoon, before the travelers reached Châlons. They should have been there by midday.

Tired from sitting so long in the crowded carriage, Louis got out at the posthouse, while the horses were being changed, for a friendly chat with the bystanders about their crops. Curious people crowded about the huge, gaudy coach with so much luggage. Who could these wealthy folks be? But Madame de Tourzel says, "We passed Châlons without being recognized." The party was allowed to go on.

Everyone in the berlin was happy and chatting gaily. Rattling along at a steady eight miles an hour, they had covered a hundred miles since leaving Paris without being stopped. They felt their troubles were over. Now it was only ten more miles to Pont de Somme-Vesle, where the Duc Gabriel de Choiseul's cavalry, the first of their military escort, was waiting. After that, all the way to the border fortress of Montmédy, they would have the protection of troops. But when the coach stopped in Somme-Vesle, and Louis looked out, except for the hostlers at the relay station, no one was in sight. Choiseul and his men, after waiting for several hours, had decided the King must have changed his mind and was not coming. They returned to Varennes by a short cut through the woods. The berlin reached Somme-Vesle an hour after the dragoons left.

"That's odd! It must be at Sainte-Ménehould we were supposed to meet Choiseul," Louis said, and he ordered his postilions to drive on. At eight o'clock, Tuesday night, they drew up before the relay station at Sainte-Ménehould to change their tired horses. Again there was no one to be seen—especially not a soldier. The road was deserted.

Louis, putting his head out of the coach to ask, "This is Sainte-Ménehould, isn't it?" was recognized by the owner of the relay station, an ardent revolutionary. Taking from his pocket some paper money with the King's picture on it, Jean-Baptiste Drouet compared the face on the currency with the one at the window of the berlin. "It's him, all right!" he muttered to himself, and rushed to the mayor with his suspicions.

"The King is trying to escape and seek refuge among the enemies of France," Drouet told the town official. "He must be arrested!"

Sainte-Ménehould was soon in an uproar. Drouet and his friend, Guillaume, were sent galloping after the two slow-moving vehicles that had left a half hour ago, flanked by mounted guards. The two horsemen followed the route taken by the fugitives, which climbed through the Argonne forest as far as Clermont. There the main road went on east, to Verdun and Metz; another turned north, in the direction of Varennes.

Drouet was about to gallop on, straight to Metz, where he assumed the King was going. It was pure chance that, at this point, he and Guillaume met Drouet's postilions, who, having driven the berlin to Clermont, were returning with their horses to Sainte-Ménehould.

"We overheard the fat man in the coach talking with the riders who replaced us," one of them said on being questioned. "He told them to take the road to Varennes."

Drouet wheeled his horse to the left. The two local men, knowing the Argonne region well, took a short cut through the forest and reached Varennes by eleven o'clock, ten minutes before the green-and-yellow berlin.

Varennes, built on the slope of a hill, consists of an upper and lower town, separated by the Aire River. Drouet and

Guillaume stopped in the upper town, at the Bras d'Or (Golden Arm), an inn situated on the street leading down to the bridge. Dashing into the tavern, Drouet demanded of its owner, "Jean Leblanc, are you a good patriot? You are! Then warn everyone in town that the King is approaching Varennes, trying to escape from France. He must be stopped. Quick! Barricade the bridge!"

Material for this was right on hand. Two big farm wagons loaded with lumber blocked the narrow bridge over the Aire when the royal coach came to a halt in the upper part of town. The race from Sainte-Ménehould had been won by Drouet, but the tired travelers in the green-and-yellow berlin didn't know this. It was dark and they woke from their naps, glad to be in Varennes, only twenty miles from Montmédy.

Now came a nasty surprise. On the outskirts of Varennes, where the next relay had been promised them, there were no horses. Thinking that the relay must be waiting for them at the Hôtel du Grand Monarque, across the bridge in the lower town, they drove down the steep street leading to the river, right into the trap Drouet had set for them. For hardly had the coach reached the Bras d'Or Inn, beyond an archway under Saint-Gengoult church which spanned the road, than cries of "Stop!" were heard. Hands grasped the horses' bridles. "Who are you?" voices demanded.

"Madame de Korff and her daughters, going to Frankfurt."

"Show us your passports."

The papers were produced, examined, and found to be in order. Forgetting that she was supposed to be a mere governess, Marie Antoinette spoke sharply through the carriage window, "That's enough now! We're in a hurry, don't delay us." At that, a lantern was flashed in at her, lighting up the children's frightened faces. By this time, a crowd had gathered around the carriage. The King's bodyguards ordered the postilions to drive on. But Drouet, pointing his pistol at the coach, shouted, "Move and I'll fire!"

Jean-Baptiste Sauce, a grocer and mayor of the town, came up to the berlin. "I cannot endorse your passports until morning," he told the travelers, "but I'll gladly put you up for the night."

Now was the time to have used force. A few shots from his bodyguards over the heads of the crowd might have scattered them. Instead, Louis good-naturedly yielded to the threats of the crowd and climbed out of the berlin. Holding Thérèse and Charles by the hand, their father led the ladies into Sauce's grocery store, which was on their left, down the road.

Sauce took his guests upstairs and into a bedroom so small the eight people could hardly crowd into it. There were some cane chairs and, in one corner of the room, a four-poster on which Madame Royale and the Dauphin were placed to rest. Tired out, the children fell asleep on the grocer's bed, watched over by Madame de Tourzel.

The royal family were prisoners again, only twenty miles short of their goal. Marie Antoinette and her sister-in-law Elisabeth sat sunk in despair. But Louis could always eat. He asked for a bottle of wine and some cheese, and chatted with Sauce, hoping to win him over.

The grocer wasn't sure Drouet was right, that this was the royal family, for Louis kept insisting he was the Baronne de Korff's servant. Fearing that they had made themselves ridiculous by stopping ordinary travelers, Sauce went out and came back with a local judge, Jacques Destez, who had seen the King several times during a visit to Paris.

Destez gave one glance at the fat man. "*Bonjour*, Sire!" he exclaimed. After that, further denial was useless. "Yes," Louis admitted, "I'm your king."

How horrible! But desperate as their situation was, it was not utterly hopeless. Choiseul, lost for hours in the woods after leaving Somme-Vesle, now came galloping into Varennes with his forty hussars. Drawing his sword, he forced his way through the crowd that surrounded the grocery store and reached the upstairs room where the refugees were huddled.

"Where is the Marquis de Bouillé?" the colonel asked.

Nobody knew, but surely he was on his way to Varennes. Two ancient cannon from the Hôtel de Ville had been dragged down the hill to a position where they commanded the bridge. Old as they were, they were still capable of barring the road leading up from the lower town against any possible rescuers. But when the troops, waiting on the other side of the river, at the Hôtel du Grand Monarque, to escort Louis XVI on to Montmédy, found they could not get to him over the barricaded bridge in the face of cannon fire, they had ridden off to tell the Marquis de Bouillé, commander of the Metz garrison, of their unsuccessful attempts to reach the King. From the commotion the soldiers could see going on across the river, they feared that His Majesty had been arrested.

General Bouillé was at Stenay, a village south of Montmédy, only sixteen miles away. With a larger force than his, enough soldiers to scatter the mob before Sauce's house, Choiseul assured the King, Bouillé would surely hurry to his rescue, and reach Varennes by four or five o'clock the next morning.

But Wednesday morning came, four o'clock passed, and Bouillé did not come. Instead, the ringing of the tocsin, the general alarm, from the bell tower of the church, brought the peasants hurrying into Varennes from their outlying farms. By five o'clock, a crowd of several thousand people had collected outside Sauce's shop. Another hour of suspense dragged by . . . and there came, not Bouillé, but Romeuf and Bayon, two deputies from the Assembly, bringing with them an order for the King to return to Paris.

One hope remained, to gain time and linger until Bouillé, notified of the King's arrest, could reach Varennes with his troops. "We must eat something before starting," Louis said to the deputies.

This much was allowed the royal family. They sat down to breakfast, and ate as slowly as possible–Bouillé, where was Bouillé? The people outside were shouting, "To Paris! To Paris!" Finally, no further delay was possible.

The King, with a resigned sigh, rose from the table. "Very well, let them harness the horses," he told Grocer Sauce.

At half-past seven in the morning, his sleepy son in his arms and his little daughter clutching tightly to his coat, Louis led the ladies down to the berlin and they started for Paris. A quarter of an hour later, the dragoons from Stenay galloped into Varennes. If the King could have delayed his departure that long, they might have saved him.

Unable to get over the barricaded bridge, protected by the cannon in the upper town, the dragoons rode along the east bank of the Aire, looking for a ford by which they could cross the stream. Unfortunately, the Marquis de Bouillé had remained in Stenay and left the rescue of the King up to his son Louis, who was unfamiliar with the Argonne region. Young Bouillé did not know that, several miles from Varennes, the road to Clermont, along which the royal family had been led away, crossed to the east bank of the Aire–that is to say, the side on which his hussars were at present. They could have caught up to the procession without fording the stream.

"If Monsieur de Bouillé had not entrusted the mission to a youth of twenty, the Revolution might have turned out very differently . . ." comments Madame de Tourzel sadly. For, strangely enough, Louis Bouillé never thought of consulting a map. Seeing no way to cross the Aire River, he and his cavalry wheeled their horses around and returned to Stenay, leaving Louis XVI to his fate.

* * * *

Begun that unfortunate Wednesday morning, the journey back to Paris was a dreadful ordeal for Thérèse and her family. She sat bolt upright, her hand in Aunt Babet's, staring out of the coach window with big, frightened eyes.

The heat of the day and the dust from the road were bad enough. Added to these discomforts as the carriage crawled along through clouds of dust, under the scorching June sun, was the fatigue of the exhausted occupants, who had not been to bed since they left the Tuileries two days ago. But even more crushing was their feeling of disgrace at being led captive a second time to Paris. The escort surrounding their carriage changed continually, those who dropped out being replaced by hordes of drunken peasants from each village through which they passed. So as not to hear the insults hurled at them, the weary, perspiring travelers shut the windows of the coach and rode along, almost suffocated by the heat. They had driven the hundred and twenty-five miles from Paris to Varennes in twenty-one hours. The trip back lasted four days.

Châlons, where they stopped Wednesday evening, provided the only night's rest since they had left Paris. The next day, Thursday, fresh insults awaited them. A man stuck his head in the carriage window and actually spit in the King's face.

At Épernay, the prisoners were joined by three more deputies, sent by the Assembly to travel with them the rest of the way. Maubourg climbed into the cabriolet with the Queen's maids, but Aunt Babet must take Thérèse on her lap, his mother hold Charles, to make room for Pétion and Barnave

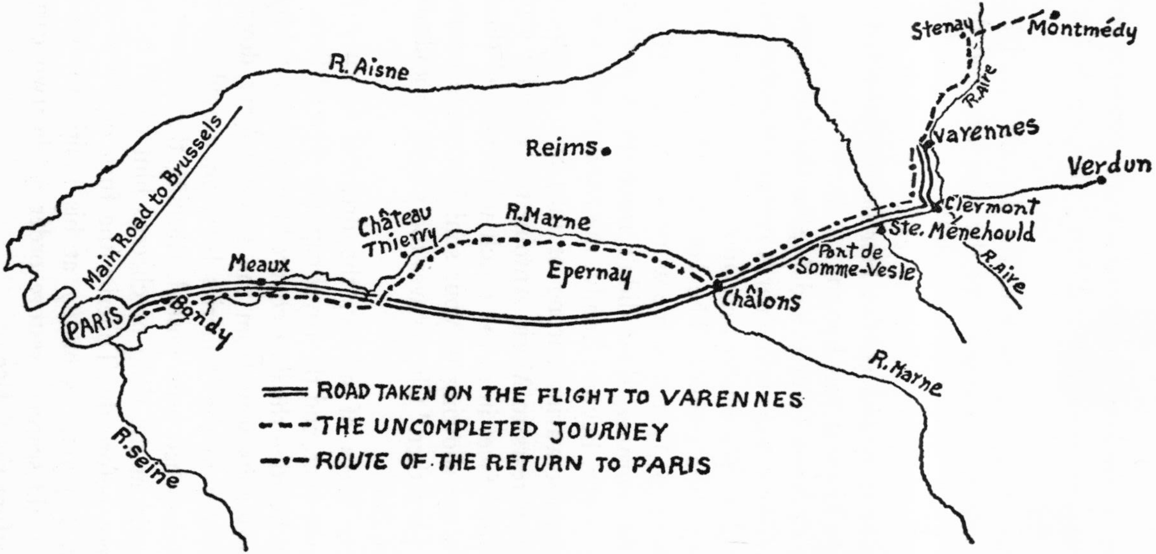

Map of the route followed by the Bourbons in their flight to Varennes—and of their unhappy return to Paris.

in the berlin, where now eight people were packed together. "All of us covered with sweat and dust," Madame de Tourzel wrote.

The Queen refused to speak to the deputies, until Pétion maliciously asked her the name of the man who had driven them out of Paris. "Wasn't he a Swede?"

"I'm not in the habit of asking cabdrivers their names," Marie Antoinette replied coldly. Her heart contracted with fear. So they knew it was Fersen!

Through Château-Thierry and Meaux the sad procession passed, the King's three bodyguards chained together on the top of the berlin. The nearer they approached Paris, the more hostile became the crowds. The last day of their journey, Saturday, June 25, 1791, was the worst of all. Leaving Meaux at six in the morning, they didn't reach Paris until eight o'clock that night. Beyond Bondy, the royal family was met by a jeering, fist-waving throng of men and women, who brought angry tears to Marie Antoinette's eyes by shoving their hate-filled faces in at the coach windows and shouting at her, "No use showing us your son! Everyone knows fat Louis isn't his father." Charles was too young to understand, but Thérèse did.

After four days of misery, the dreadful journey from Varennes was over, and the royal captives entered Paris. Not a sound was heard as the dust-covered berlin, followed by the cabriolet, made its way from the Etoile barrier down the Champs-Elysées to the Tuileries between crowds of silent people. Notices had been posted, warning that anyone who shouted insults at the King or cheered him would be hung. Nevertheless, before the Tuileries the fury of the populace broke out. Lafayette, shouting at his militia to use their bayonets, could scarcely restore order as the two carriages drew up before the palace.

The door of the berlin opened. The King and Queen

stepped out. Then came the children, their aunt, and governess. At eight o'clock on Saturday night, the royal family, half-dead from heat and fatigue, disappeared into the palace-prison they had left, so full of hope, at midnight on the previous Monday, only five days ago.

As soon as the door closed behind them, shutting out the roar of the mob, the Queen, no longer "that arrogant Austrian" but a pale, shattered woman, flung herself exhausted into a chair and tossed aside her hat.

"Mama, what makes you look so different?" Thérèse exclaimed. Then she knew. Marie Antoinette would never need to use powder on her coiffure again. During the drive back to Paris, her hair had turned white.

7

NO LONGER FREE

If only by being late they hadn't given Choiseul the idea they weren't coming. . . . If only Louis hadn't climbed out of the berlin and shown himself so often. . . . If only Fersen hadn't furnished them with such a luxurious coach that it attracted attention at every stop. . . . Perhaps that had been their worst blunder, for the Comte de Provence traveling with the Comte d'Avaray, and his wife Josephine with her friend, Marguerite Gourbillon, escaped separately, in two humble hackney cabs, and reached Brussels safely. But then the ease with which the King's brother was able to leave France caused people to say that Monsieur must be in cahoots with the Revolutionary leaders.

Well, here the royal family was, back in the Tuileries, and the Assembly was determined that they should not escape again. The guards at the palace were doubled. Sentries, wearing on their hats red, white, and blue cockades, the Revolutionary colors, were to be seen everywhere, even on the roof.

Charles, a cheerful little extrovert, soon recovered from the horror of those dreadful five days. But returning from Varennes, Thérèse, a high-strung child, had again seen a man's head borne on the end of a pike, that of the Comte de Dampierre who had tried to come to their defense. She dreamed of it often and woke from the nightmare sobbing, "Mama!" But, invariably, it was Aunt Babet or Madame de Tourzel, who, rushing in, rocked the frightened girl in her arms until she stopped crying.

To the half-forgotten memory of their drive from Versailles to the Tuileries was added the horrors of the journey from Varennes. "Madame Royale was never to forget what she had seen," wrote Pauline de Tourzel. "Always a serious little girl, after that, she seemed to be old for twelve and far too nervous for a girl her age."

Even the children realized that the Tuileries was now a prison. Louise de Tourzel tells how the royal family was compelled to stay indoors, because the Assembly had opened the palace grounds to the public:

> The Queen was forced, at the end of July, to give up her walks. She had gone for a breath of fresh air with Madame Royale to the Dauphin's little garden, situated at the end of the terrace. She was grossly insulted [by the crowd]. Four of the guards came to her rescue. They surrounded Marie Antoinette and her daughter, and brought them back to the palace. The Queen refused after that to go out again.

But the King told the Assembly he was happy to have the people of Paris use his garden. So the government asked another favor of the feeble monarch. On September 10, 1791, Louis XVI, much against his will, was forced to sign a paper and France had a constitution. Still, the King's repeated concessions didn't satisfy the radical element that had gained control of the Assembly. The extreme Left, the Jacobin party, under the leadership of Maximilien de Robespierre, wanted to have a republic.

It was then that a new Marie Antoinette, her spirit stiffened by adversity, emerged. When Thérèse went down to see her mother these days, she usually found her writing letters. They were appeals for help. All of Europe was shocked by what had happened in France. The French Revolution was a threat to absolute monarchy throughout Europe, and in August, 1791, Austria and Prussia mobilized their armies to come to the rescue of the French king. Because only an outside force could aid them now, Marie Antoinette was writing to her brother, the Emperor Leopold of Austria, and to King William of Prussia, imploring them to hurry and save Louis XVI and his family.

She also wrote, in invisible ink and cipher, to Axel von Fersen, in Brussels. He wanted to return to France, and be near her, but his part in the flight to Varennes was known, and, terrified at what would happen to him, if he were seen in Paris, she begged Axel not to come. Instead, Marie Antoinette sent him a gold ring on which were engraved three fleurs-de-lis (lilies) and the words, *Lâche qui les abandone* (Shame on him who forsakes them). She wore the ring for two days, and kissed it many times, before dispatching it to him.

Wearing her ring on his little finger, Fersen replied "I live only to serve you." And he was willing to risk his life to prove it. He had thought of a new plan of escape. This time, the royal family must flee by ship to England.

Such a matter was too dangerous to entrust to writing. So, eight months after the drive to Varennes, on February 13, 1792, the Swedish Count, disguised in a red wig, arrived in Paris. He waited at the house of a friend, Baron de Goguelat, in the Rue Pelletier, until eight o'clock at night. Then he went to the Tuileries. Axel was known by sight to many of the court officials and servants, but the darkness hid him. He managed to slip past the sentries into the Cour des Princes. Knowing of an unguarded door that led to the Queen's apartment, and having a key to it, he let himself into the palace.

Fersen was tiptoeing down a dimly-lighted corridor, patrolled like every foot of the palace by guards, when he heard steps approaching. A sentry! He dodged back into the shadows, but too late, it was a young girl and she had seen him.

"Oh!" Madame Royale let out a scream. Axel put his hand over her mouth. "*Hss!* Don't give me away!" he pleaded.

In his red wig, Thérèse didn't know him. "Who are you?" She gazed up at the odd-looking stranger with frightened eyes.

"Axel von Fersen. I'm here to see your parents. There's a price on my head, little one, if I'm caught they'll shoot me. Thérèse, you're a big girl, thirteen. Can you keep a secret? Promise me that you won't tell anyone you've seen me."

"I promise."

"Thanks, dear!" Leaning down, Fersen gave Madame Royale a hug and a swift kiss. Then he disappeared down the hall.

That evening, the Queen sent word to her ladies that she was ill. No one was to come near her, except a trusted maid who brought her food. For twenty-four hours Marie Antoinette and Axel were alone. What happened during that time, no one knows—only that it was six in the evening of the following day before the Queen told her husband of Fersen's arrival. Then the King came down to his wife's apartment and talked with the Swedish Count. But he would not agree to another attempt to escape.

"Louis has promised [the Assembly] not to run away again," Axel noted regretfully in his diary, "and he is such an honorable man."

Next day, the Queen's eyes were red from weeping, and Fersen was gone. Besides Papa, only Thérèse knew that the Count had been in Paris. And nothing could have induced her to tell.

* * * *

Louis XVI still had the right to veto under the constitution. A devout Catholic, he refused to sign a bill exiling to the penal colonies all priests who had not sworn loyalty to the government. So on June 20, 1792, the anniversary of his flight to Varennes, when the King of France, disguised as a servant, had tried to run away from his own subjects, the Assembly sent twenty thousand rioters, wearing the bonnet rouge and armed with pikes, to break into the Tuileries and throw a scare into Fat Louis, to prevent him from showing such independence again.

Hearing shouts of "Down with Monsieur Veto!" in the courtyard, and the noise of smashing woodwork as axes broke down the palace door, the King met the ruffians that swarmed into the Tuileries with calm courage. Forced into a bay window with his sister Elisabeth, he was kept a prisoner there for four hours. Louis refused to make any promises. But he good-naturedly put on a bonnet rouge (the red cap adopted by the French revolutionists because it was worn by the Greek galley slaves after their emancipation) handed to him by one of the crowd.

Meanwhile, in another room of the palace, Marie Antoinette and her children were facing the intruders from behind a large table the guardsmen had dragged before them as a barricade. As the door was broken down, and the crowd poured in, Thérèse shrank terrified against her mother. It was like that dreadful time when they had stood together on the balcony at Versailles—a lot of wild-eyed, ragged men and women filing by on the other side of the table, shouting insults and threatening them with pistols and knives. So as not to see their hate-filled faces, the frightened girl hid her face in Marie Antoinette's gown.

Pauline de Tourzel, in her *Souvenirs de Quarante Ans*, tells what happened next. A man asked, "How old is your daughter?"

PLAN OF THE TUILERIES AND ITS SURROUNDINGS IN 1792

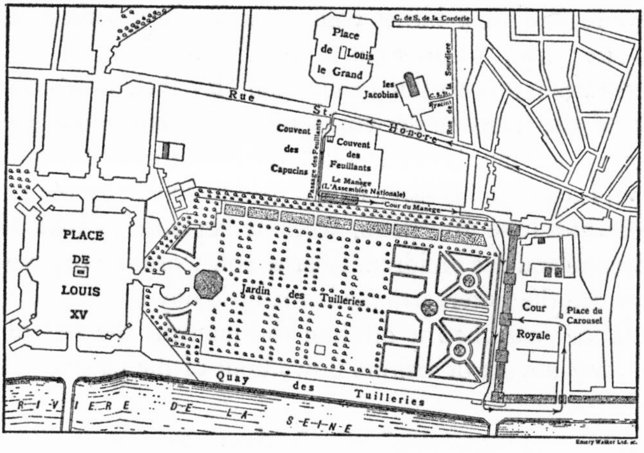

Place de Louis XV: the present Place de la Concorde, scene of the guilliotine, where Louis XVI, Marie Antoinette, and Princesse Elisabeth were beheaded.

Place du Carrousel: Napoleon's Arc du Carrousel (spelled "Carousel" on this old map) stands today on the site of the Cour Royale, main entrance to the Tuileries. The palace was burned in May, 1871, during riots after the Franco-Prussian War. Across from the Place du Carrousel is the Louvre, not shown on the map.

Place de Louis le Grand: now the Place Vendôme.

Le Manège: former riding-school of the Tuileries (spelled "Tuilleries"), used by the National Assembly as a meeting hall. It stood on the spot where the Rue Castiglione (the former Passage des Feuillants) joins the Rue de Rivoli. At the time of the French Revolution, neither of these streets existed. The great gardens of the convents and the private houses of the Rue Saint-Honoré stretched right up to the line now occupied by the Rue de Rivoli, and were separated from the Tuileries only by a long, narrow courtyard, known as the Cour du Manège. The arrows show the route taken by the mob, when they invaded the palace on June 20, 1792.

Couvent des Feuillants: where the royal family spent the nights of August 10, 11, 12, 1792, while the Assembly decided their fate.

"Old enough to be shocked at what she has seen," the Queen replied in a bitter voice that Pauline, writing sixty years later, said, "I still seem to hear."

After stealing everything they could lay their hands on, the dregs of the Paris underworld finally streamed out of the Tuileries, leaving broken windows and smashed furniture behind. Louis and his sister Babet, held prisoners by the rabble all that hot June afternoon, were at last able to join Marie Antoinette and the children. Charles still wore the red woolen liberty cap the rioters had made the little boy put on his head. His mother snatched it off him the moment the last of the long, dirty stream of visitors flowed out of the palace.

* * * *

An Austrian-Prussian army was invading France along the Moselle, under the Duke of Brunswick; and Axel von Fersen, with the best of intentions, now did Marie Antoinette more harm than had any of her enemies. He wrote a dispatch he had Brunswick sign, warning the Revolutionary leaders that Paris would be burned to the ground if any harm came to the royal family.

This was enough to unite the French against the foreign foe. The enemy was marching on Paris, and little encouragement was needed to stir up a fresh mob against the feeble King and his arrogant Austrian wife. Six hundred ardent democrats had arrived from Marseilles, dragging their cannon all the way and singing, "*Allons, enfants de la Patrie!*" Rouget de Lisle's new marching song, "La Marseillaise," would become the hymn of the Revolution. With the help of these toughs from the south of France, the Jacobins in the Assembly felt themselves to be strong enough to storm the Tuileries again.

Seven weeks separated the two attacks. At dawn on August

10, 1792, Marie Antoinette and her daughter, Thérèse, stood at the window of the Tuileries, listening to the tocsin. It reminded them of Varennes. In every belfry the church bells were ringing, calling all of Paris to arms.

At six o'clock, the Queen urged her husband to go down and review the troops who were to defend the palace and give them courage. A few fiery words were needed. But none of the royal family had slept much that night. The King had not gone to bed, only dozed a little in a chair. So when he went down to the Cour des Princes and faced the National Guard, the militia saw, not a resolute leader like Napoleon, who would have inspired them, but a ridiculous-looking stout man, bewildered and disheveled. Louis XVI never looked less royal. As he waddled past the massed ranks of soldiers, the men who were to risk their lives for him thought, "*Le Gros Cochon* (the fat pig)! Must we die for such a fellow?"

A few stammered words and Louis fled back into the palace to face his wife, who had been watching him from a balcony with the two children. Marie Antoinette was sick with disappointment. But Thérèse ran to throw her arms about dear Papa. So bedraggled! So forlorn! She loved him with all her heart. All the more now that people were being "rude" to him.

Outside, in the Carrousel, the crowd was growing denser. The men from Marseilles and their cannon had arrived. Since the National Guard, in spite of their promise to defend the palace, were frankly deserting, Comte Roederer warned the King that the Tuileries could not long be defended. He urged him to take refuge with his family in the big oval riding hall of the palace, situated to the north of the gardens, where the Assembly was meeting.

"Only among the deputies will you be safe," Louise de Tourzel quotes Roederer as saying. "Your Majesty, there isn't a minute to lose. In another quarter of an hour, you won't be able to leave the Tuileries."

The King rose wearily from his chair. "All right, we will go," he said.

Marie Antoinette cried out in protest. Putting her arms around the Dauphin, the child she loved more than her own life, she pleaded, "Louis, are you mad? If you leave here, you'll be giving up your throne. I don't care about us, but don't abandon the Tuileries, I beseech you, for the sake of Charles, France's future king!"

But her husband had made up his slow mind. He continued down the stairs, past the guards, who looked at him in amazement—a coward who surrendered before the first shot was fired—and out of the palace. What could the rest of them do but follow him? So after the King came the Queen, holding her two children by the hand, Aunt Babet, the Princesse de Lamballe, and Madame de Tourzel.

It was the duty of the governess of the Children of France never to leave them. So Pauline de Tourzel tells how the Marquise accompanied the royal family, leaving her seventeen-year-old daughter behind. "I was forbidden to follow Mama. They left in such haste that she only had time to kiss me. . . . From the window of the King's bedroom we watched them cross, on foot, the garden of the Tuileries. It was a sight to break your heart."

According to Pauline's mother, Louise de Tourzel, only the adults "walked sadly." The sudden relief from their long confinement indoors made the children gay. Thérèse and Charles ran ahead, shuffling their feet through the dead leaves on the gravel path that had dropped from the chestnut trees in the park. "It's only August, the leaves are falling early this year," Papa remarked, as casually as if they were taking a pleasant family stroll.

None of them realized how fatal that short walk would be. "We will soon be back," were Marie Antoinette's last words to those who remained at the Tuileries. She believed it, probably, and so did the others. But, as Madame de Tourzel says, "Only one of them was to see the Tuileries again."

* * * *

The royal family was homeless now and a nuisance to the Assembly. When the King and Queen appeared in the crowded riding hall, asking for protection, the deputies did not know what to do with them. Finally, a place was found for the prisoners to sit in the press box, a grated cage unbearably hot and so small the seven people could hardly squeeze into it. During the next twelve hours the Tuileries was looted and partly burned by the mob. The guards and the royal servants were butchered. Louis and his family could not go back there. So, at night, they were sent to sleep in an empty building nearby, the former Couvent des Feuillants, where, in four dirty cells, some cots were placed.

For three ghastly days, huddled together in that hot reporter's cage, the ruling family of France listened to their fate being decided. Misfortune failed to curb Louis' appetite. Several times a day he asked for food and wine, and ate heartily. Then, while the debate went on that cost him his throne, the King napped for several hours, snoring loudly. Marie Antoinette looked at her husband in disgust. Seated in the rear of the box, her son on her lap, she ate hardly anything.

Then, blessed relief, their sufferings seemed to be coming to an end, for the Assembly got around to discussing what to do with Fat Louis. It was finally decided to send him and his family to the Temple, the former residence of the Comte d'Artois that, after the King's brother fled from France, the city of Paris had confiscated. At six in the evening, on August 13, 1792, two carriages came to take them there. The royal family crowded into the first one with the Princesse de

Lamballe, Madame de Tourzel and her daughter, for, to Thérèse's joy, "sister Pauline," who had escaped from the Tuileries, was going with them.

The trip took three hours, the coachman having been told to drive slowly so that all of Paris could enjoy the sight of "l'Autrichienne" being carted off to jail. Louise de Tourzel wrote, "Crossing the Place Vendôme, the carriage stopped to let the King see the statue of Louis XIV overturned two days ago, as had been all the other statues of our kings." It was nine o'clock and dark before they reached the Temple palace, where Marie Antoinette had often been entertained by her brother-in-law.

Led at first into Artois' town house, the King and Queen naturally assumed this was where they would live. Louis bustled about, assigning to Aunt Babet, the Princesse de Lamballe, the Marquise de Tourzel, and Pauline their rooms. It was not until after supper that they had a rude awakening. "The Dauphin, exhausted with fatigue, fell asleep while I was trying to feed him a bowl of soup," Madame de Tourzel wrote, "and I asked to be allowed to take the tired little boy to his room and put him to bed."

"Come, I'll show you the way," said Pierre Manuel, the city official who had brought them to the Temple. Snatching up the sleeping Charles, Manuel went off with him in his arms—but not up the stairs to the palace bedrooms, to the consternation of the others.

Where was the man taking him? The Dauphin's governess and his frightened relatives "were in a panic," Louise de Tourzel remembered, as they hurried after Manuel carrying the child, along endless vaulted corridors and down steep winding stairs that finally brought them to the Temple courtyard. There two stone towers rose, a small one leaning against a tall, grim dungeon with a pointed roof and four peaked corner turrets. At the sight of them, a shudder went through Thérèse, the girl didn't know why. She longed to turn and run.

"You'll see," Mama was saying to Louise de Tourzel, "that's where they'll put us, in the Big Tower. I've always had a horror of that place. A thousand times I begged the Comte d'Artois to pull it down."

Charles, who liked the picturesque, medieval tower, had not done so, and it was too late now.

8

DEATH ONE BY ONE

IT WAS INDEED in the Big Tower that the royal family was to be imprisoned. "Didn't I tell you?" Marie Antoinette exclaimed. But first the square gray keep of the Knights Templar, with stone walls ten feet thick, and narrow, barred windows, must be made doubly secure. While a wall eighteen feet high was being built around the larger edifice, the prisoners were housed for two months in the Little Tower. Attached to the big dungeon, the smaller and lower building had been occupied by Jacques Berthélemy, archivist of the Templars, who was turned out.

The keeper of the archives had lived comfortably on two floors of the Little Tower. But they were cramped quarters for twelve people used to the great expanse of the Tuileries. On the second floor, cooped up in rooms fifteen feet square, Thérèse and her mother slept together; Charles with Madame de Tourzel; Aunt Babet with the Princesse de Lamballe. Pauline and the Queen's two maids were put in a tiny kitchen, next to the guardsroom, where the men's loud talking kept them awake most of the night. Above the ladies, in Berthélemy's sleeping quarters on the third floor (where Louis took down the archivist's pictures from the wall, so "my daughter should not see such indecent things"), the King was installed with his valets, Hue and Cléry.

The royal family was truly prisoners now—no letters, no visitors, not even newspapers. But they had one consolation, they had their devoted little court about them, consisting of the Princesse de Lamballe, the Marquise de Tourzel, Pauline, and a few faithful servants. The Temple prison was in charge of the Commune, the city government of Paris, and Madame Royale, writing of their imprisonment three years later, tells how nearly all of these last friends were taken away:

> On the night of August 19, six days after our arrival, an order came from the Commune to remove from the Temple all the people not of the royal family. The guards told us they would return after being questioned. We kissed them good-by, hoping to see them next day. But next day, we were told that they would not return and had been taken to La Force prison.

There had been a sad parting between Marie Antoinette and Louise de Lamballe—the young, Italian-born widow, who, having escaped to England, had returned to be with the Queen. Placing the Dauphin in his mother's arms, his governess describes how she ran from the room, "forcing myself not to look back at my dear little Prince. . . ." And, to the last minute, Thérèse and her "sister Pauline" clung to each other.

With the departure of these close friends went the royal family's final link with Versailles. François Hue was sent away, and the King was left with only one valet, Jean-Baptiste Cléry. The ladies would have to wait on themselves. For the hard work, the Commune supplied a man named Tison and his wife—a dirty, surly couple who were really spies.

Yet the prisoners were not utterly friendless. Louis Turgy, a former waiter at the Tuileries, had loyally followed them to the Temple. He worked in the kitchen, and on the days when Turgy went to market to buy food, he brought back news of the war. How to convey it to the prisoners was a problem. Even at meals, they were closely watched by the guards. But Princesse Elisabeth and Turgy invented a language of signs.

Charles, too young and talkative to be trusted, was not let in on the secret, but Thérèse was told by Aunt Babet how to interpret Turgy's hand signals. If, in the course of serving them, the waiter rubbed his right eye, the Duke of Brunswick was advancing. Did he scratch his ear? That was bad, the Allies were in retreat. But what the prisoners were eagerly watching for was to see Turgy stroke his hair with his right hand (the left one was reserved for adverse news), for that would mean the invading armies were approaching Paris and they would be rescued.

This hope was all they lived for now. And it was a completely false one. In fact, the nearer Brunswick got to Paris, the greater their danger grew, for, fearing that the city would be captured, the revolutionists butchered hundreds of persons accused of being accomplices of the invaders. Thérèse writes how she burst into tears on hearing a guard threaten her father. "Verdun has fallen, the last fortress on the road to Paris," the man said to Louis. "If the enemy get here, we'll all die, but you'll be the first one."

On September 3, 1792, Madame Royale, seated on a stool beside the table, was watching her parents playing trictrac, when they heard voices outside shouting Marie Antoinette's name. Cléry went to the window, to find out what was the matter. He later described in his memoirs how he stepped back in horror, on seeing what was down in the courtyard, on the end of a pike.

"What is it, Cléry?" Marie Antoinette asked. The valet says he could not answer her, but one of the guards did,

"Well, since you wish to know, go to the window and look out." Thérèse started to obey instead, but the jailer, stepping in front of the girl, pushed her back. "Not you, your mother," he said.

"Me? Why?" asked the Queen.

"It's Lamballe's head," the man informed her. "They want you to see it, our answer to Brunswick. You'd better show yourself, if you don't want them to come up here with it."

With a cry, Marie Antoinette fainted. While Louis and Elisabeth tried to revive her, Cléry tells how he quickly drew the curtain across the window so that Madame Royale should not see the rabble of drunken maniacs in the courtyard below, who had come to show her mother, on a pike, the still-bleeding head of her murdered friend.

Seventeen days later, Brunswick was defeated at Valmy by the army of the Republic, and with the retreat of the Allied armies back to Belgium went the royal family's last hope of being rescued. The fact that Paris was no longer threatened gave the revolutionists added confidence. On September 21, 1792, they announced the monarchy ended and France now a republic. They even took from Louis XVI his title. Because everyone in France was equal now, the former king was not to be addressed as Sire or Your Majesty in the future, but as Citizen Louis Capet, the family name of Hugh Capet, an early French king.

"Capet? Why call us that?" Louis exclaimed. "Our family name is Bourbon."

* * * *

On October 26, the alterations on the Big Tower being completed, the "Capet family" was moved into it. Their jailers occupied the first floor of the four identical stories. The former King and his son were lodged above them. A folding cot for Charles was placed in his father's room. Cléry slept in another room, close by. The ladies were put on the third floor. It consisted, like the others, of four small rooms. The first served as an antechamber, where guards remained on watch day and night, sleeping by turns on a folding cot. Above the King's room was the Queen's, with Thérèse's bed in one corner. Aunt Babet and the Tisons occupied the two remaining ones. But all of the royal family, as well as the Tisons and the guards, must use the Tower's only toilet in one of the corner turrets.

The fourth floor was empty. Above it, around the pointed roof of the Tower, ran a gallery where the prisoners were allowed to walk. A winding stairway, inside one of the turrets, led up to it. On each landing two thick doors, one of iron and the other of wood, fastened with bolts, locks, and chains, made escape impossible.

Back in the old days at Versailles, surrounded by a horde of courtiers and servants, the King and the Queen and their children had shared little family life. In this gloomy fortress, shut off from the outside world, their troubles drew the helpless people closer together. Mornings, Papa taught Charles Latin, history, and arithmetic, while Mama gave Thérèse singing, drawing, and Bible lessons. Before lunch, the whole family left the damp Tower, to go down and take a walk in the sunless courtyard, now closed in by a high wall. Charles flew his kite or played ball with Cléry, but it wasn't much fun with the soldiers, their guns loaded, watching them from the turrets in the wall. In the afternoon, Papa took a nap; Mama, Aunt Babet, and Thérèse did needlework; and after supper, when the children had been put to bed, Louis, his wife, and sister played backgammon or cards. So the days passed. But there were iron bars at the windows, and they had no privacy. The guards were always watching and listening.

December dragged around, and Madame Royale says, "An

PLAN OF THE TOWER OF THE TEMPLE

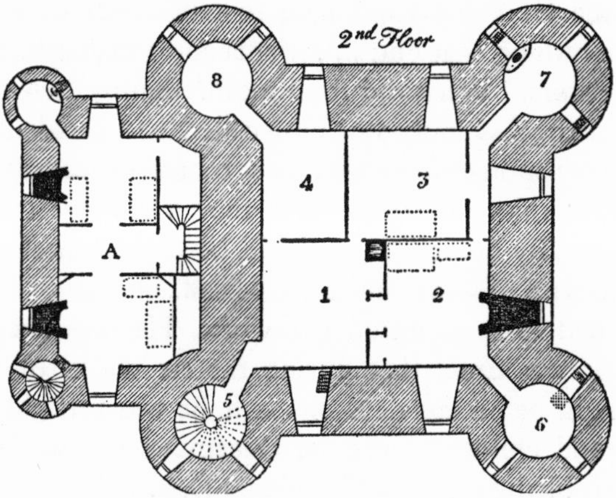

1—hall for the guards. 2—Chamber of the King and the Dauphin. 3—Cléry's room. 4—Diningroom. 5—Staircase. 6—Closet. 7—Water-closet. 8—Firewood.

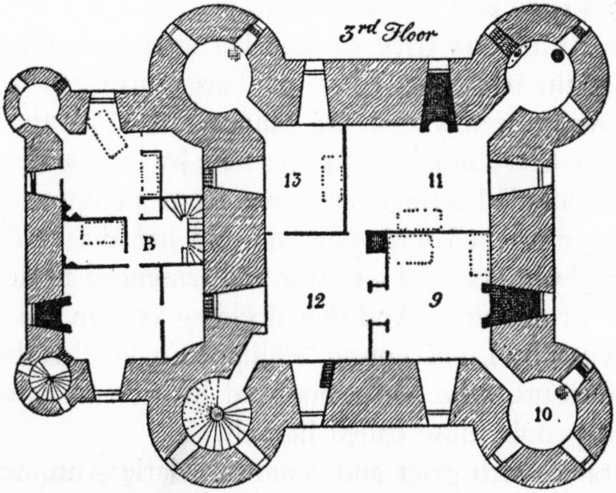

9—Chamber of the Queen and Madame Royale. 10—Their closet. 11—Princesse Elisabeth's room. 12—Hall for the guards. 13—Occupied by Tison and his wife.

order came from the Commune to take from us all knives, scissors, anything that cut. . . . Mama and I managed to hide a pair of scissors." What did it all mean? Simply that the Convention, as the Assembly was now called, had decided to bring their former monarch to trial as a traitor, in secret intrigue with the enemies of France, and they were not taking any chances that, by committing suicide, he should cheat them out of the pleasure of chopping off his head.

Louis had long expected the worst. He was prepared to die. But it was cruel that during the six weeks of his trial, which might be his last days on earth, he was forbidden to see his wife and children, even on December 19, his daughter's fourteenth birthday, or on Christmas Day.

There were no more meals together, no more walks. Charles was sent upstairs to live with his mother. The children couldn't understand it. Thérèse kept asking, "Where is Papa? Is he ill?" And Mama would reply, "No, but he has to go every day and answer a lot of questions. When Papa gets back, he's tired and needs to go to bed."

Marie Antoinette tried to hide her anxiety from the children. But the news that Cléry or Turgy managed to convey to her was invariably bad. On January 18, 1793, the last day of the trial, Cléry sent the Queen a note by means of a piece of carefully-hoarded string, let down from an upper window. In a cipher pricked with pins, he told her the verdict. The King had been declared a traitor and sentenced to death by a majority of one vote. And that deciding vote in the Convention was cast by Louis' cousin "Philippe Egalité," as the former Duc d'Orléans, who had renounced his title to cater to the common people, now called himself.

Prostrated with grief and remorse, Marie Antoinette realized to what a great extent she was responsible for her husband's imminent execution, for it was undoubtedly the bitterness still felt by Orléans because of her mock wedding

MARIE ANTOINETTE'S STATE BEDROOM, VERSAILLES, WHERE HER DAUGHTER WAS BORN. (BOTTOM). MARBLE COURT, VERSAILLES, SHOWING THE BALCONY WHERE THÉRÈSE STOOD BESIDE HER MOTHER AND FACED THE ANGRY MOB.

Photograph: Bulloz, Paris

MARIE THÉRÈSE CHARLOTTE
by Kucharski

Photograph: H. Roger-Viollet, Paris

MADAME ROYALE AND THE DAUPHIN
by Vigée Le Brun

Photograph: H. Roger-Viollet, Paris

MARIE ANTOINETTE AND HER CHILDREN, THÉRÈSE AND CHARLES
by Vigée Le Brun

Photograph: H. Roger-Viollet, Paris

BUST OF LOUIS XVI
by Houdon

Photograph: Giraudon, Paris

COMTE DE PROVENCE
by Duplessis

Photograph: Giraudon, Paris

ELISABETH OF FRANCE
(Aunt Babet)

Photograph: Bulloz, Paris

MARIE THÉRÈSE OF FRANCE
by A. U. Wertmüller

Photograph: H. Roger-Viollet, Paris

LOUIS CHARLES, THE SECOND DAUPHIN
by Vigée Le Brun

Photograph: Bulloz, Paris

AXEL VON FERSEN
by Pasch

Photograph: Giraudon, Paris

PRINCESS MARIE THÉRÈSE CHARLOTTE OF FRANCE

Photographed by the author

BRIDGE OVER THE AIRE RIVER, VARENNES, WHICH THE ROYAL FAMILY NEVER CROSSED IN THEIR ATTEMPTED FLIGHT FROM FRANCE

Photographed by the author

SITE OF SAUCE'S GROCERY STORE WHERE THEY TOOK REFUGE, VARENNES, FRANCE

Photograph: Giraudon, Paris

THE RETURN OF THE ROYAL FAMILY FROM VARENNES TO PARIS, AFTER THEIR UNSUCCESSFUL FLIGHT FROM FRANCE

Photograph: Bulloz, Paris

THE ROYAL FAMILY WALKING IN THE YARD OF THE TEMPLE PRISON, AND CLÉRY PLAYING BALL WITH THE DAUPHIN

(*Contemporary Print*)

Photograph: H. Roger-Viollet, Paris

MADAME ROYALE
(by Vigée Le Brun)

Photograph: Bulloz, Paris

THE TUILERIES, PARIS

BELVEDERE PALACE, WHERE THÉRÈSE LIVED IN VIENNA

COMTESSE D'ARTOIS

COMTESSE DE PROVENCE

ARCHDUKE KARL LUDWIG JOHANN VON HAPSBURG
by Von A. Einsle

ARCHDUKE KARL
LUDWIG JOHANN

CHARLES FERDINAND,
DUC DE BERRY

HENRI V, COMTE DE CHAMBORD

COCO, THÉRÈSE'S DOG
(*Contemporary Print*)

at the Trianon long ago that was sending her husband to the scaffold.

The children were not told that Papa was to die. But on the evening of January 20, about eight o'clock, when a guard came to tell them that the Commune had given permission for the condemned man to see his family, Thérèse suspected by the tears in her mother's eyes that they might be seeing Papa for the last time. Holding tightly to Aunt Babet's hand, she followed Mama and Charles downstairs to a room, separated by a glass door from the one occupied by the former King's guards, so they could watch everything that went on.

In this room, dimly lighted by one candle, the jailers could see "Louis Capet" seated between his wife and sister. His daughter leaned lovingly against him, his son sat on his knee. Capet seemed to be doing most of the talking. The guards couldn't hear what he said, only a low murmur, broken by sobs and long silences. The children wept a great deal. So did the women. At ten o'clock, his usual bedtime, Louis rose. The others followed suit. When they came to the door, Cléry was waiting outside in the hall. Later, he wrote of how he witnessed a touching scene. Clinging to her father, Thérèse asked, "Papa, we'll see you tomorrow?"

"Yes, at eight o'clock."

"Why not at seven?" the girl begged, hoping for one more precious hour with this man who had been a poor king but such a "*bon Papa.*"

"All right, at seven then. Now good night!" Gently, Louis freed himself from his daughter's arms, kissed them all, and hurried away before he broke down and wept.

None of the family slept much that night. Lying in bed beside Aunt Babet, Thérèse cried herself to sleep, for her father had told them he was going to die, that was why he was going away in the morning. She awoke at six o'clock. Hearing footsteps coming up the stairs, the girl sprang out of bed. Papa!

He had promised they would see him again. But it was only a guard, come to fetch the condemned man's prayer book. Seven o'clock struck, then eight. Her father did not come as he had promised. Perhaps his jailers wouldn't let him. Or he couldn't endure another good-by. At nine o'clock, she heard a commotion down in the courtyard, the sound of drums and orders being shouted, then carriages driving away.

Burying her face in the pillow, Thérèse saturated it with tears, for she knew that the person she loved the most in the whole world, and who loved her dearly in return, had gone to the guillotine.

* * * *

With the death of his father on the scaffold, the Dauphin became Louis XVII. The Convention, fearing that the royalists might rescue the little King, would have liked to have used the "national razor" (the guillotine) on him. Not quite daring to do that, since to behead a helpless child would revolt people, Maximilien de Robespierre, leader of the Committee of Public Safety which, without trial, sent victims to the scaffold, decided to take the son of the proud Austrian woman from her and put the boy where he could do as he pleased with him. So on July 3, 1793, at ten o'clock at night, when Charles was fast asleep, six deputies from the Commune, on orders from Robespierre, came into Marie Antoinette's cell and demanded her son.

The Queen sprang up, aghast. "Take Charles from me?" she cried. "Oh, you wouldn't be so cruel!" Thérèse stood beside her mother, terrified, Aunt Babet began to cry, as the men stepped over to the bed where the boy, suddenly awakened, lay looking up at them with frightened eyes.

"Oh, please, don't separate us!" begged the Widow Capet.

"Charles is only eight. He needs his mother. What are you going to do with him?"

"Merely put him back downstairs in his father's old rooms," one of the deputies said. "He's too big a boy to remain here with you women. He needs a man to bring him up."

"You have someone in mind?"

"Yes, Antoine Simon, the concierge at the Temple."

"Not that ignorant former cobbler? Why, he can't even read or write!" exclaimed Marie Antoinette in horror. Thérèse, remembering the anguish of the distracted woman, records:

> One hour was passed in resistance on Mama's part, in threats from the guards, in tears and protestations from us all. At last they threatened to kill my brother as well as me, if Mama said any more, so she was forced to yield. They ordered us to get Charles up and dress him, which we did with trembling hands, and they went off with the screaming, struggling boy. We could hear his sobs as he was carried into the darkness down the stone stairs.

Charles wept for two days. Noises could easily be heard from one floor to another in the ancient Tower, and the prisoners on the third floor heard him hammering with his little fists on the iron door of his cell and yelling to be let out.

What was happening to Charles? Would they ever see him again? The women were forbidden now to walk in the garden. They could get a breath of fresh air only by climbing to the top of the Tower, where the embrasures in the parapet had been blocked up so they could not look out. His mother, aunt, and sister were in the same prison with Charles, but if the boy was ill, they couldn't go to him. If he was led away to the guillotine, they would never know it.

Tedious now were the hours that Mama, Aunt Babet, and Thérèse sat sewing, with little to say to one another. Losing her son was what finally broke Marie Antoinette's spirit. She was only thirty-seven, but her hair white, her once-lovely face haggard, the Widow Capet looked like an old woman.

"Mama, you've lost Charles, but you have me," her daughter longed to remind her. The old hurt feeling of being rejected returned. It had been Charles' merry chatter that had made Marie Antoinette's prison life bearable. Thérèse knew she could never take the place of the laughing boy who had gone. She was shut out, even from her mother's grief.

Yet, her daughter was to give Marie Antoinette all she wanted now, a glimpse of her son, for it was Thérèse who discovered the little hole. She had climbed up the spiral stairs in the corner turret one day to feed the pigeons. On the roof the girl found a break in the boards that blocked up the turrets of the tower. Through it she could look down into the courtyard where the Dauphin was taken each day, but not at the same hour.

A few minutes later, Thérèse burst into the room where her mother and aunt were seated. "Come quick!" she cried. "I think we can see Charles!"

The three of them ran excitedly up the stairs, and as they peeked through the hole, they saw the boy pass. "After that, we climbed to the top of the tower very often," Madame Royale relates, "because Mama's only pleasure was to see Charles through a little crack, as he passed at a distance. She stayed there for hours, waiting for a glimpse of him, not knowing at what moment he would appear."

What the women saw shocked them. It was amazing how quickly the youngster, forgetful as eight-year-olds are, adapted himself to his new environment. Within a week, a red liberty cap on his head, Charles was playing ball with the soldiers who stood guard over his mother. It broke Marie Antoinette's heart. She no longer wanted to live.

So it was "without emotion," her daughter was to write, that, at one o'clock on the morning of August 2, 1793, when they were all asleep—the Commune liked to do things unexpectedly, at night—the unhappy woman was awakened by knocking. Rising from her bed, the Widow Capet opened the door to four gendarmes who had come to take her to the Conciergerie, a prison where people condemned to the guillotine were kept.

"Cut short the good-bys," the guards ordered.

Before the men, who refused to leave her, the former Queen dressed and made a small parcel of her clothes. In a minute she would leave this grim fortress, where she had lived for a year and endured so much. But it still held her beloved son, and Marie Antoinette had something to say to his sister. Why did she turn to a girl of fourteen? Not to the older woman? Well, there was no knowing what the revolutionists would do to Babet, but Thérèse, hardly more than a child, might be allowed to live. And in her daughter Marie Antoinette sensed some of her own indomitable spirit.

"Always look after your brother," she said, handing Thérèse a locket that contained a lock of Charles' blond hair. "I believe that someday, God willing, this terrible republic will be overthrown and my son may yet reign. The Bourbons have ruled France for two hundred years. It mustn't all end with Papa. Thérèse, promise, if anything happens to me and to Aunt Babet, you'll take care of Charles?"

Tears rushed to the girl's eyes. That her mother should think only of her brother, and not of her, at this moment of parting! "Yes, Mama," she managed to say.

Marie Antoinette failed to notice the hurt expression on her daughter's face. She kissed her and Elisabeth and hurried from the room, toward the circular staircase that led down from the tower. In her haste, the Queen, forgetting to stoop going through the low doorway, hit her forehead against the stone arch.

Thérèse cried out in alarm, "Mama, did you hurt yourself?"

"Oh, it's nothing," came the indifferent reply, and her mother vanished down the winding turret stairs.

9

COURAGE PLUS

THÉRÈSE WAS IMPRISONED now on the third floor of the Tower, with only her Aunt Babet for company. "In a few days, when the guards came to get some things for Mama," the girl wrote later, "my aunt and I asked to follow my mother [to the Conciergerie], but the men refused, nor would they tell us what was to become of her."

It was only through the kitchen helper, Louis Turgy, that Thérèse and Elisabeth learned anything. After his escape to England, François Hue wrote in his memoirs:

> At the risk of my life, I managed to slip into the Conciergerie and, by making friends with Madame Richard, wife of the prison turnkey, gathered news of the Queen. For several weeks I reported to Turgy, who, in turn, succeeded in telling the captives in the Temple that the prisoner at the Conciergerie, while kept in solitary confinement in a wretched cell, was still alive.

But the notes written in invisible ink soon stopped. Turgy, suspected, was dismissed from the Temple and Hue was arrested. Thérèse and Babet no longer heard anything about Marie Antoinette.

And what had become of Charles? Every day, Thérèse and her aunt climbed to the roof of the Tower, hoping to catch a glimpse of him. But the little King no longer appeared below in the courtyard. His sister and aunt knew only that he was alive and still in the same prison with them, when they heard Charles' voice through the cracks in the floor. They knelt by the hour, listening.

The royal ladies were being treated like criminals. "We were locked in day and night," Thérèse remembered. "The guards came three times a day to bring us food, inspect the barred windows, and search us. We blushed with shame, forced to undress by Simon's foul-mouthed wife, before the men, who, often drunk, made rough jokes."

Pens, ink, and paper were taken from the helpless women, for fear they might smuggle notes outside. Even their tapestry-work was confiscated. "The excuse given by Pierre Chaumette, prosecutor of the Commune, who was in charge of our prison," Thérèse wrote, "being that we could weave secret messages into the design." Tison, the man who cleaned their room, was sent away; and no one, except a boy who brought them wood and water, was allowed to enter their cell. Concerning those dreadful days, she reported:

> Hébert [Chaumette's assistant] told my aunt that equality was the first law of the French Republic, and since no other prisoners had servants, he was going to take away Tison. After that, we no longer had anyone to wait upon us. We had to make our own beds and sweep the room, which took a long time, so little were we used to doing it at first. In order to treat us still more severely, we were deprived of small comforts. For example, the armchair used by my aunt. When our meals arrived, they were handed in through a wicket in the door, so we could not see who brought the food. We were forbidden to go up on the Tower, and they took away our sheets, fearing that, in spite of the thick bars, we might get down from the windows.

My aunt, who had a burn on her arm, had difficulty in getting ointment to dress it. One day when she asked for fish, eggs, or other food suitable for fast days, Aunt Babet was told, "Citizeness, you don't seem to realize what has happened, there is no difference now between the days of the week. Only fools believe in that nonsense." My aunt did not ask again. She made me eat whatever they brought me, as I had not reached the age for abstinence, but Aunt Babet kept the whole Lent, although deprived of Lenten food. She ate no breakfast; at dinner, she took a bowl of coffee with milk [it was her breakfast she had saved]; and in the evening, she ate nothing but bread.

One morning, the princesses were making their beds, when they heard the bolts drawn, the door of their cell opened, and two gendarmes entered. "Thérèse Capet, you're wanted downstairs," one of them said.

Elisabeth put an arm protectively about the trembling girl. "May I go with my niece?" she begged.

"No, she's to go alone."

"Will she come up again?"

"Yes, the girl will return."

Thérèse, sick with fear, hung back. Through the open doorway, she could see the spiral staircase, so narrow two persons could hardly pass on it, down which her father had gone—and then her mother. Thus far, those who had been led away, down those winding turret stairs, had not come up again. But she did not dare disobey the guards. So, after kissing her aunt, who was trembling violently, the girl courageously followed the men out of her cell, to the head of the steps leading down into the dark. There she stopped. Her frightened voice echoed under the vaulted stone ceiling. "Where are you taking me?"

"You'll see." Grabbing the girl by the arm, one of the guards shoved her roughly down the steps.

The staircase seemed endless. But, finally, they reached the second floor. As they passed Charles' cell, the door was open, and Thérèse caught sight of her brother, whom she had not seen for three months. She ran forward to embrace him. But Madame Simon barred her way and ordered the girl to go into the next room, where a sandy-haired man was seated behind a table.

"Sit down, Thérèse Capet," said Chaumette, the prosecutor of the Commune. And he began questioning Marie Antoinette's daughter about her mother, hoping to get the girl to say something damaging they could use against the Queen.

After three hours, unable to get Thérèse to say anything evil of her mother, Chaumette sent the girl back to her cell and had her aunt brought downstairs. Of this interview, Thérèse wrote later:

> Arriving, I kissed Aunt Babet. They told her to go down, which she did, and they asked her the same questions they had asked me; she replied about as I did. My aunt returned at four o'clock. Her questioning lasted only an hour and mine lasted three. That was because the men saw they could not intimidate her, as they had hoped to do to a person of my age. But the life I had led for more than four years had given me courage.

After this, the princesses' monotonous prison life went on in the same manner for seven dreary months. Their only consolation was that they had each other. They read and reread Elisabeth's religious books and La Harpe's *Travels*, the only books the prisoners had. For several weeks nothing alarming had happened at the Temple. They had begun to hope that their tormentors had forgotten them, when on the evening of May 9, 1794, as the two women were going to bed and were half undressed, they were startled to hear a key grate in the lock.

Hurriedly getting back into their clothes, they turned to

confront the two jailers who entered. "Citizeness, you're to go with us," one of the men said to Elisabeth.

"And my niece?"

"She'll be attended to later."

Her heart was thumping against her ribs, but, turning to the fifteen-year-old girl she was leaving, Babet tried to speak cheerfully. "Chéri, don't be afraid. I'll be back soon."

"No, Citizeness," the man said, "you're not coming back."

* * * *

One after another, Thérèse had lost all her companions in captivity—her father, her mother, her brother, and her aunt. Of the last, she wrote:

> I was brokenhearted when I found myself separated from Aunt Babet. She looked on me always as her daughter, and I considered her as my second mother. We had absolutely the same character, and resembled each other very much. I did not know what had become of her, nor would anyone tell me.

When would they come for her? Now, at night, when she heard the guards making their rounds through the Tower, their heavy steps echoing on the stairs, and the bolts of her door being drawn, the trembling girl no longer had her "second mother" to whom she could cling. Thérèse was alone . . . and she remained so for thirteen months.

What she suffered no one can imagine! In 1809, Napoleon had the Temple prison torn down. Before he did so, the Tower was bought by a speculator, who made it into a tourist attraction. Crowds of curious people flocked in to see the cells where their beheaded king and his family had been kept. On the wall were two lines Marie Antoinette had drawn with a pencil one day when she was measuring the heights of her little daughter and son, and had written: "March

27, 1793, four feet, ten inches; three feet, two inches." The sight-seers could also read what Capet's daughter had scratched with a needle on the wall: "Marie Thérèse Charlotte is the most unhappy person in the world. My God, watch over me from heaven!"

On July 28, 1794, when Robespierre was liquidated, the young prisoner, hearing the sound of drums outside the Temple walls, thought that now it was her turn—that they had come to take her to the Conciergerie. "I was terrified," Thérèse wrote, "but when they brought my supper, I did not dare ask what was going on."

Beyond her prison walls, heads were rolling. The moderates had gained control in the Convention, and Barras, commander of the Republic's armed forces, sent the tyrant Robespierre to the guillotine, where Robespierre had sent so many others. Once he was in power, Barras replaced Robespierre's men at the Temple with his own keepers. Christophe Laurent, a Creole from Martinique, became head jailer, with Jean Gomin as his assistant.

On November 8, 1794, the day of Gomin's arrival, Laurent took him to see the royal prisoners. The two men climbed the steep, winding stairs to the second floor of the Tower and stopped before an iron door.

"Here is the brother," Laurent said, "in what used to be the room of his father's valet. I've done what I could to clean it. When I came here in July, his cell was crawling with rats. No one had cleaned the place for six months. Not since Simon and his wife left the Tower, last January. It made me sick to go in."

Laurent unlocked the iron door, and the two men entered a tiny room with one small window. On an iron cot lay a tall boy with chestnut hair, long arms and legs. Beside him, on a table, was his meal of watery soup and black bread that he hadn't touched. Laurent asked him, "Charles Capet, why don't you eat?"

The boy did not reply.

"He refuses to speak," Laurent said, "probably because he hates us all. He's very sick. But, Gomin, you should have seen the poor child when I found him. He had been left alone for six months, except when at night his jailers handed in his scanty supply of food and water through a revolving shelf in the door. We cut his hair, trimmed his long nails, and took off his clothes full of fleas and vermin. Then we pried open the window, closed for a year, and remade his bed with clean sheets. It had not been changed in six months." Laurent turned back the thin blanket to show Gomin the boy's long, spindly legs covered with tumors. "I don't think we can save him, but Dr. Pierre Desault from the Grand Hôspice, the best hospital in Paris, comes every week to clean his sores."

"He needs nourishing food," Gomin said.

"I've told the Commune so, but they say that Little Capet and his sister must live like other prisoners, on the same wretched fare we give to thieves and murderers. I don't dare disobey orders, but I do what I can for the poor boy."

"How old is he?"

"The prison records say nine, but he looks older, doesn't he?" The two men looked down at the boy, too tall for his age. "It's pitiful." Laurent sighed. "I've heard that at Versailles the Dauphin was a handsome lad, always happy and smiling. I wonder, could this be another boy? He looks more like a child of twelve or fourteen. Well, come along, Gomin, and see his sister."

The men climbed to the third story of the Tower and, as before, found their way blocked by an iron door. Laurent opened it with a key he carried, and they went in. Thérèse was seated by the one small, barred window, knitting. She did not look up or take any notice of the men.

"This is my assistant, Citizen Gomin," Laurent introduced his companion. But the girl answered not a word. Nor did she speak to her new jailer for about a week, although, in his rounds of the prison, he visited her every day.

Finally, Gomin decided on a bold step. The Princess' pretty face was haunted with fear. Otherwise, she reminded Gomin of his own blond, blue-eyed daughter, and he wanted to help her. He was always the last to leave Thérèse's cell, as it was his duty to lock the door. One morning, when Laurent was already on the stairs and had his back turned, Gomin handed the teen-age prisoner some paper and a pencil, and asked her to write down anything she wished to have.

Madame Royale looked up in surprise. Gomin was the first keeper who had spoken kindly to her. The others, most of them, had been so impertinent that, unless forced to do so, she never replied. Now, when, after her long silence, Thérèse tried to speak, the words wouldn't come. With great effort, she said in a hoarse voice, "I need matches."

Gomin, when he brought them to her, saw to his dismay that the poor girl had neither fire nor light. They had taken away her matches. For six months she had lived alone in a cold cell, unable to light a fire in the stove or heat water to bathe herself. She didn't even have a candle. When it grew dark, she went to bed.

Thérèse's big blue eyes thanked him, when Jean Gomin brought her such simple necessities as candles and matches. She never spoke to him before the other jailers, for fear of getting him into trouble, but several days later, when he was going out after the other men, the girl whispered, "I want shoes and stockings." Gomin, looking down, saw her bare toes through the holes in her shoes.

He obtained for her shoes and stockings, several cotton dresses, linen underwear, and a few books. At last, she could discard her faded plum-colored silk frock, which she had been constantly mending. It was all in rags, but the only one Madame Royale had. Gomin even gave her a little dog, Coco, that had belonged to her brother. He was a mongrel spaniel, red and ugly, but Thérèse loved him. Now she had a companion in her loneliness. But when she asked about her brother, Gomin's vague answers were not reassuring.

How could he tell her that, on the hot afternoon of June 8, 1795, the boy on the second floor of the Tower had died? For two days his body lay in the room directly under hers, but Thérèse didn't know it. The Commune announced that Charles Capet was dead. And after dark, two nights later, the little corpse of the Dauphin had been secretly buried in the cemetery of Sainte-Marguerite in Paris.

If it *was* the Dauphin, Gomin thought. Strange things went on in this grim, silent prison. But Laurent had been dismissed and replaced by a new head jailer, Etienne Lasne, it was said, because he had dared to call the Commune's attention to the fact that the sick boy in the Tower looked too big to be the Dauphin. Gomin, the son of a poor upholsterer, was badly in need of his job at the Temple. "Hear all, see all, say nothing—otherwise, you don't get ahead, do you?" Gomin thought to himself. So when Madame Royale questioned him about her brother, Gomin, careful not to make Laurent's mistake, held his tongue.

10

SWEET TASTE OF FREEDOM

THE NEWS of the Dauphin's death shocked France. The children of Louis XVI and Marie Antoinette had almost been forgotten. People were surprised to learn that they had been shut up in prison for three years. On June 18, 1795, when the citizens of the city of Orléans heard of the reported death of the boy Capet, they sent the Convention a petition, demanding that the girl Capet be set free.

Anyone making such a request as recently as a few months before would have been condemned to death. But the Revolution had spent its fury. A reaction had taken place in people's minds. Even the deputies in the Convention felt more kindly toward the sixteen-year-old girl in the Tower. Louis XVII they had feared. But his sister, who by French law could never become queen, was harmless. The question was, what to do with her? Meanwhile, the daughter of Louis Capet was allowed to resume her walks in the prison courtyard, and it was decided to give her a woman companion.

"I was so lonely," Thérèse says in her *Journal*, "that I would have welcomed anyone not a complete monster." Citizeness Madeleine (Renée) La Rochette, wife of Citizen

Bocquet de Chanterenne, 24 Rue des Rosiers, who was selected to live with Madame Royale, was no "monster," but a well-educated woman of thirty who spoke English and Italian. Her husband was in the police force. She was a spy, reporting daily to the Convention, but Thérèse, never suspecting this, opened her heart to the lady. At last, she had someone who would tell her the truth.

Marie Antoinette had been dead for a year and eight months, but her daughter didn't know this. "Where is my mother?" Thérèse asked; and Renée replied sadly, "My dear, you no longer have a mother."

"And how is my brother?"

"Dead."

"And my aunt?"

"Dead, too."

Stunned by the shocking news, Madame Royale realized that she was an orphan, alone in the world. She burst into tears. But when her grief had somewhat spent itself, the girl begged to hear the details. Renée told her how Marie Antoinette and Princesse Elisabeth had been beheaded on the Place de la Revolution, where Louis XVI met his death, and that Charles, dying in the Tower, was buried in the cemetery of Sainte-Marguerite. The death of Elisabeth of France had been especially horrible. Executed with twenty-five other aristocrats, she had been killed the last, to make her suffer the most. The sound of the guillotine knife, falling twenty-five times, was too much for her. Elisabeth fainted.

"Poor Aunt Babet!" Thérèse sobbed. "She never harmed anyone. Of what could those wicked men accuse that sweet woman?"

Now that the tragic facts were known to her, Madame de Chanterenne did her best to comfort the poor girl. Mornings, Renée gave the young Princess English and Italian lessons. She even encouraged her to write down an account of her imprisonment in the Tower, the famous memoirs frequently quoted in this book. Thérèse liked to draw and paint. Madame de Chanterenne got her some paper, India ink, and brushes. She was shocked by the girl's harsh voice, grown hoarse from not speaking for thirteen months and, to limber up Madame Royale's throat muscles, had her read aloud from the works of Racine. Afternoons, the two walked in the courtyard. Coco, the little spaniel, followed them; as did a white goat, a gift from Renée, of which Thérèse grew very fond.

As soon as it became known that Madame Royale was allowed to go down to the courtyard again, the top windows of the houses along the Rue des Cordeliers, overlooking the Tower wall, became filled with royalists. François Hue, Louis XVI's former Gentleman of the Bedchamber, brought them there, and they smiled and waved at the daughter of their late king, until Lasne, head keeper of the prison, warned Hue that such demonstrations of affection must stop.

But others succeeded in showing their loyalty. On September 3, 1795, Madame Royale was visited by the Marquise de Tourzel and Pauline. Only by a miracle had Thérèse's former governess and her daughter escaped being beheaded in La Force prison with the Princesse de Lamballe. Released from jail, they had been trying for two months to get into the Temple. Louise de Tourzel wrote:

> As soon as we were released from prison, we tried to get news of Madame Royale. It seemed to be impossible. M. Hue tried too, and came to report to me the little he was able to learn. . . .

Later, of their first visit, she says:

> Madame came to meet us, kissed us tenderly, and took us up to her room. Almost at once, she began telling us about the saddest moment in her life, when she was separated from her father whom she had loved with all her heart. We were amazed at the change in her. We had left Madame frail and delicate-looking.

Now, after three years of captivity, we were astonished to find her tall, handsome, and healthy. Heaven had given her the courage to overcome unparalleled hardships.

"Your thirteen months alone must have been ghastly," Thérèse's former governess said to her. "My dear child, how were you able to bear them?"

"By following the advice Aunt Babet gave me, to keep busy," the girl replied. "I was occupied every hour of the day in dressing myself, in tidying up my room, in mending my clothes, and reading. I had only Aunt's religious books, La Harpe's *Travels* that I'd read a thousand times, and some knitting, which bored me dreadfully, for they refused to give me more wool. When I finished the scarf, I unraveled it, and started over again. But I could at least keep myself clean. I had soap and water, and plenty of time to think and pray and find a new strength."

"How did you get along without exercise?"

"I swept the room every day, and after we were forbidden to go down to the garden, Aunt Babet made me walk up and down very fast for an hour every morning, with my watch in my hand, to keep up my circulation."

Hearing of Madame de Tourzel's visit, the Baroness de Mackau, Thérèse's second governess, also obtained permission to come to the Tower. Madame de Mackau was sick and feeble after a long imprisonment. Being told of her arrival, the Princess ran downstairs to meet her, and was in the Baroness' arms before the old lady had crossed the courtyard. "It's three years, one month, and one day, since I've kissed you," she cried.

After that, the Marquise de Tourzel and Pauline, or the Baroness de Mackau, took turns visiting Madame Royale each week. Thérèse wrote Pauline after the second visit:

The pleasure of seeing you again has greatly helped to relieve my sorrow. During the long time that I was separated from you, my thoughts were often with you. To the sufferings I had to endure was added my anxiety over you. I did not hear of your second captivity. Since then, you have tried to share mine, or at least to see me. Had I not already cared for you as I do, this proof of your devotion would attach me to you forever. I love you, and shall continue to do so all my life.

It was from Pauline that Thérèse learned she was to be set free. The Emperor Francis II of Austria, Marie Antoinette's nephew, was Madame Royale's first cousin. What was more logical, the Convention decided, than to hand over the girl to her maternal relatives? France and Austria were still at war. And it happened that five of their deputies had been captured by the Austrians. So Paris suggested to Vienna that Capet's daughter be exchanged for them. Negotiations between the two countries were under way, but progressing slowly, when on the afternoon of October 5, 1795 an event occurred that hastened matters. Louise de Tourzel wrote:

Pauline and I were greatly upset when Gomin came to tell us that, from the top of the Tower, he had heard cannon shots coming from the direction of the Rue Saint-Honoré. He thought a riot had broken out there. He advised us not to wait any longer, or we would not be able to get home. We left hurriedly, promising Madame to return the next day, if possible.

Crossing the Pont Notre Dame over the Seine was a terrible ordeal for the frightened women. Cannon were thundering in the Rue Saint-Honoré, only a few blocks away. Next day, when Louise de Tourzel and Pauline returned to the Tower, they were full of their dangerous trip home. A royalist insurrection had broken out. It was put down in a half hour, though, by the Convention's artillery, under the command of a little Corsican officer twenty-five years old. By placing his cannon on the steps of the church of Saint-Roche, Captain Napoleon Bonaparte scattered "with a rain of grapeshot" the royalist column advancing up the Rue Saint-Honoré.

For the first time, Thérèse heard the name of a man unknown to her, but who was to change her life and the history of all of Europe. "Because of what he did yesterday, the Convention has made Captain Bonaparte a general," Madame Tourzel told her.

The royalists had been headed for the Temple, to try to capture the prison and free Marie Antoinette's daughter. Aware that their attempt had almost succeeded, the Convention decided to exchange the girl to their advantage before she was kidnaped. The negotiations with Austria were hurriedly concluded. On November 28, 1795, Minister of the Interior Bénézech came to inform Madame Royale that she was to be set free, and ask her whom she wished to have go with her to Vienna.

The Marquise de Tourzel was ill, Pauline about to be married, so Thérèse suggested the Baroness de Mackau. "And I should also like to take with me," she told Bénézech, "those former faithful servants of my father's, Hue, Turgy, and Cléry."

Unfortunately, the plans for her journey worked out differently. The Baroness de Mackau, too old to go, begged that her daughter, the Marquise de Soucy, accompany Madame in her place. Thérèse did not care for Jacqueline de Soucy, who insisted upon taking her little boy with her. Turgy, ill at the time, said that he and Cléry would come to Vienna later. And, to Thérèse's annoyance, her request to take Renée de Chanterenne was refused.

The Convention also insisted that she leave her prison after dark. They were afraid to have the daughter of Louis XVI and Marie Antoinette pass through Paris by daylight. The mere sight of her might start a counterrevolution. So at eleven o'clock at night, Bénézech came to the Temple to fetch the girl who, with Gomin, was waiting on the ground floor of the Tower. The outer gate was opened by the guard. The night was dark, the streets about the Temple deserted, no one saw "Thérèse Capet," after three years, four months, and six days, leave her prison.

Bénézech, Thérèse, and Gomin, carrying her bag, walked to the Rue de Bondy. There, in a berlin drawn by eight horses, Jacqueline de Soucy and Captain Mechain, a guard, were seated. Madame Royale took her place on the back seat, beside Madame de Soucy. As they drove off, Bénézech looked at his watch. It was just past midnight. A new day had dawned, December 19, 1795.

It was Thérèse's seventeenth birthday.

* * * *

An hour after the berlin started, another coach left Paris. In it were François Hue; Madame de Soucy's son; Meunier and Baron, servants from the Temple; and Thérèse's dog. Coco had not gone with his mistress. For fear that his barking might draw attention to her departure, the little dog was shut up, but not forgotten. He found a place in the second carriage.

Five days later, the two vehicles arrived, within a few hours of each other, at Huningue, on the eastern frontier of France. It was Christmas Eve. At ten o'clock that night, Thérèse was in her room, Number 10, on the second floor of the Tavern du Corbeau, writing to Renée de Chanterenne an account of her journey. Lamenting the fact that "Renette" was not with her, she said:

> Fancy, my dear Renette, Madame de Soucy has taken her son and her maid with her, although I was refused a serving woman. I have tried to get to the bottom of the intrigue which prevented your coming with me. I think Monsieur de Mackau had something to do with it. He wished his sister to have the appointment. I want to pour out my feelings freely to one I love, but she is not the person I should select for that—

Quoting these words in his *Souvenirs d'Un Page*, Comte d'Hézecques breaks Thérèse's letter off abruptly at this point. Was it because, at that moment, the second carriage arrived from Paris, and Coco bounded into the room, followed by François Hue? When her father's former Gentleman of the Bedchamber had been taken from the Temple to La Force prison, to spend several years in and out of jail, all of the royal family were still alive. This was the first time Hue had seen Madame Royale since. Overcome with emotion, he wept as he kissed her hand.

The identity of the pretty girl who was traveling incognito under the name of Sophie was suspected in Huningue. The next day was Christmas, a religious holiday the French Republic did not allow to be celebrated, but Madame Joseph Schuldz, the wife of the innkeeper, could not resist giving the daughter of her former monarch a present. As soon as she heard that Thérèse was up on Christmas morning, Madame Schuldz went to the Princess' room with her children, Marie nine and Conrad ten, each of them carrying a bouquet of flowers. They had been hard to find in December.

To her embarrassment, the penniless daughter of a king had no money to give the children or tip the servants at the inn. Thérèse gave a scarf to little Marie, a handkerchief to young Conrad, and kissed them both good-by, when, at four o'clock on the afternoon of December 26, 1795, First Secretary Bacher of the French embassy in Switzerland came to drive her into Bâle (now Basel), to meet the Prince de Gâvre and Baron Degelmann, Austrian Minister to Switzerland, who were to receive Madame Royale on behalf of the Emperor of Austria.

Since France and Austria were still at war, Thérèse's exchange for the five deputies of the Convention captured by the Austrians was to take place on neutral ground. Everything was ready for the ceremony at Bâle, in Switzerland. A rich merchant, Reber by name, had lent his house, just over the Franco-Swiss border, for the exchange. And it had been arranged that, on the Princess' arrival, the prisoners taken by Austria, now at Fribourg, should be brought to Riechen, near Bâle, on the Swiss bank of the Rhine.

Waiting to conduct Thérèse to her mother's country, François-Joseph Rasse, Prince de Gâvre, had been at the Reber house for a half hour, when her carriage drove up. It was a dark night and raining. The Princess alighted in the mud, walked up the damp path with Monsieur Bacher, and entered the house, dripping wet. The Austrian envoy was in the parlor. The Prince de Gâvre handed the French diplomat a formal receipt "for Marie Thérèse Charlotte, daughter of Louis XVI, last king of the French." Then Bacher hurried off to Riechen, to free the French prisoners.

There was nothing now to detain Madame Royale. At nine o'clock, having said good-by to Gomin and Mechain, who were returning to Paris, she took her place with the Marquise de Soucy and the Prince de Gâvre in a carriage the Emperor of Austria had sent to fetch her.

The skies had cleared. The night was cold, the moon shining, as the imperial coach entered the city walls of Bâle by the Porte Saint-Jean. They heard singing and shouts of "*Vive la République!*" as the carriage passed the Hôtel des Trois Rois. In the taproom of the inn, the French prisoners were celebrating their freedom. One man was shouting louder than the rest. And Madame Royale was hurried past the inn, so she wouldn't know that the person who had done her so much harm, the owner of the relay station at Saint-Ménehould, was within a stone's throw of her.

By an astonishing coincidence, among the prisoners surrendered by Austria was Jean-Baptiste Drouet, the man who by recognizing Louis XVI on the fatal drive to Varennes had caused the arrest of the royal family. A deputy of the Convention, serving in the French army, Drouet had been captured by the Austrians at Mauberge, on the Flemish border. How horrible it would have been if he and Thérèse had met! But, fortunately, the girl didn't get even a glimpse of the prisoners for whom she was exchanged.

Madame Royale, to escape the crowds, was taken through Bâle in the night. Crossing the Rhine, her carriage followed along its German bank to Füssen castle in the Tyrol, where Thérèse stopped briefly with the Elector of Trèves, Prince Clèment de Saxe, Madame Royal's great-uncle, the brother of her father's mother. Then she visited for two days in Innsbruck with her aunt, Marie Antoinette's sister, the Archduchess Elisabeth. After which, little suspecting the intrigue over her, she continued down the Danube to Vienna. For a girl of seventeen, riding along with a mongrel dog in her arms, had become a prize to be fought over by two kings, Francis II of Austria and Louis XVIII of France, as the Comte de Provence was calling himself since the reported death of his nephew, the Dauphin.

Hearing of her release from prison, Thérèse's uncle, in exile at Verona, Italy, had vowed that she should never reach Vienna and fall into the clutches of the Emperor Francis, whom he hated. Provence's close friend, Antoine de Béziade, Comte d'Avaray, was sent to Innsbruck, to try to stop Madame Royale there and insist upon her coming to join her uncle in Italy. But, in December, the Brenner Pass over the Alps is blocked with snow. Comte d'Avaray, unable to get through to Innsbruck, was forced to return to Verona and tell the King that the girl had gone on to Vienna, arriving there on January 9, 1796, twenty-one days after she left Paris.

"Well, Avaray, Francis won the first round," Provence said, "but I'll win the second." And he sat down to write his niece a letter.

11

THOSE MARRYING HAPSBURGS

FREE, after more than three years in jail, Thérèse's heart felt as though it were singing. She rode through Austria, her mother's country, smiling happily out of the window, unaware that her cavalry escort surrounded the coach for her protection. Armed with loaded pistols, they were there on the Emperor's orders, to prevent any attempt by Thérèse's uncle to kidnap her.

Francis II of Austria knew how much it would enhance Louis XVIII's reputation in the eyes of the royalists to have his niece with him in Italy. Many who had no use for the Comte de Provence would resign themselves to his calling himself king of France, if Marie Antoinette's daughter was by his side. And Francis had other plans for the girl. He intended to marry her to his second brother, the Archduke Karl.

The Emperor of Austria and the Pretender to the French throne, each was playing his own game, self-interest, not affection, dictating their moves. But Thérèse, ignorant of this and grateful to the Emperor who offered her a home, arrived in Austria happy to be out of France and safe with her mother's family. Francis II, the son of Marie Antoinette's brother Leopold, had married Maria Theresa of Naples, daughter of Ferdinand IV, King of the Two Sicilies, and Maria Carolina, Marie Antoinette's sister. So both the Emperor of Austria and his second wife were Thérèse's first cousins.

In Vienna, huge crowds lined the streets between the city gates and Hofburg Palace. Madame Royale of France smiled and waved in response to their cheers. When her coach with its outriders rumbled to a stop before the Hofburg, there at the entrance stood Francis and Maria Theresa, waiting to greet her. "My dear little cousin . . ." The Emperor kissed the girl and kept his arm around her as they walked into the palace.

Francis was in a rare good humor, fairly gloating over his capture of Madame Royale. And the orphaned Princess was happy, too. Her mother's family all loved her, Cousin Francis said so. Thérèse no longer felt herself alone in the world.

Her happy mood lasted until a few days later, when the Emperor drove his young cousin out to Belvedere Palace, built by Prince Eugene on the outskirts of Vienna, where she would live. There were formal gardens that reminded Madame Royale of Versailles and, in their midst, a huge, white baroque building. She became quieter and quieter as Cousin Francis hurried her from one vast room to another. This sumptuous palace, used by the Hapsburgs for state banquets and receptions, seemed to Thérèse more like a museum than a home.

Yet it was at Belvedere, where a ball had been given for the Archduchess Marie Antoinette before she left for France to marry the Dauphin, that the daughter of this marriage would live, in a small apartment under the roof, surrounded by a household of Austrians—the Prince de Gâvre, the Comtesse de Chanclos, and Madame de Dombasle. After a few days, to Madame Royale's dismay, her French entourage was ordered to return to France. Thérèse did not regret losing Jacqueline de Soucy. "She picks quarrels about nothing," Thérèse wrote Renée de Chanterenne. "Besides, I don't care for her, she bores me." But she resented Cousin Francis dismissing the others, without even consulting her.

"We're at war with France," was the Emperor's excuse. "All French people must leave Austria."

Meunier and Baron, two employees from the Temple, who had come to Vienna with Madame Royale, were sent home on January 20, 1796; the Marquise de Soucy and her son, three days later. Not even permitted to say good-by to the Baroness de Mackau's daughter, Thérèse wrote her:

> I feared that the war between the two nations would separate us. The same thing has happened to all the French [in Vienna]. Say everything that is kind for me to your mother. I thank you for the sacrifice you made in leaving your country to follow me. I shall never forget it.

It was hardest of all to lose François Hue. He came to Madame Royale in February and told her that, ordered out of Austria, he was going to join Louis XVIII in Verona, Italy. Thérèse wept on parting from the man who had meant so much to her father. But she rebelled when they tried to take Coco from her. The Prince de Gâvre had cause for complaint. The little red spaniel had bitten him. "Surely, Madame, we can get you a better dog than that." The haughty Austrian looked with disdain at the mongrel in the Princess' arms.

"No, Coco belonged to my brother," Thérèse replied firmly. "I will never part with him."

The exiled Princess was now entirely surrounded by Austrians. Their first duty was to make her forget France. She was forbidden to speak French, and must endure long hours of lessons in German and court etiquette in order to make her into a suitable consort for the Emperor's brother.

Before leaving Paris, Thérèse had been told that, on reaching Austria, she was to be married to the Archduke Karl Ludwig Johann von Hapsburg. Jokingly, Madame Royale began calling this man she had never seen her "lover." "I hear they are going to marry me to my lover," she wrote Renée de Chanterenne from Huningue, "but I hope it won't be for some time." First, the orphan wanted a year of mourning for her parents. She had been forbidden to wear black for them in prison.

Thérèse did not find it odd that a husband had been chosen for her. Royal children are seldom consulted. Kings marry their sons and daughters into whichever reigning family offers the most, from a political standpoint. Thérèse's grandmother, the great Empress Maria Theresa, had married her mother to her father to strengthen the alliance between France and Austria. The lively little Austrian archduchess of fourteen had never seen the dull Bourbon prince whom her mother picked for her to marry, untill she came to France for their wedding. Marie Antoinette had never loved Louis XVI, she hardly respected him; their daughter didn't expect anything different. As well the Emperor's brother as another. The eldest Archduke, Ferdinand, Duke of Tuscany, was already married. So it was the third son of Leopold II, the Archduke Karl, they had selected for her. She was told that Karl, a man of musical tastes, carried a spinet in his luggage, and listened to Hayden's music the night before a battle. This did not endear him to Thérèse, who had no ear for music. But at least he was young.

Over the centuries, the house of Hapsburg had increased the landholdings of the small kingdom of Austria, not by wars, but by marriage. "The Marrying Hapsburgs" they came to be called, as the insignificant family turned into a powerful dynasty that, largely through marriage, now controlled all of Central Europe.

The Archduke Karl, at twenty-four the youngest general

in the Austrian army facing the French on the Rhine, had been told what was expected of him. Prodded by his brother Francis, the Archduke agreed to return to Vienna and meet his bride, but he took his time. It was August, and the imperial family was at Schönbrunn, their summer palace on the outskirts of Vienna, before he arrived.

As his coach rolled down the avenue leading to the palace, Karl saw a girl running to catch a dog that was barking at his horses. She was almost in tears, for fear that her pet would be kicked or run over by the carriage.

The Archduke called to the coachman to rein in his team. The heavy vehicle rumbled almost to a stop, as the girl caught the barking dog. She lifted the animal up in her arms and, over his head, smiled her thanks. Dark eyes met blue eyes. Something magnetic passed between them. Then, the dog in her arms, she ran off and disappeared.

Because she was dressed in calico, her hair flying loose, Karl took her to be a servant. But an hour later, as he sat in the Empress' parlor, chatting with his sister-in-law, to his surprise, he saw the same girl enter the room, properly gowned in silk this time. She was all in black, her blond hair (so long and thick that people declared Madame Royale wore a wig) brushed back, without powder, into a knot behind. Although it was fashionable at the time for women to crop their hair short, Thérèse refused to cut hers. Hadn't all women—including her mother—been forced to cut their hair before going to the guillotine?

"Good day, Cousin." With one of her rare smiles, the sad-faced Princess went over to the Empress Maria Theresa and kissed her on the cheek.

"Who are you?" demanded Karl.

"Marie Thérèse of France," she replied in a husky voice.

This grave, lovely girl his bride? What luck! Her youth, so full of sorrow, had etched on Thérèse's face a touching beauty. The Archduke found her enchanting. He was barely polite to the Empress, he hardly glanced at the other ladies, and talked only to Madame Royale for the rest of the afternoon.

That night at dinner, which was a formal banquet in his honor, the Emperor's brother never took his eyes off his young cousin. And at the ball that followed, he danced with her almost continuously.

It was an excited girl who laid her head on her pillow that night. A princess married for state reasons, she couldn't expect love, so Thérèse had thought. But perhaps she could? Karl had loved her on sight. She loved him madly. For the first time in her life, Marie Antoinette's daughter knew what it was to be radiantly happy.

But the cautious Francis, anxiously watching events in France, had begun to doubt the wisdom of his brother marrying the daughter of a king who had lost his throne. "Young man, you've a war to fight," he reminded Karl. "Get back to the front."

Napoleon Bonaparte had come a long way from the obscure artillery captain who had scattered the royalist uprising in Paris with a "whiff of grapeshot." Now a general, in command of the Republic's principal army, he had conquered most of Italy, and was threatening to march north and attack Vienna. In Belgium, on Austria's eastern frontier, the Archduke Karl was having better success. He had managed to push the French, under Jourdan and Moreau, back over the Rhine.

So Karl was away at the front most of the time. Thérèse saw him only on furloughs. Then they rode in the Vienna woods, they danced together and, better still, the Archduke taught the sad-faced French Princess how to laugh and be gay. He was all that she had imagined a "lover" would be. Thérèse always remembered how excited, almost faint, she had felt the first time Karl took her in his arms. In prison during the years when most girls are having their first love affairs, Madame Royale, at seventeen, had never been kissed before. "It was then I began to live," she thought afterward.

The people of Vienna were delighted. The romantic story of love at first sight between the Emperor's popular brother and the orphaned French Princess appealed to their sentimental natures. An artist had sketched Madame Royale at Huningue, on her way to Austria, and her picture and that of the Archduke Karl decorated many a shopwindow throughout the Austrian Empire.

The old fortifications that had guarded Vienna against the Turks, now planted with trees, made a fine promenade. Happily dreaming of her "lover," Thérèse was walking along the ramparts with Coco one day when she realized that a man was following her. She exclaimed with joy, when he came closer, and she saw who it was—François Hue.

"I've come from Verona," her father's former Gentleman of the Bedchamber said to her, "and here's a letter from your uncle. The King has written to you several times. But, I suppose, the Emperor's police saw to it that his letters never reached you."

Not having heard from her father's brothers in five years, Thérèse had come to the conclusion that Provence and Artois had forgotten her. Tears came to her eyes as she read Louis XVIII's fatherly letter. He loved her like his own daughter, the Pretender to the throne of France wrote, and he begged his niece to leave Vienna, where her mother's family were holding her prisoner, and join him in Italy. And what was this he heard about her marrying an Austrian archduke? He begged Thérèse to remember her dead parents' wishes concerning the choice of a husband. Had she forgotten that she was engaged to Artois' eldest son, the Duc d'Angoulême?

Thérèse was trembling when she finished reading her

uncle's letter. She recalled that mock wedding at Trianon, when her mother had betrothed her to the little Duc d'Angoulême. Antoine was twelve, Thérèse nine then, she had hardly thought of him since.

"I'll bring you other letters," Hue promised, "but if I'm caught, the Emperor will have me shot, so I suggest that Your Highness use invisible ink in replying to the King. I'll be here, on the ramparts, the first Monday in every month, at half-past twelve, to take to Italy any letter that Madame wishes to send. If I touch my ear with my hand, it will indicate that I've a letter from His Majesty; and if I play with Coco, you'll know that I've safely delivered your last one to him in Verona."

So began a correspondence, unknown to the Emperor and his secret police, between Madame Royale, Louis XVIII, and after a few months, with the Duc d'Angoulême. It gave Thérèse, hungry for love, a warm, comforting feeling to know that her father's family had not forgotten her.

12

THE LAST LINK WITH MARIE ANTOINETTE

"I HAVE LOST EVERYTHING," Count Axel von Fersen wrote to his sister Sophie, the Countess Adolph Piper of Sweden, when he heard of Marie Antoinette's death. Fersen was not yet forty, but his life was over, he had nothing more to live for —or so he thought.

While the Queen was in prison, Axel had remained in Belgium, doing all he could to try to save her. He had even prepared a house for Marie Antoinette and her children at North Edgecomb, Maine, if he could succeed in getting them to America.

His attempts to rescue them failed, the royal family was too carefully guarded, and after the Queen's death, Fersen returned to Sweden. His father died the following year, and he found himself heir to a large fortune. But of what use was his wealth now? He tried to interest himself in his estates and in public life. But Axel was still living in the past, the present was empty, so the honor that had pleased him the most was being appointed by Gustavus IV ambassador to the boy king imprisoned in the Temple, for it implied Sweden's recognition of Louis XVII.

When on June 27, 1795, Fersen heard that the boy was said to have died, he wrote in his journal, "This event has overwhelmed me. He [Charles] was the last and only interest that remained for me in France, for I have less affection for his sister." But in his loneliness, all that mattered now in Fersen's life, he discovered, was to find "the last link with Marie Antoinette," as he wrote of Thérèse in his diary, and talk with her about her mother. It was the confidante Axel wanted, someone to whom he could say, "Do you remember?" So in January, 1796, shortly after Madame Royale's arrival in Austria, her mother's devoted champion left Stockholm and came to Vienna to try to see her.

Fersen was told that it would be impossible for him to get a word with the Princess alone. The poor girl had merely changed her prison from Paris to Vienna. The Austrians were not really her friends, but a new set of jailers. Only by bribery was Axel able to slip into Belvedere Palace and catch a glimpse of the daughter of Marie Antoinette. It was an unsatisfactory meeting, as he wrote on February 19:

> I went this morning with the Duke de Guiche to see Thérèse as she came from Mass. We stood in the hall as she passed at half-past ten with Madame de Chanclos. She is tall, well made, but looks more like Madame Elisabeth than the Queen. Her face is rounder than when I last saw her, but little changed. She is fair and has pretty feet, but she turns them in, in walking. Passing us she flushed and, on entering her apartment, turned to glance at us again. In her manner I recognized her mother. The impression was so strong that tears came to my eyes. I felt my knees shaking as I went down the stairs.

Thérèse had stolen a second look, and the Swedish Count was sure she had recognized him, the most loyal friend of her dead parents. But the girl had been afraid to speak or even smile. Still, Thérèse's proud way of holding her head reminded Axel so much of her mother that he vowed to redouble his efforts to help her.

Before coming to Vienna, Fersen had visited Brussels to try to get for Marie Antoinette's daughter the 150,000,000 livres that her parents had managed to smuggle out of France during the Revolution. In 1791, from the Tuileries, they had sent a chest containing gold coins and diamonds to the Comte de Mercy, former Austrian ambassador to France, now living in Belgium, and told him to give the coffer to Fersen, who would hold it for them. Instead, Mercy turned over the diamonds and gold to the Princess Albert of Saxe-Teschen, another of Marie Antoinette's sisters. Fersen wrote to her. Maria Christina replied that she no longer had the chest. Hearing of Thérèse's arrival in Vienna, she had sent it to Francis II to give to her niece.

Good! So Thérèse's fortune was in Vienna. Axel wrote to the Emperor. Getting no reply, on arriving in the Austrian capital, he went to the Hofburg and demanded to see Francis.

The interview the Count had with the Emperor on February 24, 1796, was anything but cordial. Four years of ruling Austria had turned the twenty-eight-year-old Francis into a stern, cold man. Fersen disliked him heartily. He knew the Emperor had declared war against the French, not to rescue his aunt, for once Marie Antoinette was safe, Austria would have no further excuse to invade France, but in order to annex the French province of Alsace-Lorraine.

"Certainly, I have the gold and jewels," Francis admitted. "I'm holding them in trust for my little cousin, until Thérèse comes of age."

"She is of age now, seventeen."

"In Austria, one doesn't become of age until twenty-one."

It was a lie, and the Emperor knew it, but Axel, looking into Francis' cold gray eyes, knew he was beaten. He stormed out of the room in a temper.

Frustrations such as this had plagued him for years. Where were the diamonds that Marie Antoinette had entrusted to Léonard, her hairdresser, who was to meet her at Montmédy, on the frontier? During the drive to Varennes, the jewel case had vanished with Léonard, as had the large sum of money the Queen sent to her sister in Italy. When Fersen wrote and begged Maria Carolina, Queen of the Two Sicilies, to let him have the gold, so he could bribe Marie Antoinette's way out of prison, her sister claimed that the money was lost on the way to Naples. Maybe? If he had had the gold, Alex thought bitterly, the Queen of France might be alive today.

He doubted that Marie Antoinette's daughter knew about this wealth that was hers by right. Determined to open Thérèse's eyes to the way her mother's family were using her to further Hapsburg ambitions, Fersen wrote to the Comtesse de Chanclos and asked for a talk with Madame Royale in private. To his delight, a reply came, inviting him and the Duc de Guiche, Alex's traveling companion, to come to the Belvedere Palace on March 27, 1796, at noon. That night he wrote in his diary:

The Duc de Guiche believed that we would be alone, I didn't and I was right. There was a circle of sixteen people, men and women, all seated. Thérèse was on the sofa and talked with each of us, but the conversation was general. She spoke to the Duc de Guiche about his children; to me, of Sweden and our king. Her face lighted up when speaking, her eyes and skin are superb, but she has less of her mother in her than her father. I wish it were the other way around. The reception lasted three-quarters of an hour. Then the Princess rose and we left. I noticed that she seemed embarrassed to be receiving the Duc de Guiche and myself in this manner. She kept looking at me, but Madame de

Chanclos watched her closely, no doubt under orders from the Emperor. She is treated like a child and forbidden to see whom she wishes, especially old friends. I do not think the girl is happy; I hear, in her room, she cries a great deal.

A second attempt had failed. And it was two months before Fersen found a way to see Marie Antoinette's daughter alone. He discovered that Madame Royale took her dog walking on the ramparts of the city. So one afternoon in May, it wasn't François Hue who met her there, but Axel. He found Thérèse seated on a bench, playing with Coco. She looked up when he stopped in front of her. "You didn't come here by accident," the girl said. "You've been following me. You want to tell me something. What is it?"

"That I'm your friend, here to help you." Axel sat down on the bench and began to explain how he had been in Vienna for four months, trying, without success, to get for Thérèse the fortune her parents had sent out of France. The Emperor Francis refused to give it up. Fersen doubted that he ever would. "You see what the Hapsburg are?" he concluded bitterly. "They never hand over a thing they don't have to. Do you know that your mother's dowry has never been paid?"

She sat silent beside him. . . . "I can't believe it," Thérèse said finally, in a shocked voice. "Cousin Francis is so good. He freed me from prison, he has given me a home, I'm very grateful to him."

"Do you think the Emperor would have taken you in, if it wasn't to his selfish interest?"

"Me? What can I do for him? The Revolution took everything my parents had. You say that they sent money out of France. I never heard of it. I think you're wrong, Count Fersen. I'm penniless, utterly dependent upon what the Austrians give me."

"That's what the Emperor wants you to think. On the contrary, my dear, you're a great heiress—in case of a Bourbon Restoration, of course. That's why Francis is holding you here, to get Alsace-Lorraine."

"Alsace-Lorraine? I don't understand."

"A rich province of France that's yours by inheritance from the Duc de Lorraine, your mother's father. Thérèse, don't you see what your scheming cousin is up to? The Archduke Karl marries you and Austria acquires another vast tract of land, without even a battle. Oh, they're clever, those Marrying Hapsburgs! Of course, with Napoleon doing so well in Italy, a Bourbon Restoration isn't likely, but it's worth a try."

"Oh, I don't believe it! Karl isn't marrying me for any reason but that he loves me and I love him. Until I met him, I'd never had much happiness, Count Fersen, you know that. . . . Oh, I want so much to be loved, to be happy, and begin living!"

It was the cry of a girl, only seventeen, who had been in prison for three years. "You poor child!" Axel put an arm around her. "I'm sorry I upset you. If you love your archduke, I hope it works out. I hear he's a nice young man. Thérèse, I want you to be happy. You and your brother are all I have left in the world—" The words were hardly out of his mouth before Fersen regretted what he had said. He hadn't intended to tell her.

"My brother?" said her voice, muffled against his shoulder.

"Yes, I don't think Charles is dead."

"Of course he is. He died from mistreatment and neglect, and they buried him in the cemetery of Sainte-Marguerite."

"That's what your jailers told you. But from what I hear from my agents in Paris, it is possible that the boy they buried wasn't Charles, but one they put in his place."

Thérèse showed no surprise, no joy; she didn't believe him, Axel felt sure. "When did you last see your brother?" he asked her.

"One day when Chaumette, the Commune's prosecutor, had me brought downstairs to question me about Mama. I only caught a glimpse of Charles. I wasn't allowed to speak to him. His jailer's wife, Madame Simon, hurried me into the next room, where Chaumette was waiting. Shortly after that, the Simons left the Tower. No one was permitted to see Charles. François Hue, Papa's valet, begged Chaumette to let him rejoin my brother in jail and wait on him, but he was refused."

"Of course he was. Hue would have seen at once that it wasn't the same boy, but one several years older and much taller. I firmly believe, Thérèse, that he was substituted for Charles, who was taken out of the Temple, possibly by Antoine Simon and his wife. Just how, I don't know. But I think it was the Simon couple who took him away."

"Took him away? How?"

"That's what we must find out. Thérèse, think back. On the night of January 19, 1794, when the Simons left, do you remember anything odd happening?"

The girl's face went white. "Oh, Count Fersen, I can't bear to think of those terrible days! Please don't ask me to, I'm trying so hard to forget them."

"I know, dear, and I'm sorry to upset you. But it's necessary, if we want to find your brother. Just answer a few questions—"

Madame Royale struggled for a few moments to regain her composure, then replied, "Yes, about nine o'clock, peeking out through the bars, Aunt Babet and I saw a long, white bundle being carried out. We took it to be some of the Simons' possessions, for we had been told they were leaving. My brother must have gone with them, we thought, it was so quiet on the floor below. But later we heard that only Antoine Simon and his wife had gone. Aunt Babet and I couldn't believe that Charles was down there alone. He was a spoiled little boy. Had he been left behind by the Simons, we were sure he would have wept and shouted with rage, as he did when they took him away from Mama. Why was Charles so quiet now, we wondered, if his jailers had really gone, and he was alone in the dark?"

"That proves it, Thérèse. There was a boy below you on the second floor, but he wasn't Charles. What else did you hear?"

"Next day, a pounding began."

"That was made by the men at work for two days, turning Cléry's tiny room into a sealed-up dungeon. But the sickly, imbecile boy, who was walled up there to die, wasn't your brother. I'm convinced of that, Thérèse, if for no other reason than by the fact that no one who had known the Dauphin must see this new boy. Turgy and Cléry were sent away, and the Tisons locked up, for fear they would detect the fraud and tell. Isn't it suspicious that an entire new set of jailers were appointed? Neither Laurent, Gomin, nor Lasne, who replaced Simon and his wife, had ever seen Charles."

Axel thought he had convinced her, when Madame Royale suddenly sprang to her feet. Her jailers had told her in the Tower that her brother had died. Never before had she questioned the fact, or suspected that they might be lying. It was hard for her to get used to the idea at first.

"Oh, this is ridiculous, Count Fersen! I don't believe you. My brother is dead!" Thérèse cried. "Now I must go. I can't stay here any longer. I'm not allowed to talk with old friends. Suppose someone should see us and tell the Emperor?"

She started to walk away, but he stopped her, his hand on her arm. "Before you go, Thérèse, please look at this—" Fersen took from his pocket a roll of paper. He unwrapped it, and showed her what was in the paper, several strands of coarse brown hair. "That came from the head of the boy they buried. Now, do you believe me?"

With trembling fingers, Madame Royale felt for a locket hanging around her neck. She let Axel see what it contained—a silky lock of light hair. "It's one of Charles' curls. Mama gave it to me, when she was taken away to the Conciergerie." Her voice quivered. "Yes, I believe you. They're not from the head of the same boy."

"Good! Then we can go on from there. I'm going to find your brother, Thérèse, and you're going to help me, aren't you?"

"Yes, Mama's last words to me were to look after Charles, always."

"I have to go back to Sweden, but I'll track down every clue I get. If I come across anything of interest, I'll let you know." Fersen took from his finger the ring he always wore, that Marie Antoinette had given him, and showed her daughter the motto engraved on it, *Lâche qui les abandone* (Shame on him who forsakes them). "I will never forget your mother," he told Thérèse tenderly. "Did you know that I made several attempts to rescue her from the Tower, and take your mother, you and Charles, to America? I had a house waiting for you at North Edgecomb, Maine. Now that she is gone, do you think I would desert you and your brother? You can always count upon me as your friend."

"I'll remember that, Count Fersen. Now I must go. They'll wonder where I am."

They went together to the steps leading down from the ramparts. Thérèse called to Coco to follow her, and she walked by Fersen's side until they reached the driveway where her coachman was waiting. Axel helped Madame Royale into the carriage, lifted the dog in beside her, and watched them drive away.

He was moved to tears. The sight of Thérèse had brought back memories of both her parents. She looked like her Aunt

Babet, but she had her mother's proud manner, and was a quiet, moody girl, given to long silences like her father. She didn't have Marie Antoinette's elegance. Did she have her mother's courage? Axel hoped so, for, surrounded as she was by intrigues, the girl would need it.

13

RUNNING AWAY FROM NAPOLEON

AT SEVEN O'CLOCK on the morning of April 7, 1797, the Comtesse de Chanclos hurried into Madame Royale's bedroom at Belvedere. "You're to go to the Hofburg immediately," Josépha announced. Thérèse sat up in bed, half-awake. "At this hour? Why?"

"The Emperor has sent a carriage for you. And while Your Highness is at the palace, we're told to pack for a journey."

"Good heavens, where?"

"His Imperial Majesty will explain. Please hurry, Madame. You mustn't keep the Emperor waiting."

Thérèse got up and dressed quickly. What had happened? The war with France was going badly. Winning a succession of victories, Napoleon had driven the Austrians out of Italy. The Archduke Karl, in command of the Austrian forces in Germany, had been successful against the French on the Rhine. So he had been rushed to the Tyrol, to try to stop Napoleon from marching on Vienna. To halt the French advance was impossible. All that spring of 1797, Napoleon had pushed the Archduke's army back through the Alps. The enemy were at Leoben, only a hundred miles from Vienna, the Austrians having halted there to make a last stand. Had more bad news come from the front? Thérèse hadn't seen Cousin Francis or his family for months. Then, suddenly, there was this urgent summons.

As her carriage turned in through the gates of the Hofburg, Madame Royale saw that several baggage wagons blocked the courtyard. Trunks were being loaded onto the wagons. At the entrance to the palace, six traveling coaches stood waiting.

A flunkey led the Princess to the Empress' private suite, where her cousins were gathered. Francis, worried-looking and tired, stood chatting with an aide. Maria Theresa, seated on the sofa with her children, six-year-old Marie Louise and Ferdinand, four, wore a hat and traveling coat. So did her ladies.

The blond little Archduchess ran to embrace her cousin. "Thérèse, you're coming to Prague with us!" Marie Louise cried. "Mama says that, if we don't escape before he reaches Vienna, the monster will eat us!" Francis' young daughter had been brought up to hate the "French ogre." When Marie Louise played with her dolls, she showed her hatred of the man who had brought the proud Austrian Empire to its knees by sticking pins in one she called "that vile Corsican," hoping to bring him bad luck.

The voodoo magic hadn't worked. Napoleon continued to advance, and Vienna was in a panic. The Emperor came over to tell Thérèse why he had sent for her.

"You're leaving with us this morning for Prague," Francis explained. "If Napoleon gets through the Alps, there's nothing to prevent him from marching on, straight to Vienna. We've lost twenty thousand men. We've none left to defend the city, so there's no choice for me but flight. The Emperor cannot be taken prisoner. Nor must you. I assure you, my dear girl, you're not safe here. Napoleon has no love for the Bourbons."

At this moment a lackey announced, "Your Majesty, a messenger from the front." Francis' face went white, as he replied, "Let him come in."

A young officer in a mud-spattered uniform entered and saluted. "Your Imperial Highness, I come from the Archduke Karl," he said. "He begs Your Majesty to leave at once. Napoleon has stormed the last pass in the Alps. The Archduke doesn't know how long he can hold the road to Vienna. I regret to be the bearer of such frightful news."

There was a minute of shocked silence. Then the Empress sprang to her feet. "Come, Francis, hurry!" Maria Theresa grasped her husband's arm. "Do you want us to be taken prisoners?"

Thérèse did not even have time to return to Belvedere. Twenty minutes later, seated in one of the imperial coaches with little Archduchess Marie Louise and the tiny Imperial Prince Ferdinand and their nurses, she was on the road to Prague, fleeing from Napoleon.

* * * *

The triumphant "Corsican" demanded unconditional surrender. On October 7, 1797, the Archduke Karl signed an armistice with the French at Campo Formio. The five-year war between Austria and France was over.

In November, when it was safe for the Emperor and his family to return to Vienna, Madame Royale came back from Prague with them, to find her life changed by Napoleon's conquest. To her delight, François Hue and his wife Julie, who had dared to return to Vienna, were allowed to visit her. Also, those two servants who had been so devoted during the days when the royal family was imprisoned in the Temple,

Louis Turgy and Jean-Baptiste Cléry, came to call one day and kiss the Princess' hand. Thérèse was surprised that these French friends, whom the Emperor had kept out of Austria, had been permitted to join her. She thought it was because France and Austria were now at peace. That her new freedom was granted her for another reason never occurred to her.

Cléry and Turgy had come from Paris; the Hues from East Germany. François and Julie Hue had been in the duchy of Brunswick, staying with Louis XVIII, for he had been forced to move again. In April, 1796, the Republic of Venice, frightened by Napoleon's conquest of Italy, demanded that the Pretender to the nonexistent French throne leave Verona. Where could the poor man go? Nobody wanted to shelter the penniless exile. Finally, the Duke of Brunswick, taking pity on Louis XVIII, agreed to let him stay in the little town of Blankenburg, near Hannover, where Provence rented three rooms in a brewer's house, all he could afford.

"Where is Blankenburg?" Thérèse wrote her uncle. "It must be a tiny place. I looked for it on the map, and cannot find it."

Then, on a cold December day in 1797, Madame Royale, seated shivering in big, drafty Belvedere Palace by a dying fire, looked up to find Madame de Dombasle standing in the doorway. "What is it?" she asked.

"Madame, Count Fersen, from Stockholm, is downstairs and asks to see you. Shall I send him up?"

"Yes, but first light the fire, bring candles, and something hot to drink."

When Axel entered her sitting room, he found Thérèse seated by the fireplace, Coco on her lap. "My dear Count, I'm no longer a prisoner," Madame Royale greeted him joyfully. "No more meeting you in secret on the ramparts. I'm allowed to see anyone I wish. Who do you think is in Vienna?" And she told him about the Hues, Cléry, and Turgy living nearby.

"Yes, even the Emperor knows I'm calling on you," Fersen replied, as they sipped their hot drink. He hadn't the heart to tell the poor girl that she wasn't a prisoner, being guarded and spied upon by the Austrians every minute, because they no longer cared what she did. Napoleon's victories had made a Bourbon Restoration unlikely. So the daughter of a king who had lost his throne and his head was no longer a suitable consort for a Hapsburg archduke. Instead, Axel said, "Thérèse, I came to Vienna again about that money Francis owes you. He still won't hand it over, so I went to Rastadt to see what I could get from Napoleon."

The French general was at Rastadt, drawing up peace terms with Austria. At first, he had refused to speak to the man who had planned the flight of the royal family to Varennes. But finally Napoleon consented to receive Fersen on November 28, 1797, at nine o'clock at night. An odd time, Axel thought, but apparently Bonaparte worked late.

"You've always been an enemy of the Republic, I hate to have anything to do with you," the General greeted him. "What do you want? Tell me, and make it quick."

Aides were constantly interrupting them, but Fersen had done his best, in the short time allotted to him, to try to persuade Napoleon to give back to Marie Antoinette's daughter the French crown jewels and the estates of the Bourbons the Republic had confiscated.

"Count Fersen, you're such a good friend!" murmured Thérèse, remembering how, on leaving France at Huminque, a penniless princess, she had been embarrassed at not having even a small coin with which to tip the hotel porter.

"My dear, I'm sorry to bring you bad news," Axel said. "Napoleon won't do a thing for you."

"Then I'm still dependent upon Hapsburg charity?"

"I'm afraid so." Fersen sighed. "Napoleon is returning to Paris, to prepare for a campaign against the English in Egypt.

Since he refuses to see me again, I'm returning to Sweden. But I stopped off in Vienna, Thérèse, to warn you about a Jean Hervagault, who claims that he is your brother. If the fellow tries to get in touch with you, don't have anything to do with him. He's an impostor, the son of a tailor from Saint-Lô, in Normandy. But he insists he's the lost Dauphin, that the Simons carried him out of the Tower in a basket of linen, from which a boy his own age was taken and put in his bed. What interests me, Thérèse, is what Hervagault says happened to him after he got out of the Tower. He claims the Simons handed him over to a General Frotté, who took him to Charette's headquarters in the Vendée, disguised as a girl. Hervagault has probably based his story on something he overheard. It proves what I've thought all along, Charles was abducted from the Tower by the royalists. Probably, by bribing Simon."

"Yes, there were several plots to rescue us. Your attempt to save us and take us to America, Count Fersen, wasn't the only one. Did you know that a group of French refugees built a huge log house at Asylum, in Pennsylvania, for Mama, in the hope that she could escape from France and live there in safety? These frequent attempts to smuggle us out of the tower frightened our jailers. They would wake us in the night to see if we were still there."

"It's a pity that General François Charette, leader of the resistance forces in Brittany, was executed at Nantes last year by the Republicans. He might have told us something. Still, I think I'll go to Brittany anyhow, before I return to Sweden. If Charles isn't with the royalist army of the Vendée, I'm sure they know where he is."

So several weeks later, Axel von Fersen was a Fontenoi in Brittany, at the royalists' camp, chatting with Comte Louis de Frotté, who had helped Charette in his attempt to rescue the Dauphin.

"Three years ago, the Convention wanted peace at any price, here in Brittany, and they were willing to hand over the Dauphin to get it," Frotté told him. "So Charette was able to make a secret deal with them. On the night of June 13, 1794, he sent me and a woman named Françoise Desperez, an agent of ours in Paris, to wait in a carriage on a street corner near the Temple. A man appeared, carrying a boy. Madame Desperez dressed him as a girl, and we brought him to Fontenoi. Charette took one look at the child and told us, what both Françoise Desperez and I suspected, that we had the wrong boy."

"The Convention tricked you?"

"Perhaps they were fooled, too. Someone had gotten into the Tower and, right under their noses, stolen the real Dauphin. So the Convention sent us another boy, hoping we wouldn't know the difference. There must have been an escape from the Temple, for the police were ordered to arrest, on every road in France, anyone traveling with a nine-year-old child. Several boys were arrested and then released. There was great excitement about it in the newspapers, Count Fersen, didn't you read about it?"

"No, I've been in Sweden. Then you think Louis XVII is alive?"

"I do, and that the Dauphin is being kept in hiding, to use at the proper time," Frotté replied. "Not now, with Napoleon so powerful, but later, if the Corsican should begin to slip."

14

GLORY COMES HIGH

THE TREATY OF CAMPO FORMIO was a blow to Austrian prestige. That the Hapsburgs were given Venice by Napoleon in return didn't make up for their humiliation at losing the Austrian Netherlands, that is, modern Belgium, and the German provinces on the west bank of the Rhine. The Archduke Karl, who at twenty-six prided himself upon being Austria's best general, blamed their defeat on his lack of men.

"France has passed the first conscription law in history," he told his brother Francis. "Every Frenchman between the ages of twenty and twenty-five must enlist. Why can't Austria do the same? Otherwise, how can we stand up against the French? Their armies will be enormous. They'll overrun Europe."

For months the Emperor had been pleading with the Archduke to break off his engagement to Marie Thérèse of France. Now he smiled slyly, for he saw the way to handle his brother. "Very well, I'll let you modernize the Austrian army on one condition—" the Emperor said, and he named his terms. They were bitter ones. But the Archduke, who loved military glory above all else, found them hard to resist. And the night of his personal triumph was for Madame Royale an evening of deep humiliation.

To avoid meeting the Emperor and Empress, who seemed to have grown to dislike her, Thérèse no longer attended their state dinners and receptions. But she was present the night of the Emperor's birthday ball, held at Schönbrunn.

Madame Royale was entering the ballroom when Baron Franz von Thugut, Austria's Minister of Foreign Affairs, and another gentleman passed her. "I hear our handsome Karl is about to be sent on a tour of the courts of Europe to select a king's daughter for a bride," the friend said.

"Yes." Thugut laughed. "And not a headless king."

Thérèse's heart turned to ice. But at that moment, in the ballroom beyond, the Court Chamberlain clapped his hands for attention. She heard his voice above the murmur of the guests. "Please, everyone listen." The room was so crowded that Madame Royale, at first, could not make out what was happening. Then she saw the Emperor, the Empress, and the Archduke Karl standing together. "Form a circle around us," Francis called out. "I've an important announcement to make."

"Have you all champagne?" cried the Empress gaily. "We have a toast to drink." Someone handed Thérèse a glass. She took it because everyone else did.

"Ladies and gentlemen, I've news to tell you concerning my dear brother." Francis looked at Karl, standing beside him, straight and proud. "You all agree with me, I know, that our favorite archduke is also Austria's ablest general, so, as a birthday gift to the nation and myself, I've decided to"—the Emperor paused to heighten the effect of his words—"make him field marshal general."

It was the highest rank in the Austrian army. As Francis pinned another medal on his brother's chest, already covered with military decorations, the guests lifted their champagne glasses and drank to the new field marshal general—all but

Thérèse. "Oh, no," she cried hysterically. It was all too plain. Karl was being bribed to give her up.

Dashing her glass to the floor, Madame Royale ran past the horrified guests and through the long corridors to the entrance of the palace, where, in a trembling voice, she summoned her carriage. "To the Danube," she told the coachman. When they reached the quay, the Princess got out and ordered, "Go home, I wish to be alone." The man drove away quickly. Thérèse decided that he must think she had come there to meet a lover.

The brokenhearted girl walked out onto the bridge over the Danube and, leaning against the parapet, for fifteen minutes or more looked down into the water. How cold and black the river looked! Soon Madame Royale would know how the water felt, for when she could get up sufficient courage, she was going to jump off the bridge.

"Have courage!" the priest had said to Marie Antoinette, as she mounted the steps of the scaffold.

"Courage?" the Queen replied scornfully. "It doesn't take courage to die, it takes courage to live."

Her daughter had learned that, during her three years in prison. But now Thérèse's courage had run out. The thought of Karl married to another girl was bad enough. Added to that was her humiliation at being rejected for the second time—first, by her mother, now by her Austrian cousins. It made Madame Royale feel alone and insecure again, and so bitter, she no longer wanted to live. Placing her hands on the parapet of the bridge, she tried to pull herself up—

Someone seized her shoulders and dragged her back. The weeping Princess tried to shake off the hands and begged, "Leave me alone!" But the man moved her firmly away from the parapet. Thérèse saw it was François Hue. She realized now why her coachman had driven off in such haste. It had been to fetch her friend.

In spite of her struggles, Hue led Madame Royale firmly over to the carriage, pushed her in, and sat down beside her. "To Belvedere, hurry," he ordered the coachman.

"Let me out!" Thérèse sobbed. He held her in a firm grip, but the voice of her father's former Gentleman of the Bedchamber was gentle as he said, "What were you trying to do? Commit suicide? Highness, I'm ashamed of you! Why, even during those three terrible years in prison, you never tried to kill yourself. What happened?" His words brought everything back to the brokenhearted girl and she cried, "Karl is being sent all over Europe wife-hunting. I'm no longer good enough for him. François, did you know this?"

"Yes, and I'm sorry, for your sake. There, Madame, you mustn't catch cold." He took off his coat and wrapped it about Madame Royale's bare shoulders. Her teeth were chattering. She had on only a thin chiffon gown, and, on fleeing the palace, had forgotten her evening wrap. "Now tell me what happened," Hue urged.

"They've made him field marshal general–" And Thérèse was crying again. "Oh, his brother Francis knows just how to handle him! Karl would agree to anything to get military honors. All he cares about, really, is the army."

Hue couldn't deny that. "Just cry yourself out," he said. "Just cry." And Madame Royale cried and cried. She couldn't stop. The carriage rolled on through the darkness. After a while she asked, "Do you like Karl?"

"No, not much."

"Why?"

"He's a weak-kneed, conceited fool."

She pulled away. "I love him as I never loved anyone in my life. More than I did Mama, Aunt Babet, or even Papa, so I can't understand it. We were engaged to be married. At least, I thought we were."

"The Archduke will never marry you. Forgive me for

hurting you, Madame, but it's better to speak frankly. It isn't that he doesn't love you, but the Emperor won't let him. Napoleon wouldn't like it. And it's Napoleon that the kings of Europe must cater to now. Why, they're all wondering if Napoleon has a sister—"

At that moment, the carriage creaked to a stop. They had arrived at Belvedere. "Madame, where is your pride? You should leave Austria," Hue said, as he helped her out.

15

STABBED TO THE HEART

Thérèse caught cold that night by the Danube. For two weeks she was ill with a sore throat, a high fever, and what was worse, a broken heart. The Hues moved into Belvedere Palace, and Julie nursed the Princess tenderly. The Archduke Karl sent an aide every day to inquire about Madame Royale's health. He couldn't understand what had happened to Thérèse the night of the Emperor's birthday ball. "Her Highness had a headache and went home," was what Madame Hue told him. And by the time that Madame Royale was well enough to receive visitors, the Emperor had shipped his brother off to visit the courts of Italy and Spain, where there were several unmarried princesses.

"Madame, you should be gone when the Archduke returns," Hue said earnestly. Ever since that night on the bridge, he had been urging Thérèse to leave Austria.

"All right," she finally agreed. "But where can I go?"

"To one of your mother's sisters. The Queen of the Two Sicilies–"

"Cousin Francis' mother-in-law? Aunt Carolina doesn't want me any more than he does. She's too afraid of Napoleon.

And Aunt Elisabeth is so hateful. Oh, I wouldn't be happy with her!" Thérèse shuddered, remembering the two miserable days she had spent in her aunt's gloomy old castle at Innsbruck.

The Archduchess Maria Elisabeth, the beauty of the family, had become embittered after she was disfigured by smallpox. Nor among Marie Antoinette's four other sisters was there one to whom Thérèse could turn—Maria Christina, married to Prince Albert of Saxe-Teschen, had died that year; Maria Amalia, the wife of Duke Ferdinand of Parma, was insane; Maria Anne, the abbess of a convent in Prague, was ill with consumption; while Maria Carolina, consort of Ferdinand IV, King of the Two Sicilies, was about to be chased off her throne by Napoleon. Not one of Marie Antoinette's family could give her daughter a home.

"Then, Your Highness, that leaves only the Bourbons," Hue said. "Have you thought of living with your father's aunts?"

"Oh, not with Adélaide and Victoire!" Thérèse protested, remembering the old ladies' letters, filled with wails of poverty. Since escaping from France, Louis XV's daughters had existed on charity at the court of Naples, until Napoleon's conquest of Italy sent them fleeing to Trieste. They were living in a wretched boardinghouse there—Adélaide crippled with arthritis, Victoire dying of cancer. Thérèse couldn't add to their burdens.

"If only your Aunt Clotilde could take you." Hue sighed. They both knew that was impossible. Louis XVI's eldest sister was married to Charles Emmanuel IV, King of Sardinia. He had fled to that island in the Mediterranean, abandoning to the French his possessions on the mainland (Savoy and Piedmont). Living in fear that Napoleon would force him to abdicate, Aunt Clotilde's husband would hardly risk provoking the French by harboring a Bourbon.

"Then, that leaves only your father's brothers," Hue said. "The Comte d'Artois is out of the question. He is in Edinburgh, Scotland, barely getting along on the pittance the English crown gives him. But perhaps Louis XVIII—"

Thérèse's face brightened. As she had preferred her father to her mother, so the thought of living with the Bourbons rather than the Hapsburgs appealed to her. "Yes, dear Uncle Provence—" Madame Royale exclaimed. There was someone who loved her! She hadn't seen him for a long time, but recently the Pretender had been writing her such sweet, fatherly letters. She knew he was poor, living in wretched lodgings in Brunswick, but wouldn't it be better to go where she was loved and wanted than to remain in Austria, where she was in the way? She wouldn't go happily, though. . . .

Thérèse hesitated several weeks before she finally said sadly, "All right, François, do as you like. Write and tell my uncle I'll join him."

"You know what else he wants?"

"That I marry the Duc d'Angoulême? How ridiculous!"

"It was your mother's fondest wish."

"Merely to spite the Duc d'Orléans, who wanted me to marry his son, Louis Philippe. You're mad, François! Do you expect me to feel bound to Antoine by that mock marriage at Trianon eleven years ago?"

"Remember, Your Highness, you stood up before a priest, your tutor, the Abbé d'Avaux. That ceremony you treat so lightly may be more binding than you think."

"You know perfectly well that I hardly remember my cousin. I haven't seen Antoine since he was a boy and we played together as children at Versailles." Thérèse spoke crossly. "François, why do you continue to torment me?"

"How, Your Highness?"

"With this continual talk about my marrying the Duc

d'Angoulême! If I can't have the Archduke Karl, I shall never marry."

Hue looked shocked. "Believe me, Madame, it's a princess' duty to marry, not for love, but for political reasons. You can help His Majesty a great deal by becoming his nephew's wife."

François had struck just the right note. "I can help my uncle? He needs me?" Thérèse asked eagerly.

"Very much, Your Highness. To have the daughter of Marie Antoinette beside him, as his nephew's wife, will win over a great many people to the Pretender's cause."

"All right, then, I'll even marry the Duc d'Angoulême—" Madame Royale jumped up. She never remembered running, blinded by tears, up the stairs. But here she was, in her room, flung across the bed, and sobbing her heart out.

Julie came in and sat down beside her. "Chéri, you don't have to marry the Duc d'Angoulême, if you don't want to," she whispered.

"Oh, what does it matter?" Thérèse sighed. "I might as well, if it will make everyone happy."

Again the young orphan was reaching out, in her hunger for affection, to those she felt loved and needed her. Besides, royal princesses usually marry their cousins. And for months Antoine had been courting her in letters from Germany.

For several years, the sons of the Comte d'Artois had been with Condé's royalist army, which joined any one of the Allies fighting Napoleon who would support them—England, Austria, or Russia. But now Charles Ferdinand de Berry was with his father in Scotland; Joseph Antoine d'Angoulême was in Germany with his Uncle Provence. Since the Austrian police had stopped confiscating their letters, Antoine and Thérèse had been corresponding regularly. One that she had recently received from him was so sweet that, when Julie left her,

Madame Royale dried her eyes, took Antoine's letter out of the drawer of her desk, and reread it. He wrote:

> The feelings which my dear cousin have graven upon my heart constitute both my happiness and my torment. I cannot submit without sorrow to the delay of hopes [their marriage] of which I dream night and day. It [the delay] is like wresting from me the days I would so gladly consecrate entirely to your happiness.

What an ardent love letter for a quiet, shy boy to write, Thérèse thought, for that was how she remembered her cousin. He must have changed. She was curious to see Antoine again, and had repeatedly urged him to come to Vienna. He hadn't come. That was strange, too.

* * * *

The Archduke Karl went dutifully to look over several possible brides. To his relief, nothing came of his visits, and he returned to Vienna determined not to be bullied any longer by his older brother. He would go to Thérèse and they would . . . What? He couldn't marry her. Francis had made that plain enough. Even loving her was forbidden.

"But somewhere, somehow, we'll be together," the Archduke promised himself vaguely. Perhaps the Emperor would make him governor of Venice, the new province Napoleon had given Austria. He and Thérèse would live in a palazzo by a canal. But Karl knew that dream was impossible. To become governor of Venice, he must resign from the army. He loved being the top field marshal. Karl was a born soldier. He couldn't imagine any other life.

Still, the Archduke told himself that somehow he would persuade Francis to let him marry the girl. So Karl's vacillating heart was dealt a cruel blow when, on his return home, he was told that Madame Royale was leaving Vienna to join her uncle, the French Pretender. He couldn't believe it!

The first time the two young people met after the Archduke's return from his futile bride hunt was at a ball. As he gazed at Thérèse across the room, Karl knew he would never love anyone else. The musicians began to play, and he took an impulsive step forward—Then he stopped, for the Emperor was looking at his brother sternly. Shortly after, the Swedish ambassador having asked Madame Royale to be his partner, she was lost in the swirl of dancers.

Karl turned to his brother, the Duke of Tuscany, and asked, as casually as he could, "Is it true that Thérèse is leaving us?"

"Yes," Ferdinand replied, "to marry her cousin, the Duc d'Angoulême."

So he had lost her! Karl wanted to collapse sobbing in a chair. Instead, he rushed from room to room, searching for Thérèse everywhere. When he finally found her by the refreshment table, their eyes met for a long, agonizing moment. Hers, to Karl's surprise, were as reproachful as his and as sad. Couldn't his darling realize that he still loved her? That it was Francis who had separated them? Not trusting himself to speak to her, the Archduke hurriedly left the ball.

Two days later, the young Field Marshal General was back with his troops, where he was urgently needed. In May, 1798, Napoleon had gone off to Egypt with his army, to try to cripple England by cutting her trade with India. All of the French fleet, but two ships, was destroyed by Nelson off Alexandria, leaving the French general marooned in Egypt. The peace of Campo Formio had been but an armistice. Austria was at war with France again—and with the Russians—trying to regain Italy in Napoleon's absence.

Field Marshal Karl returned to the front an angry young man, especially when he learned that it was common gossip in

Vienna that the Emperor Francis had even considered marrying off Madame Royale to Napoleon, only to find that he was already married.

* * * *

Thérèse, having made her hard decision, was eager to join her uncle. Never a girl to do things by halves, she wrote him: "I am much touched by your kindness in arranging a marriage for me. As you have selected Cousin Angoulême for my husband, I joyfully consent with all my heart. Your choice could not have fallen on a man more agreeable to me. I hope the marriage will soon take place."

It was not until May 3, 1799, however, when Madame Royale had been in Austria for more than three years, that she was able to leave Vienna. The delay was owing to the fact that Provence had no proper home to offer his niece. Since fleeing from France, the Pretender had stayed for a while in Turin with his father-in-law, Victor Amadeus III, the late King of Sardinia, then at Verona. Finally, he found a refuge in Germany. But in February, 1798, the French forced Prussia to ask him to leave Brunswick. Where could he go? Provence was in despair. Then Paul I of Russia offered him a home.

The Czar's hospitality was because of the fact that, in June, 1782, badly dressed and ill at ease, the son of Catherine the Great had visited Versailles. Marie Antoinette and her friends made fun of him. But the Queen's daughter, a charming child of three, had climbed on his knees and said, "You are a nice man. I like you. You must come and see us often."

"No, I can't come again," Paul replied. "I live far away, in Russia."

"Then, someday," Thérèse said, "I'll come to see you."

Now, sixteen years later, remembering what the little Princess had said, the Czar took Louis XVIII in and gave him an annual pension of 200,000 livres, which he agreed to increase by 120,000 more when Madame Royale came to Russia.

Provence had expected to live in St. Petersburg. To his humiliation, he learned that the refuge the Czar offered him was in a small provincial town in Courland, named Mitau (the present Yelgava in Latvia, S.S.R.), on the Lielupe River that flows into the Gulf of Riga, an arm of the Baltic Sea. He would be buried alive in such an isolated spot. But the penniless Pretender had no choice. He went to Mitau in March, 1798. Unfortunately, that didn't end his troubles. Before his niece could join him, he must settle a delicate matter.

Louis XVI's two brothers had married sisters, the daughters of Victor Amadeus III, the late King of Sardinia. After fleeing from France, the Provences and the Artois spent a brief time with the King of Sardinia at Turin. Then they went their separate ways. Neither the Pretender nor Charles had lived with their wives for years. Marie Josephine de Provence was at Budweis, in Czechoslovakia; her sister, Marie Thérèse d'Artois, at Klagenfurt, Austria. Louis XVIII's pathetic little court consisted of the Comte d'Avaray and a few old friends. They were all men, and before he could invite his niece to become a member of his household, the Pretender knew that, for appearance sake, he must persuade his wife to join him.

It wasn't easy. The Queen of France, as the Comtesse de Provence delighted in calling herself, had long resented the way her husband neglected her. Now that he needed his wife desperately (and the 84,000 livres a year her cousin, Charles IV of Spain, gave her), Josephine of Savoy took her revenge by making her husband wait for more than a year before she would agree to go to Mitau. And then she would come only if her inseparable companion, Marguerite Gourbillon, came with her. "Never!" replied the King, for Josephine was too fond of the bottle, and Madame Gourbillon, a coarse, illiterate woman, whose husband was employed at the Lille post office, encouraged her.

The bickerings between husband and wife went on until April, 1799, when the Queen finally consented to travel to Russia without her devoted friend, and Provence could happily start planning the wedding. He obtained from the Pope the permission necessary for a marriage between cousins, and Madame Royale, accompanied by the Hues, Cléry, and Turgy, left Vienna on May 3 and arrived at Mitau on June 4, early in the morning.

The King and his nephew drove out five miles from town to welcome her. When the coaches met on the highway, and stopped opposite each other, Provence descended from his. It took him some time and considerable effort, for he had grown very stout.

Thérèse, light as a gazelle, in spite of a month spent in her carriage, jumped out, ran across the road to the uncle she had not seen in eight years (not since the night of June 20, 1791, when the drive to Varennes began), and flung her arms around him. "Dear Papa . . ." she cried. His brother reminded Madame Royale so much of her dead father that she burst into tears.

Provence kissed her. Then he drew from behind him a short, frail creature, whose long arms and legs, and silly grin, made him look like a monkey.

"Your fiancé," he announced.

Thérèse gasped, as the small, ugly youth kissed her hand. She had expected the son of the handsome Charles d'Artois to be better looking. Antoine was completely the opposite of what she had imagined. Now Thérèse knew why he hadn't come to Vienna. Her uncle hadn't wanted her to see him.

16

FIRST LOVE DIES HARD

LOUIS XVIII WAS OVERJOYED to have his niece fall in with his plans. He had insisted that the Duc d'Angoulême write to his cousin in Vienna twice a week. Provence had composed the love letters himself, and made his nephew copy them, he was so anxious that Antoine should make a good impression on Thérèse and the marriage not be broken off.

The former castle of the Dukes of Courland, where their wedding would take place, was situated on the left bank of the Grosbach River, on the road to Riga. Most of the old, dilapidated building was a military hospital, but the Czar had placed one wing at Louis XVIII's disposal, and he began decorating rooms in it for the young married couple. Provence sent to Riga for a tapestry frame and colored silks, for François Hue had told him that Thérèse liked to do needlework, and he ordered from London a hundred-guinea harpsichord. Not until the instrument had been delivered did he learn that his niece didn't care for music. He sold the harpsichord—and made eight hundred rubles on the transaction, money the Pretender needed badly.

Soon he had everything ready to receive the bride. When she arrived on June 4, 1799, Madame Royale was given no time to recover from the fatigue of her month's journey from Vienna and possibly change her mind. Six days later, on the tenth, the anniversary of the funeral of her alleged brother, she was married to the Duc d'Angoulême.

Louis XVIII's wife had reached Mitau the day before her niece. Except for her, few of the bridegroom's family would have been present at his wedding. His father, the Comte d'Artois, and Antoine's younger brother, Ferdinand, were unable to come from Scotland because of the cost of the journey; his mother, the Comtesse d'Artois, who had never shown much affection for her boys, pleaded ill-health; and it would have been better if Antoine's Aunt Josephine had stayed away.

On June 3, the King had driven several miles out of Mitau to meet the Queen, whom he hadn't seen in seven years, not out of eagerness to greet his wife, but to make sure that Marguerite Gourbillon wasn't with her. To his horror, there the woman was, in a carriage with the servants. Provence, furious, had Madame Gourbillon lodged in the Riga jail, until he could ship her back to Budweis.

It was only on arriving in Mitau that Josephine discovered what had happened to her "belle amie." Her Majesty, in front of her husband's shocked entourage, went into hysterics. Refusing to enter the castle, the Queen declared she would return with her dearest friend to Czechoslovakia.

The King put an end to this disgraceful scene by having his wife carried bodily into the building and locked in her room, where, sulking, she had been ever since. Josephine, however, had managed to smuggle in several bottles of liquor. On the morning of the wedding, she was roaring drunk, pounding on the door, and shouting to be let out.

"Ignore Her Majesty," the King ordered the Cardinal de Montmorency, "and begin the ceremony."

Assisting the Cardinal was the Abbé Henry Edgeworth, Louis XVIII's chaplain. Both of these prelates had followed the French Pretender into exile. Wearing the diamond necklace the Czar had sent her for a wedding present, Thérèse knelt with Antoine before an altar decorated with white lilies (the Bourbon flower) and listened reverently to the Abbé Edgeworth, the Irish priest who had risked his life in order to accompany her father to the scaffold and console him in his last moments.

Tears came to the bride's eyes when Antoine slipped a ring on her finger. It was Papa's wedding ring. Inside it were engraved the initials M.A.A.A. (Marie Antoinette, Archduchess of Austria) and the date of their wedding, May 16, 1770. Before leaving for the scaffold, Louis had asked Cléry to give his watch and wedding ring to his wife. Marie Antoinette had sent them to the Comte de Provence, for him to keep and give to the Dauphin. Instead, her uncle gave them today, as a wedding present, to the Dauphin's sister.

Otherwise, Marie Thérèse of France was the poorest princess ever married. Had the Revolution not occurred, the daughter of Louis XVI and Marie Antoinette would have brought her husband vast tracts of land and a rich dowry. Now the royal exiles were entirely at the mercy of the whims of two monarchs. They had nothing to live on but what they received from the Czar of Russia and the King of Spain.

Still, what girl isn't happy at her wedding? The new Duchess d'Angoulême was the usual radiant bride at the banquet which followed the marriage ceremony. It was that night, after her husband left her, that Thérèse, disillusioned, cried herself to sleep. Why hadn't someone told her? She loved children. She had married expecting to have a large family. The knowledge that she might never have a baby was more than she could bear.

* * * *

Having shared Marie Antoinette's dislike of the Comte de Provence, Axel von Fersen was shocked when he heard that Thérèse had joined her uncle. He imagined the poor girl believed in the sincerity of his affection, and hoped to find in him a second father. But did she know that the Convention had been willing to exchange all of the royal family before her mother's death? They had written to Provence—and he had not replied.

Fersen believed the Pretender would someday be unmasked and the world would know what he had been during the French Revolution, an ambitious, unscrupulous traitor. It was the unspeakable Hébert, suspected of having been Provence's hired agent at the Commune, who had made up the accusations that sent Marie Antoinette to the scaffold. And Axel was convinced that he had married the Queen's daughter to his nephew merely for his own self-interest.

Worried about the girl he had grown to love, the Swedish Count came to Mitau in May, 1800, and took a room in the village. He was shocked at the change he found in her. What three years in prison had failed to do, ruin Thérèse's good looks, a disappointing marriage had accomplished in a year's time. There was a pathetic droop to her lips, for she had discovered that Antoine could never have written those love letters. The sickly Angoulême had inherited the physical defect from which both his uncles suffered, Louis XVI temporarily, Louis XVIII incurably. A weak, homely young man with defective eyesight, he was hardly the proper mate for a beautiful, virile girl.

But Axel von Fersen hadn't come to Mitau to commiserate

with Thérèse about her marriage. In regard to that, he could do nothing. He wanted to talk with her concerning her brother. But on the morning he went to the castle, he first asked to see Louis XVIII. Etiquette demanded that he must present to the King the compliments of his own Swedish monarch.

He found Provence studying a map. All Europe was anxiously watching Napoleon, who had made a dramatic return from Egypt, overthrown the Directory, and made himself First Consul, sole ruler of France. Following this he had led his army across the Alps into Italy, and was regaining all the territory lost by France during his absence.

"My nephews are fighting here, with the Austrians." Louis pointed a fat finger to Pontaba, in Italy. So Thérèse's husband had rejoined Condé's army? Antoine was hardly the soldier type. It must have taken considerable urging from his uncle, Axel thought, to make him leave his beloved books and his dogs.

Fersen had expected to chat briefly with the Pretender and leave, but they were hardly seated before Provence said, "My niece tells me that you think her brother is alive. I doubt it very much, but the hope has made Thérèse so happy that I'll be glad to do all I can to help you find the boy."

Looking at the plump, middle-aged man before him, his round face benign and smiling, Axel had to steel himself to remember that they used to say in Paris, "*Faux comme Monsieur* (as treacherous as the Comte de Provence)." He replied, "You have agents in Paris, Your Majesty, working for a Bourbon Restoration. I'd be glad of any information they could send me as to what happened to the little King." Then, as soon as he decently could, the Swedish Count rose and said good-by.

Louis XVIII followed him to the door. "I assure you," he said earnestly, "that I've only assumed the title of King until my nephew is found. If that should happen, I'll gladly turn over the throne to him."

Fersen doubted that Provence would be so generous. He detested hypocrisy. And he hurried down the hall to the Angoulêmes' apartment, feeling a little sick.

He found Thérèse just returned from the main section of the palace. It was part military hospital, part prison. She went there every day with the Abbé Edgeworth to take care of the wounded soldiers, although she hated nursing. It meant touching men crawling with lice, bandaging stumps, and soothing the dying, tossing in delirium. But the Duchess made light of the long hours she spent in the wards smelling of gangrene. "I talk to the French prisoners about France, poor dears, they're so homesick." She sighed. "Well, enough of that, Count Fersen. You wrote me that you had news of my brother. What is it?"

"Not much. Every year it gets harder to trace him," Axel replied. "So many people who might have told us what happened to Charles are dead. Chaumette and Hébert, for instance. In April, 1794, Robespierre had them beheaded. Simon was allowed to live three months longer. After he left the Tower, my Paris agents tell me, Simon became an inspector of army baggage wagons. But he knew too much. In July, he, too, mounted the scaffold. And, Thérèse, that isn't all. . . . After Simon and his wife left the Tower in January, 1794, for six months, until Laurent came in July, no one was allowed to see the little prisoner, walled up alone in his dark cell. Then on May 6, 1795, Laurent called in a Dr. Desault to take care of what was by then a dying boy. A month later, on June 5, Desault himself died, three days before his patient's death. His family insist he was poisoned. Perhaps Desault was asked to kill the boy and refused. Or he may have suspected he wasn't the Dauphin and been about to talk."

"How horrible!" exclaimed the Duchess.

"There's something stranger still," Axel went on. "Before Desault came, the sick boy, for a long time, had refused to speak. Was it because Charles, through mistreatment, had become sullen? Or had a deaf mute been substituted for him? It is believed the boy talked some to Desault. The doctor took down what he said, but, after Desault's death, his notes were never found. And the chemist Choppart, from whom Desault bought his medicines, also died, most mysteriously."

"So many deaths! Count Fersen, is this what you came to Mitau to tell me?"

"No, my dear, but to reassure you. I'm more convinced than ever that the boy who died in the Tower five years ago, while you were imprisoned there, wasn't your brother. I'm told that Roberspierre said, 'If the royalists try to rescue Louise XVII, we'll show them a boy so half-witted they'll give up all idea of making him king.' "

"All right, then, if the boy who died in the Tower wasn't Charles, where is he?"

"Thérèse, you remember I went to Brittany to see if your brother was with the royalist army? He wasn't, their attempt to rescue him failed. But General Frotté believes that Charles was smuggled out of the Tower and is safe somewhere. The Convention would have been afraid to kill him, for, by having the little King die a violent death, they would make a martyr of him. Frotté agrees with me that Charles was abducted, by whom, we don't know, and is being kept in hiding to use when necessary, and a sickly, idiot boy, who would die anyway, was put in his place."

"Oh, if that were only true!"

"His kidnapers meant to produce Charles before now. But Napoleon's rise has interfered with their plans. Since there's no hope of a Bourbon Restoration, your brother, I believe, has been sent to America."

"To America? What make you think so?"

"Because on May 1, 1794, a year before the Convention announced that the Dauphin had died, an artist named Bellanger was allowed into the prison to sketch him for a whole day alone, although the rules were that no one must go near the boy without a jailer. I believe that was when the real Dauphin was carried secretly out of the Tower. And it explains why the boy whom the Convention handed over to the royalists on June 13, 1794, hoping to make a secret deal with them, and Frotté took to Charette in Brittany, wasn't Charles. The young King had been gone from the Tower for a month."

Fersen, who wanted so badly to believe that the Dauphin was alive, and to comfort Thérèse, had good news for her. "Now, I'm told that Bellanger has appeared in Philadelphia with a boy he says is the Dauphin," he informed the Dauphin's sister. "My dear, I served with Rochambeau's forces during the American Revolution. I have written to friends of mine in Philadelphia, asking them to hunt up Bellanger and his boy. I hope and pray we find Charles safe in America, and that this isn't all a hoax. I'll let you know what I hear from Philadelphia."

It was nice having Thérèse so near him in Russia, Fersen thought. It was a pleasant sail across the Baltic from Stockholm to Riga, then only a short drive inland to Mitau. He would see her often. But Napoleon had begun his conquest of Europe. His victories would affect the lives of both the Swedish Count and the Duchesse d'Angoulême. One of them would become the victim of a political crisis in his own country, and the other to roam Europe, a fugitive—but that's getting ahead of our true account of the dramatic events in her life that made Marie Antoinette's daughter as much of a tragic and gallant figure in history as her famous mother.

17

THE FRENCH ANTIGONE

THE SNOW WAS FALLING, the wind howling about the dreary old castle of the Dukes of Courland. It was January 21, 1801, the eighth anniversary of Louis XVI's death. Thérèse had eaten breakfast early, intending to spend this sad day in prayer and thoughts of her father, whom she would never cease to mourn, when she heard stumbling steps in the hall. Her uncle, crippled with gout, hobbled painfully into the room, leaning on a cane.

"My dear, what shall we do?" he exclaimed. "We're ordered to leave Mitau. And General Dreisen says our pensions are to stop. What will we live on?"

Louis XVIII had been existing precariously on the 200,000 livres Czar Paul gave him annually, Thérèse's 120,000 livres, and the 84,000 livres a year Queen Josephine received, begrudgingly, from her cousin, Charles IV of Spain. It was barely enough to support the army of Bourbon hangers-on who had flocked to Mitau to live off the Pretender.

"I can't believe it!" Provence exclaimed. "Since Napoleon has conquered most of Europe, the Russians are frightened to death of him. But, Thérèse, dear, I thought Paul was your friend. How can he do this to us? It's humiliating! I'll be the laughingstock of Europe, turned out of Russia on a moment's notice!"

Uncle and niece sat stunned. What could have caused the change in the Czar? Was it entirely his fear of Napoleon? Or had Paul, after supporting Louis XVIII and his quarreling little entourage for three years, in memory of the old days at Versailles, had enough of them?

The old castle at Mitau, now they must leave it, looked good to them. It was drafty and uncomfortable, but it was better than being turned out into the snow in the middle of January. Here, at least, they had a roof over their heads. Thérèse didn't mind for herself, any change from her monotonous life at Mitau would be a relief, but she was worried about her uncle's health. Greatly overweight and crippled by gout, could he stand the fatigue and cold of a long journey through the snow of a Russian winter, to where . . . ? Who wanted them?

Poland was finally decided upon, and the anniversary of her father's death that Thérèse had expected to spend in seclusion she spent frantically packing. At eight o'clock on the morning of January 22, 1801, two carriages left the courtyard of the castle. In the first was the King, the Duchesse d'Angoulême, Abbé Edgeworth, Comte d'Avaray, and the Duchesse de Sérent. The second contained the Hues, Turgy, the servants, and Thérèse's dog Coco. Queen Josephine, who hated the endless Russian winters, was in Hamburg with her beloved Gourbillon, as usual.

The King and his niece were obliged to travel slowly, owing to the bad state of the Russian roads in the middle of winter. Scarcely had they begun their journey before the servants' carriage upset. Larne, the cook, broke his collarbone and had to be sent back to Mitau. It was bitter cold, and they must cross the vast Lithuanian plains, covered with ice and snow. Nights were spent in dirty wayside inns, crowded with drunken peasants. A blizzard was raging on the fifth day. The high wind, driving clouds of snow before it, frightened the horses and blinded the drivers. The carriages sank so deep into the drifts at times that the crippled King was obliged to alight and, supported by his niece, with the icy wind cutting their faces, painfully wade through snow more than a foot deep. At last, after ten exhausting days, they reached Memel.

Desperately in need of money, in Köningsberg, the next large town, Thérèse was forced to sell her diamond necklace, the Czar's wedding gift, for 2,300 ducats. But it was there she heard the good news that, thanks to the Duchess' appeal to the Queen of Prussia, a friend of her mother's, the Pretender was to be allowed to live in Warsaw. In those days Poland belonged to Prussia.

The exiles rented the Vassiliovitch house, in Cracow Faubourg, and settled down. Their dangerous trip from Russia was over. And their six-weeks journey to Poland, through the deep snow of Lithuania, had won for them the sympathy of all of Europe.

Thérèse's courage and tenderness toward her uncle throughout the trip brought words of praise from the Comte d'Avaray. "The Duchess never complains," he wrote. "She is an inspiration to us all."

In Paris, a print was sold showing Louis XVIII trudging through the snowdrifts, leaning on Thérèse's arm, with Coco bounding along beside them. Entitled the "French Antigone," after the devoted niece in the Greek classic, this was the first political propaganda picture. It did so much for the Bourbon cause that Napoleon had his police confiscate every copy they could find, but the engraving was clandestinely distributed. Great sympathy was felt for the invalid King and his gallant niece, forced to risk their lives by traveling across Russia in the middle of winter.

Louis XVIII had not been long in Warsaw when, on March 23, 1801, Paul I of Russia was assassinated. The new Czar, Alexander, sent word to the Pretender that he would restore part of the pension his father had given him and Louis could return to Mitau. Remembering the winters there, Provence was in no hurry. He remained in Warsaw for more than three years. The royal exiles were desperately poor. The Duchesse d'Angoulême was often at a loss to make ends meet. Then Prussia, too, grew tired of them. Where else could they go but back to Russia? It was December, 1804, when they returned to Mitau, Napoleon had dealt the Bourbon cause what seemed to be a fatal blow by restoring the throne in France and crowning himself Emperor.

Over the next three years the country around Riga became a battlefield between the French and Russians. In April, 1807, Mitau began to fill with sick and wounded prisoners from Napoleon's Grand Army, who had been captured by the Czar's troops. Typhus broke out in the wards. But the Abbé Edgeworth, who had nearly perished on the scaffold because of his devotion to the royal family of France, was not afraid of a mere fever. Caring for the sick men, the elderly priest caught typhus himself.

Condé's royalist army had disbanded in discouragement, and Antoine, on rejoining his wife at Mitau, was alarmed to find her nursing the Abbé. He warned her of the danger of infection.

"I'm not afraid," Thérèse replied. "I must do what I can for the poor man, after all he did for Papa."

It was hard to persuade the Duchess, once she had entered the contagious ward of the hospital, to leave the room in which her father's confessor lay dying. She gave the Abbé Edgeworth his medicines and sat by the old priest's bedside for five days, fanning the flies away. He grew steadily weaker and on May 22, 1807, died in her arms.

She emerged, exhausted, from his sickroom to be confronted by a family crisis, for again they had been told to look for another home. After the Peace of Tilsit, the Czar informed the Bourbon Pretender he must leave Russia, Napoleon might object to his presence there. Where could the French exiles go but to England? Napoleon's conquests had made it impossible for them to live on the Continent. So in July, 1807, Provence went to Yarmouth to see if the British would take him in.

They would do so only if the French Pretender agreed to live in England as a private citizen. He had to resign himself to that and, as the Comte de Lille, became the guest of the Catholic Marquis of Buckingham, who lent Provence his country place, Gosfield Hall, in Essex. There, in August, 1808, Queen Josephine and the Angoulêmes joined him.

To her Uncle Provence, who had given her a home when no one else in the family wanted her, Thérèse would always be fiercely loyal. "I will follow my King wherever he goes and share his misfortunes. He takes the place of all those I have lost," she wrote to the Queen of Prussia. In Provence, Thérèse had found again the father she had loved so dearly. No matter what happened to her uncle, she would stand by him. Rejected by her mother, and by her Austrian cousins, for the first time Thérèse felt herself needed. She knew she made the Pretender respectable.

Gosfield Hall was a big Tudor mansion, built in the reign of Henry VIII. Queen Elizabeth I had visited there twice. Vacant for eleven years (the Marquis of Buckingham preferred his estate at Stowe), only part of the house was livable. Finding it hard to heat and too isolated, the royal exiles began to look for a home nearer London.

Always grateful to anyone who did anything for her, Thérèse suggested to her uncle that, before leaving Gosfield Hall, they thank the Marquis for his hospitality by building in the park a Grecian temple dedicated to gratitude. Round like the Temple of Love at Trianon, it was surrounded by five elm trees. The first was planted by Louis XVIII, the second by his wife, the third by his niece, the fourth and fifth by his brother's sons, Angoulême and Berry.

In April, 1809, they moved to Aylesbury, in Buckinghamshire, forty miles from London. There, the Pretender first rented Hartwell House from Sir George Lee for the sum of five hundred pounds a year. Later, he bought the estate, for Napoleon was so firmly seated on the throne of France that there was little chance of his returning to Paris.

But hope dies hard. The French exiles closely followed the news from across the Channel in the English newspapers. That spring of 1809 Napoleon had invaded Austria for the fourth time, and once more Field Marshal Karl Ludwig Johann von Hapsburg was trying to prevent the French from taking Vienna. In May, when the Archduke won the battle of Aspern, Napoleon's first military defeat, all of Europe rejoiced. "The Archduke Karl is the only general who can stand up against Napoleon," people said. But the Archduke lost at Wagram (July, 1809), and Napoleon advanced down the Danube and entered Vienna.

The Emperor had long considered divorcing Josephine, and taking a younger wife, so as to have an heir. Now the once-humble Corsican astonished everyone by marrying into one of the oldest and proudest royal families in Europe.

"Oh, I can't believe it!" the Duchesse d'Angoulême exclaimed when she heard that, seventeen years after her mother's death, another Austrian archduchess was to sit on the throne of France. For the girl Napoleon selected as his second wife was Thérèse's cousin, Marie Louise, eighteen-year-old daughter of Francis II of Austria.

Thérèse remembered the little girl she had known in Vienna. Marie Louise hated the French who had put her great-aunt, Marie Antoinette, to death. Four times "that vile

Corsican" had humbled the Austrians and driven her family into exile. Yet, when asked to marry the forty-year-old "monster," more than twice her age, Marie Louise meekly submitted to her father's wishes.

The British press reported that Napoleon, too busy to come to Vienna for his wedding in the church of the Augustines, had chosen a "close friend" to represent him on March 11, 1810, and marry the Archduchess by proxy. In England, a few weeks before the event, the Duc d'Angoulême looked up from his newspaper one morning at the breakfast table to say, "Thérèse, listen to this! Who do you think is to be the proxy bridegroom?"

His wife finished pouring herself a cup of coffee. Thinking it might be one of Napoleon's generals, she sipped her drink and replied indifferently, "Who?"

"Your old lover, the Archduke Karl."

"Antoine! You're joking?"

"Indeed, I'm not. Karl is to take Napoleon's place and kneel at the bride's side before the altar. The two men, once bitter enemies, must have become very friendly."

Thérèse sat stunned. She couldn't speak, and something died inside her. It was her love for Karl. That he should so demean himself! "I'm not surprised. Doesn't Karl always do what his brother Francis says?" she replied coldly. "Antoine, don't let's mention the Archduke again. I've long ago forgotten him."

"A woman never forgets her first love."

He's jealous, Thérèse thought, and leaning across the table, fondly patted her husband's hand. "Well, I have," she said. It wasn't quite true. Thérèse had not completely gotten over loving Karl—well, not until this minute. She hated a turncoat.

18

COULD IT BE MURDER?

Before settling in England, Louis XVIII had considered making his home in Sweden. But the enthusiasm for the Bourbons there had cooled. Fersen regretfully wrote the Pretender that he would not be welcomed in Stockholm. Axel was having his own troubles. Gustavus IV, a Bourbon supporter, declared insane in 1809, had been forced to abdicate. In his place ruled his uncle, Charles XIII, an ardent admirer of Napoleon. Fersen, with his hatred of the French, was not in accord with Sweden's new foreign policy.

No longer a favorite at court, Axel decided to leave Stockholm for a while. He would have preferred to go to France, and talk with some people there about the lost Dauphin. But, afraid that he would be arrested by Fouché, Napoleon's chief of police, if he were seen in Paris, Fersen decided to go to England. He wanted to talk to a Lady Edward Atkins in London. She was helping him in his search for Louis XVII.

A pretty red-haired woman, Charlotte Atkins had been an actress before her marriage, specializing in boys' parts. Being in France at the time the royal family was imprisoned, Lady Atkins became interested in rescuing them. Fersen had first heard of the Englishwoman when she wrote him that, masquerading in her favorite role as a boy, she had managed to slip into the Conciergerie and speak with the Queen. Charlotte urged Marie Antoinette to escape—she even hired accomplices to help her do so—but the Dauphin was too carefully guarded, and the Queen refused to leave France without him. Instead, she begged Lady Atkins to try to save her son.

Charlotte hadn't done so because she didn't think that, after January 19, 1794, the little prisoner on the second floor of the Tower was the Dauphin, any more than Fersen did. But Sir Edward Atkins had died, leaving his widow wealthy, and Charlotte spent her money generously in searching for the real boy. Now what had brought Axel to London that spring of 1810 was a letter from Lady Atkins saying that she had heard something concerning "our little king" too dangerous to write.

"What is it, Charlotte?" Fersen asked, as soon as they were seated in her drawing room.

"Something I heard from an agent of mine in Paris, Little Jules . . . of course, that's not his real name. Axel, it worries me. Tell me what you think of it. But, first, have a cup of tea." As Lady Atkins poured the drink, her hand trembled. "Jules writes me that, after the royal family left the Temple and it became a political prison, the head jailer, to occupy the prisoners' time, let them cultivate gardens. Well, it seems that one of them, a Comte d'Andigne, imprisoned there in June, 1801, while working in his plot of ground by the Little Tower, dug up the skeleton of a boy."

"A boy? You're certain?"

"Yes, dead about seven years. Quicklime had destroyed the flesh. But the skeleton was intact. Oh, Axel, I'm so upset! The body had been hurriedly buried, without a coffin. Everything points to a crime having been committed. Do you think it was the Dauphin? That someone murdered him?"

"Come, come, my dear Charlotte, don't jump to conclusions. There have been other boys, children of the jailers, who have died at the Temple."

"Oh, no, the skeleton wasn't that of an ordinary child, the son of some keeper. If so, why did they bury him quickly, without a coffin? Why didn't they send the little corpse to a cemetery? I'll tell you why, Axel, because they couldn't bury him anywhere else. That boy was murdered."

"Why haven't we heard of this before?"

"Comte d'Andigne, who found the skeleton, was warned not to talk. It was reburied immediately."

"And he kept the secret for nine years? That's a long time. Why did he finally tell?"

"To ease his conscience. Comte d'Andigne is dying."

"He said he had found the skeleton of a boy, but he didn't say they were the Dauphin's bones? Good! Then, Charlotte, I'd forget about this. Have you told anyone else?"

"I tried to tell the French royal family. I thought they should know. I went out to Hartwell, but neither the King nor the Angoulêmes would see me. Then, after considerable effort, I succeeded in getting an appointment with the Comte d'Artois, who lives here in London. I waited in his parlor for an hour. Finally, Artois sent down word that he was confined to his room with a sprained ankle, the result of a hunting accident, and unable to hobble downstairs to talk with me. The wretch! I'm sure it was merely an excuse not to see me. The only member of the family I managed to get an interview with, and who would listen to me, was the Duc de Berry. He agrees with me that we should search for that skeleton."

"I wish we had heard of this nine years ago. It's pretty late now."

"Perhaps not. You know that Napoleon is having the Temple prison torn down. One of the workmen may dig up that little skeleton. I think it's a valuable clue. Oh, Axel, I'm frantic! It's the first time I've thought our boy might be dead!" Tears glistened in Lady Atkins' eyes. "You're going to Hartwell, of course. Will you tell his sister about the Comte d'Andigne's discovery and ask her what she makes of all this?"

Fersen promised he would. But on the day that he drove out to Aylesburg, the Swedish Count was not at all sure that he would mention to Thérèse what Lady Atkins had told him.

When Axel reached Hartwell House, a couple of miles from Aylesburg on the Oxford road, it proved to be a curious blend of two architectural periods. About 1755, on an old Elizabethan mansion, Sir William Lee had built an eighteenth-century addition, making Hartwell Elizabethan on the north, Georgian on the south. Fersen arrived on a Sunday morning, after Mass. The Duchesse d'Angoulême caught sight of him as she was leaving the chapel.

"Oh, it's good to see you!" Thérèse cried. Her arm through his, she took Fersen upstairs and into a room overlooking the garden, where her uncle, more obese and infirm than ever, chatted with the Swedish Count for several hours, talking chiefly about his new hobby, raising camellias.

At three o'clock in the afternoon, the household assembled in the dining room for the main meal of the day. The Duchesse d'Angoulême sat in the Queen's place at table, for her aunt, a hopeless alcoholic, dying of dropsy, no longer left her room. The food was plain. Nor was there much of it. An exiled monarch must watch his expenses. Dinner was followed by coffee in the drawing room, conversation, and whist. The ladies played cards; the King had a game of billiards with Count d'Avaray, his close friend and secretary. The strictest etiquette prevailed. Each time her uncle entered or left the room, Thérèse rose and made him a low curtsy.

Such royal airs in the midst of genteel poverty Fersen found absurd. Louis XVIII had turned into an English country squire. He prided himself on his erudition. Fond of the Latin authors and often quoting Horace, the Pretender spent most of the day translating into French Gibbon's *Decline and Fall of the Holy Roman Empire* and pottering about in his garden. Politics were seldom discussed. He seemed to have given up all hope of returning to France.

The Angoulêmes, too, had settled into a monotonous routine. Antoine was not an easy person to live with, his wife had found. He was taciturn and dull. Unlike his brother Ferdinand, Antoine did not care for social life. He was too frail to engage in hunting or outdoor sports, and the theater bored him. He read incessantly, books on theology, philosophy, history, and the classics.

Thérèse tried her best to accommodate herself to this somewhat depressing companion. She was frankly bored, but she had cast her lot with these people for better or worse, and, although it had been mostly worse, she made no complaints. She did needlepoint and occupied herself with charity work.

London was filled with French émigrés who had fled there after the Revolution. The valuables the aristocrats were able to smuggle out of France had long ago been sold. The titled gentlemen had opened restaurants; the noble ladies had become dressmakers and milliners. Their constant appeals for help made heavy inroads on the 20,000 pounds a year the Comte de Lille, and his brother, Artois, received from the British government. Since, to maintain his prestige, Louis XVIII also supported about him a huge "French court in exile" (Fersen was shocked at the hordes of people lodged at Hartwell House at the Pretender's expense), it was necessary to practice the strictest economy.

Thérèse seldom had any new clothes. What did it matter? She never went to London, except to worship in the chapel on George Street built by the French émigrés. The English aristocracy ignored the Comte de Lille. There were few visitors to Hartwell. Artois and his son, Ferdinand, came occasionally. But Thérèse, who could be a bitter enemy as well as a loyal friend, refused to have anything to do with another Bourbon exiled in England—Louis Philippe, now Duc d'Orléans, the eldest son of Philippe Egalité. Could she forget that, but for the vote of his cousin, Philippe Egalité, her father would have escaped the scaffold?

After living rent-free on the British crown at Holyrood Castle in Edinburgh for three years, Monsieur (as Artois was now called, being second in line for the French throne), no longer able to endure the damp climate of Scotland, had rented a modest house on South Audley Street in London. For twenty years he had been devoted to Louise, Comtesse de Polastron, who had escaped from France with him. When she died on March 27, 1804, Charles was heartbroken. The death of his wife at Klagenfurt, in Austria, the following year, didn't affect him at all. His marriage to Marie Thérèse of Savoy had been only a marriage of convenience.

His younger son had a flat at 39 George Street. Short and stocky, but with great charm, Charles Ferdinand de Berry was by far the more attractive of Artois' two children. He was an amateur painter, who played the flute and liked to go to the opera. The sad result of a broken home, due to the Revolution, Antoine was only thirteen, Ferdinand eleven, when they fled from France with their parents the day following the capture of the Bastille. After which, serving with Condé's royalist forces, the brothers had lived mostly in army camps.

When Condé's army disbanded, the Duc de Berry settled in London. There he had fallen in love with an Englishwoman, Amy Brown, by whom he had a son and two daughters. It grieved Ferdinand that his uncle wouldn't let him bring them to Hartwell.

"I don't want to meet your common-law wife," Provence shouted at him, "or your illegitimate children."

"They're not illegitimate," Berry retorted. "I'm legally married to their mother." But as Ferdinand and Amy had been wed by her father, the Reverend Joseph Brown, a Protestant clergyman, his Catholic uncle refused to consider them married.

Such distressing family rows occurred every time Berry came to pay a "duty call" on his uncle. The presence at Hartwell of Axel von Fersen, who lightened the family tension with his wit and charm, was a relief to everybody. Besides, he was a reminder of happier times at Versailles. So, although it meant another mouth to feed, the Swedish Count was urged to stay on.

Mornings, Fersen would stroll out to the garden, to find the King picking the camellias he carried every day up to his ailing wife. Or Axel would help Angoulême feed his aviary of birds. He had become very fond of Thérèse's quiet, self-effacing husband. Antoine was devoted to his uncle, with whom he had lived in exile a great deal longer than he had with his father. And he dearly loved his wife. Antoine admired Thérèse's greater intelligence, and he was grateful to her. His mother had abandoned him when he was fourteen. His wife had given the shy, homely man the only feminine affection he had ever known.

Was she happy? That was what Fersen asked himself as, in the evenings, Marie Antoinette's daughter sat doing her eternal tapestry, while the others played cards. Certainly living with a drunken invalid aunt, a gouty old uncle, and a taciturn husband was enough to dampen anyone's spirit.

On one of their afternoon walks, Thérèse brought up the subject Fersen most wished to avoid. "Ferdinand says that a Lady Atkins in London told him that a skeleton—possibly that of a boy—was dug up beside the Little Tower. Why didn't you tell me?"

"Because I didn't think it was important."

"Nothing to worry about?"

"No, they could be animal bones. No doctor saw them. I'm sure that Charles is safe in America. Not with the artist, Bellanger, though. Thérèse, my friends in Philadelphia went to see that boy. The description they wrote me of him doesn't in any way resemble your brother. But I've heard of another boy in America. At Versailles, do you remember a couple named Jardin?"

"Certainly. He was Uncle Provence's valet and married one of Mama's maids. They had a little girl named Louise."

"Well, I hear from America that in March, 1794, the Jardins appeared in Albany, New York. They had with them a girl and a boy, who was younger, about nine. Thérèse, I'm sure he is your brother. From Albany, the Jardins went to Ticonderoga, on Lake George. Before they left, they told friends that only the girl was theirs, and they were going to leave the boy with the Iroquois Indians."

"Oh, how wonderful!" the Duchesse d'Angoulême exclaimed, her face radiant. "Do you suppose Charles is still there?"

"He may be," Fersen assured her. "I'm going to New York State to find out."

But Axel never went to America. When he returned home, the Count became involved in Swedish politics. Charles XIII, having no son to succeed him, had adopted as his heir a Danish prince, Carl August of Augustenburg. A rough, genial fellow, the young Dane made himself immensely popular with the Swedes, all except a small group headed by Fersen, who remained loyal to the deposed Gustavus IV, exiled in Switzerland.

In May, 1810, Crown Prince Carl made a tour of the provinces. At Qvidinge, in Scania, while reviewing some troops, he was stricken, apparently with apoplexy, and fell from his horse, dying immediately. The Prince's body was brought to Stockholm on the twentieth of June, for burial in Riddarholm church. Dressed in his state robes as Lord High Steward of Sweden, Fersen rode in his six-horse coach, with an escort of cavalry, to meet the coffin outside the city gates. When the funeral procession entered Stockholm, his gilded coach with the royal crown on its roof preceded the hearse.

A large crowd had gathered to watch the cortege. No sooner did the Lord High Steward's carriage appear than an angry roar went up, for the rumor had spread that the Crown Prince, who had lunched before the military review at the home of Axel's sister, Countess Sophie Piper, had not died of apoplexy, but from poison, placed in a chicken pie by the Lord High Steward. The crowd began to throw stones at Fersen's coach. The windows were smashed. His face bleeding from cuts made by the broken glass, but erect and proud, Axel rode on, jeered at and insulted.

At the end of a street named the Stora Nygatan, as the procession turned right toward Riddarholm church, the people stopped Fersen's carriage and dragged the coachman from his seat. The door of the Lord High Steward's carriage was wrenched open. He was pulled out. He managed to escape across the street and took refuge in a café. With the howling pack at his heels, Fersen ran up the stairs to a room on the first floor. He slammed the door shut and locked it. But his attackers followed. They broke the door down and hurled themselves upon him. Axel's sword and his medals were torn off and thrown out of the window. Bruised and bleeding, he was hurled down the stairs.

His military escort tried to quiet the mob by hustling the Lord High Steward, his state robes spattered with blood, across the street to the courthouse. They put him safely in prison and promised a trial. But the pursuing mob refused to wait. They had already condemned the poor man. The door of his cell was broken open, and Axel was pulled out. He stumbled and fell. Instantly, the howling pack was upon him. He was seized by the legs, dragged out of the courthouse, and tossed over the railing of a balcony, to fall to his death on the stone pavement of the yard below. He lay two hours, dead on the stones, before someone had the decency to cover his body with a coat.

The date was the twentieth of June. Exactly nineteen years ago, the most ghastly day in Fersen's life, Marie Antoinette had failed to reach the frontier. Ever since, it had been a sad anniversary for him and for Marie Antoinette's daughter. That June of 1810, the Swedish Count was especially on Thérêse's mind. They hadn't heard from him at Hartwell since his return home. Axel had been warned by friends not to come back to Sweden because his life might be in danger, and she was worried.

So one morning two weeks later, when Thérèse looked out of the window and saw Antoine below, at the front door, taking some mail from the postman, she ran down the stairs. The Duchess met her husband in the hall. "Anything from Stockholm?" she asked eagerly. Then she saw that Antoine was reading a letter the mailman had brought and his face was ashen. "What is it?" she demanded. He didn't reply. . . . And before her husband finally spoke, Thérèse knew. She would never see Fersen again.

"Axel—" Antoine began—and broke off.

"He's dead?"

"Yes, murdered!"

19

NEWS IN THE NIGHT

"I've had to endure so much. Can I stand this?" Thérèse asked herself. Her courage failed her when she realized that she could no longer count upon the man who, for her mother's sake, had tenderly watched over her. But the Duchesse d'Angoulême had little time to indulge in her grief. Added to her other duties now was running Hartwell House, crowded to the roof with Bourbon hangers-on, for the King's devoted secretary, Antoine de Béziade, Comte d'Avaray, ill with lung trouble, had gone to Italy for his health.

By November, 1810, Thérèse also had doctors and nurses to supervise. Queen Josephine was dying. Thérèse disliked her aunt, who had been hateful to her mother, but she was good to her, and the Queen's last words to her niece were, "My dear, all you need to go to heaven is a pair of wings."

Strangely enough, on November 13, 1810, Josephine's husband, after years of neglect, took her death hard. When the English government, which steadfastly refused to recognize him as king of France on the grounds of not having received sufficient proof of Louis XVII's death, buried his wife in Westminster Abbey with the same honors as those accorded to a reigning queen, the Comte de Lille was too grief-stricken to attend her funeral.

A loss which affected him even more was that of the Comte d'Avaray, who died in Madeira, on June 3, 1811. The King was very rude at first to Pierre de Blacas d'Aulps, an impoverished French count whom Avaray had met in Florence and sent to Hartwell to take his place as secretary. Then Blacas became the new favorite, for it was becoming too painful for the Pretender to walk, even leaning on a cane. As a result, the King seldom left his armchair, and he needed someone who would listen patiently to the long stories he liked to tell of his youth at Versailles.

Every morning, Provence and Blacas read the papers together. By the fall of 1812, the news in them grew more encouraging. Napoleon made the mistake of invading Russia. The Russians set fire to Moscow, forcing the French, from lack of supplies, to retreat through the snow, back to Germany. After Napoleon's defeat at Leipzig (October, 1813), a restoration of the monarchy in France appeared to be certain. But, perhaps, not with a Bourbon as king.

The report that the Allies were considering placing Napoleon's infant son on the throne sent the Comte d'Artois and Ferdinand hurrying to Hartwell. There was a worried family conference.

"You should join the Allied armies on the Continent," the Duchesse d'Angoulême told them. "What will people think of the Bourbon princes, if you let other men fight for you?"

Neither Ferdinand nor his father wished to leave their whist games in the fashionable London clubs and their nights at the opera. Antoine protested that he had always loathed being a soldier. "What a spineless lot!" Thérèse thought, looking at her relatives in disgust. The possibility of a Bourbon Restoration had snapped the Duchesse d'Angoulême out of the state of lethargy in which she had been since her marriage. Her eyes flashed. Color had returned to her cheeks.

Artois and his sons were not cowards. The recent execution of their cousin, the Duc d'Enghien, showed what Napoleon would do to a member of the Bourbon family, if one of them was caught on French soil. But Thérèse told them, "It is a risk you must take. Oh, I wish I was a man!" And she shamed them into enlisting.

In January, 1814, the Comte d'Artois and the two dukes left England to join the Russian, Austrian, English, and Prussian armies invading France. Artois went to Holland; Berry to Normandy; and Angoulême joined the British, under Wellington, at St. Jean de Luz, in the south of France. The Duke of Wellington had the greatest contempt for the Bourbons. He was attacking Bordeaux. And he sent Antoine to the rear of his army, with the baggage wagons, and forgot all about him.

The people of Bordeaux had intended to resist the British, but they changed their minds when they heard that the Duc d'Angoulême was with Wellington's troops. Most of them were royalists and, to the surprise of the English, they came pouring out of the town wearing the Bourbon emblem, a white cockade. At the sight of Antoine, the inhabitants of Bordeaux fairly mobbed him. Cheering crowds followed the Duke to the Hôtel de Ville, where the flag of the Bourbons, a springling of gold fleurs-de-lis on a white ground, was run up, replacing the tricolor.

Bordeaux was the first important French town to surrender. Even Wellington was impressed.

When the news reached Hartwell, on March 25, 1814, there was wild rejoicing. Over and over, Thérèse wanted to hear of Antoine's triumphal entry into the city. "The Duchesse d'Angoulême was so delighted at her husband's success, the unusual excitement injured her health," writes the Comtesse de Boigne, sister of Rainulphe d'Osmond, the Duc d'Angoulême's aide-de-camp, in her memoirs. "The Duchess had had so few opportunities for pleasure of this kind that she was unable to bear it." At last, Antoine had done something of which his wife could be proud.

* * * *

Two nights later, Hartwell House was dark and everyone in bed. About midnight, the Comte de Blacas was awakened by a loud knocking. The servants, asleep in their attic rooms, couldn't hear the noise. Wondering who could be at the front door, the King's secretary put on his dressing gown and went downstairs to find out.

On opening the door, Blacas saw a messenger holding a letter. "What do you mean, waking us all up?" he began crossly. But when the man said, "It's from His Highness, the Prince Regent," Pierre eagerly snatched the envelope from his hand.

He raced up the stairs to the Pretender's room. "Sire, I'm sorry to waken you," his secretary said, "but a letter has come from Prince George."

Louis sat up in bed and ordered, "Give it to me." Tearing open the envelope, he read by the light of Blacas' candle that Paris was captured; the "usurper," forced to abdicate, was being sent off to exile on the island of Elba, in the Mediterranean; and the Allies had chosen him to be king of France.

It was the moment that Provence had schemed and longed for all his life. He tumbled excitedly out of bed. "I must go and tell the Duchess," he cried. His first thought was to share the news with the woman who had made all this possible.

Wrapped in a dressing gown Blacas brought him, the stout old man, forgetting in his joy the pain in his legs, waddled as fast as he could down the hall to his niece's room and awakened her. "They want me to be king!" Provence sobbed. "Oh, I never thought I'd live to see this day!"

"Uncle, dear, I'm so happy for you." Thérèse hugged him. "When do we leave for Paris?"

"At once, my love," Provence replied.

But excitement brought on a severe attack of gout. It was April 20 before the King was well enough to start with his entourage.

The ride to London was a triumph all the way. The poor relation had become the royal cousin. The Prince Regent, George III's eldest son, who until Napoleon's defeat had ignored the presence of the French royal family in England, drove out from London and met Louis XVIII halfway, at the Abercorn Inn, in Stanmore. The two monarchs dined together. Then the Prince climbed into the King's carriage, its horses and postilions decorated with the white cockade of the Bourbons, and rode with him into London.

They passed through Hyde Park and Piccadilly between crowds of cheering people. The Union Jack and the French fleur-de-lis flag fluttered side by side on the buildings. At the Crillon Hotel, where the new King of France spent three days, the Prince Regent decorated Louis XVIII with the English Order of the Garter and received, in exchange, France's Cordon Bleu. And on April 23, 1814, their last night in London before they sailed for France on the royal yacht *Sovereign*, escorted by eight British warships, the Regent gave a magnificent banquet at Carlton House in honor of Louis XVIII and the Duchesse d'Angoulême. English society had snubbed the exiles at Hartwell. But now everyone wanted to see the daughter of Louis XVI and Marie Antoinette, who, at the death of her uncles, would become queen of France.

As the Duchess entered the hall leading to the dining room, the gentlemen bowed, the ladies curtsied. Then they stared in surprise. Thérèse had stopped and turned pale, for she had come face to face with a portly middle-aged man wearing a brown wig and side whiskers.

The Duc d'Orléans bowed and offered his arm. The Duchesse d'Angoulême drew back. She realized, to her horror, that the son of "Equality Philip," the scoundrel who, to save his own neck, had risen in the Convention and voted for her father's death, was to be her dinner partner.

"My dear," Uncle Provence spoke sharply, "surely you remember your cousin, Louis Philippe?"

Did she remember him? If her mother hadn't changed her mind, she might have married the creature! Philippe Egalité, known as the Red Duke for his radical views, had been guillotined by the revolutionists, receiving what he richly deserved for his betrayal of his family and his caste. And the son was no better, in Thérèse's estimation. But this was no time to show her true feelings. The Bourbons must present a united front.

"I'm sorry; I felt a bit faint," the Duchess apologized. On the arm of the man she hated, she went in to dinner.

20

RETURN OF THE LILIES

FRANCE, tired of Napoleon's incessant wars, welcomed the Bourbons back. The tricolor banners of wide red, white, and blue stripes disappeared; and on May 3, 1814, from almost every window in Paris there floated white-and-gold fleur-de-lis flags.

It was noon before the procession entered the city by the Porte Saint-Denis. A troop of cavalry that had escorted the royal family from Calais, on the French coast, led the way, followed by an open carriage drawn by eight white horses. Artois and his sons, Angoulême and Berry, rode on horseback beside it. On the back seat sat Louis XVIII with the Duchesse d'Angoulême.

They were greeted with shouts of "*Vive le Roi!*" But the crowds that lined the streets gazed with surprise at the huge fat man, a plumed tricorne hat perched on his old-fashioned white wig, his swollen legs wrapped in red velvet gaiters. Only fifty-nine, but greatly overweight and suffering with gout, Louis XVIII looked like a crippled old man. There was nothing regal about him.

The Parisians gazed with even more critical disapproval at

the woman seated beside him. The Duchess's face was partly hidden by an open parasol, but the people of Paris saw that her expression was sad, and they were disappointed. The crowd had expected Marie Antoinette's daughter to be younger and prettier. They forgot how many years had passed. Thérèse's hair, blond when she left the Temple at seventeen, had darkened to a drab chestnut. She was thirty-five, pale, and too thin.

Why didn't the Duchess wave at them and smile? "A princess must always smile," Marie Antoinette had told her daughter. Certainly this day of the triumphant "return of the lilies (the Bourbons)" was an occasion which called for the King's niece to appear at her best, to smile and look pretty. But how could she smile? The last time Thérèse had ridden through Paris, she was being taken past jeering crowds, with her parents, her brother and aunt, to a grim prison. Remembering those dreadful days, the Duchesse d'Angoulême rode along tensely, fighting to hold back the tears.

Passing the Conciergerie, the jail from which the Queen of France was taken to the guillotine in a garbage cart, Marie Antoinette's daughter almost fainted. And the nearer they came to the Tuileries, the more agitated she became, for Thérèse was returning to live in her family's first prison.

As she entered the palace, where Napoleon's imperial bees had been replaced everywhere by the Bourbon fleurs-de-lis, memories came flooding back—the horror of things that had happened there twenty-two years ago. Some young girls stood waiting with bouquets of lilies for her. Madame hurried past them. "I'm very tired," she pleaded. "Please, show me to my room."

To Thérèse's consternation, they led her to the Pavillon de Flore, overlooking the Seine, where she had lived as a girl, on the floor above her mother. "Entering the apartment reserved

Copyright Country Life, London

LULWORTH CASTLE, DORSET, WHERE THE ROYAL FAMILY TOOK REFUGE IN ENGLAND, WHILE NAPOLEON RULED FRANCE

Copyright Country Life, London

HARTWELL HOUSE, AYLESBURY, ENGLAND, WHERE THEY HEARD THE GOOD NEWS OF THE BOURBON RESTORATION

CHARLES X OF FRANCE

MARIE THÉRÈSE

LOUIS ANTOINE, THE DAUPHIN

Photographed by the author

SCENE OF FERSEN'S MURDER, COURTHOUSE, STOCKHOLM, SWEDEN

Photographed by the author

HOUSE INTO WHICH FERSEN TRIED TO ESCAPE, STORA NYGATAN, STOCKHOLM, SWEDEN

Photograph: Giraudon, Paris

THE ROYAL FAMILY (MAY, 1814) *Reading from left to right: Comte d'Artois, Louis XVIII, Duchesse d'Angoulême, Duc d'Angoulême, Duc de Berry*

LOUIS XVIII, THE FORMER COMTE DE PROVENCE

Photograph: H. Roger-Viollet, Paris

LOUIS ANTOINE, THE DUC D'ANGOULÊME
by Baron Gros

Photograph: H. Roger-Viollet, Paris

MARIE THÉRÈSE CHARLOTTE, THE DUCHESSE D'ANGOULÊME
by Baron Gros

Photographed by the author *Photographed by the author*

FORMER BRAS D'OR INN, VARENNES, FRANCE, WHERE THE ROYAL COACH WAS STOPPED. (RIGHT) VILLENEUVE L'ETANG, THÉRÈSE'S PARIS HIDEWAY.

Photographed by the author

CHATEAU DE RAMBOUILLET, WHERE CHARLES X AND HIS SON, THE DUC D'ANGOULÊME, ABDICATED

LA DUCHESSE D'ANGOULÊME

LE DUC D'ANGOULÊME

MARIE CAROLINE, DUCHESSE DE BERRY

LOUIS PHILIPPE

Photographed by the author

CHÂTEAU DE CHAMBORD

Gift of the French people to the baby Duc de Bordeaux

Photograph: H. Roger-Viollet, Paris

HENRI, DUC DE BORDEAUX, AS A BOY
by Grenedon

Photograph: H. Roger-Viollet, Paris

CHARLES X, THE FORMER COMTE D'ARTOIS
by Langlois

Photographed by the author

FROHSDORF CASTLE, NUESTADT, AUSTRIA, THÉRÈSE'S LAST HOME, WHERE SHE DIED

Photographed by the author

GOSFIELD HALL, HALSTEAD, ESSEX, FIRST REFUGE OF THE BOURBONS IN ENGLAND

Photographed by the author

Photographed by the author

FRÄULEIN GISELA FELS, WHO TOLD THE AUTHOR ABOUT THE CHAMBORDS, WHOM SHE KNEW. (RIGHT) STATUE OF THE ARCHDUKE KARL, HELDEN PLATZ, VIENNA.

VENDRAMINI PALACE, VENICE, HOME OF CAROLINE AND HECTOR LUCCHESI-PALLI. (RIGHT) CAVALLI PALACE, ON THE GRAND CANAL, VENICE, WHERE THE DUCHESSE D'ANGOULÊME AND THE CHAMBORDS SPENT THE WINTER.

Photographed by the author

MONASTERY OF CASTEGNAVIZZA, WHERE THE BOURBONS ARE BURIED, GORIZIA, YUGOSLAVIA

INTERIOR OF THE BOURBON CRYPT UNDER THE MONASTERY. MARIE THÉRÈSE'S TOMB IS ON THE RIGHT

for her," writes Madame de Gontaut, "she burst into tears, it was Marie Antoinette's old rooms!"

The return to Paris brought back no such bitter memories to Louis XVIII, who had lived through neither the twentieth of June nor the tenth of August at the Tuileries. In a suite on the first floor, he was asleep, snoring happily, in the bed that two weeks ago had been Napoleon's.

* * * *

The Comtesse de Boigne described the return of the Bourbons to Paris: We went to see the entry of the King from a house in the Rue St. Denis. The crowd was very great, and most of the windows were decorated with white flags. I must own that the people in the open carriage did not correspond to my hopes. The Duchesse d'Angoulême was the only one of the royal family whom the people remembered in France. My cousin asked me if the Duc d'Angoulême was the son of Louis XVIII? And how many children he had? But everyone knew that Louis XVI, the Queen, and Madame Elisabeth had perished on the scaffold. For everyone the Duchesse d'Angoulême was the Orphan of the Temple.

That was why Provence had married his nephew to Marie Antoinette's daughter. None too sure of himself, he needed the Duchesse d'Angoulême by his side. He was as dependent on her as he had been leaning on Thérèse's arm to surmount the drifts when crossing the snowy plains of Lithuania. Before making an important decision, Louis XVIII usually said to his ministers, "Let's first see what Madame thinks about that—" Marie Antoinette's daughter was what her mother had hoped she would be, the uncrowned queen, the most important lady of France—but after the enthusiasm over "the return of the lilies" abated, a none-too-popular one. The Paris shopkeepers especially, remembering fondly the extravagant

Empress Josephine, deplored Madame's lack of interest in clothes.

Glad to be of help to her uncle, when it was her duty to act as his hostess, the Duchesse d'Angoulême put white ostrich plumes in her hair and adorned herself with the crown jewels. No one could look more regal. The Comtesse de Boigne writes of seeing Madame at the opera, "She was beautifully dressed and covered with magnificent diamonds. She bowed [to the audience] very graciously. Without being pretty, she was very distinguished-looking." But, usually, Thérèse dressed simply, still wearing the dowdy clothes she had brought from England. Madame de Boigne continues:

> Disliking social life, the Angoulêmes put in an appearance at the theater, the races and balls, only when they had to do so. The Duke was so uncomfortable in a drawing room that as soon as he entered his one desire was to get out. But he was by no means the nonentity that people thought him to be.

The Duchess busied herself with charity work. She read all the appeals for help sent her, before giving them to Louis Turgy, the ex-waiter at the Tower, who, having faithfully followed Madame to Austria, Russia, and England, had become her secretary. And she knitted continuously for the poor. "But never on Sunday." However, as her good deeds were mostly done anonymously, the Duchesse d'Angoulême received little credit for them. She was disliked and maligned, as was Marie Antoinette in her day, although in a different manner, and with far less cause.

While in prison, too proud to weep before her jailers, Thérèse had learned to control her emotions until it became a habit. Her cold, reserved manner antagonized people. "In reality, Madame was kindly," the Comtesse de Boigne says, "but she managed to make the French believe that she hated them (for murdering her parents), and in the end they hated her." The antagonism was mutual. How could Thérèse like the French who celebrated January 21, the day her father was executed, as a national holiday?

"Madame cared little for her mother's memory," the Comtesse de Boigne tells us. "All her devotion was expended on her father." Yet Thérèse seldom spoke of him. She so revered his memory that the mention of Louis XVI's name or the word "scaffold" upset her for days. How could she forget those terrible three years in jail? The sound of a key turning in a lock or a bolt being drawn made her jump.

Twenty-two years had passed, still everything at the Tuileries reminded Thérèse of the Revolution. She refused to enter the rooms where her father was forced to wear the bonnet rouge, and she had trembled, standing behind a table with her mother. But from her windows she would see through the trees the former site of the guillotine. With a horror that would never leave her, she imagined the procession up the scaffold steps of all those she had loved.

The Duchesse d'Angoulême had forbidden her coachman ever to drive her across the Place de la Revolution (now the Place de la Concorde), where her parents and her beloved Aunt Babet were beheaded. But one day she went with Pauline de Tourzel (the Comtesse de Béarn) to see the site of the Temple Tower. When they reached the spot, Pauline exclaimed, "Gracious, I wouldn't know the place!" The ground was level where the Tower had stood. Three years ago, in 1811, Joseph Fouché, at that time Napoleon's chief of police, and now Louis XVIII's, had persuaded the Emperor to tear it down. Only part of Artois' palace was still standing.

"They say that Fouché so feared the Tower," Pauline said, "he was afraid to walk past that great black silhouette."

"I don't wonder," replied Thérèse. "Pauline, I'm going to buy what remains of the Temple and turn it into a Benedictine convent. Only the prayers of those good nuns can purge this place of all the evil committed here."

The Duchess walked off down the Rue des Archives that had been cut through the site formerly occupied by the Big Tower, and stopped before the Hôtel de Ville of the Third Arrondissement (district) of Paris, built over the old garden.

"They found the boy's skeleton buried close to the Little Tower," Thérèse said. "It must have been about there, by the north wall of the town hall."

Pauline saw that she was crying.

A few days later, the Duchesse d'Angoulême had a weeping willow, the tree of mourning, planted over what *might* be her brother's grave—although she continued to hope, as Fersen had said, that Charles was safe in America.

The Duc de Berry didn't think so. He was the only one of the royal family who thought the Dauphin was murdered. "Not stabbed, it wouldn't do to leave any telltale drops of blood in his cell or on the stairs. The poor child was probably strangled," Ferdinand said. "What does it matter how they got rid of him? With poison? A knife? Or someone's hands? Those were Charles' remains that the Comte d'Andigné found by the Little Tower. And it was the body of the boy they put in his place who was buried in the cemetery of Sainte-Marguerite."

Such talk from his brother always made Antoine lose his temper. He agreed with Uncle Provence that there had been no boy substituted for the Dauphin. "You're imagining things, Ferdinand," Antoine said. "Thérèse's brother died of consumption in the Tower. The two doctors, Pelletan and Dumangen, who performed an autopsy the day after his death, didn't find a trace of poison."

"Of course not. People must be made to believe that the Dauphin had died a natural death, so a dying boy was substituted for him. Antoine, you know that Charles was inoculated for smallpox. Did Pelletan and his assistant find any vaccination marks? The autopsy was a farce, but it enabled the murderers to fulfill the formalities required by law. They had a corpse they could decently bury."

"Ferdinand, you're mad!" exclaimed Antoine.

"No, I'm not," his brother replied. "The murderers covered up their crime well. But they haven't fooled me."

21

THE LAST PERSON TO SEE HIM ALIVE

THÉRÈSE REFUSED to believe that Charles had been murdered. The thought was too dreadful. She continued to hope he was safe in America. And now that she was in Paris, the Duchesse d'Angoulême decided to seek out everyone still living who had known her brother. She first sent for Gomin, the jailer at the Temple, who had escorted her to the Swiss border.

So many years had passed that Jean Gomin (made concierge by Madame at the Château de Meudon) was no longer afraid to speak frankly. "I never knew the Dauphin," he reminded her, "but I had seen pictures of him, and Laurent and I suspected at once that our prisoner was another boy. Madame, I believe the Simons carried off your brother. The old man is dead, but his wife is alive, bedridden for eighteen years in a Paris nursing home. You should go and have a talk with her."

So on December 13, 1814, the Duchesse d'Angoulême went to the Hôpital des Incurables in the Rue de Sèvres and asked the Sisters of Saint Vincent de Paul, who ran the old people's home, if she could speak with the only person living who might know what had happened to her brother.

"Certainly, Your Highness," replied the head nun, Sister Lucie, "come right this way." She led the Duchess down a hall and into a room where the hard-faced former jaileress lay in bed, very ill with chronic asthma. Thérèse did not tell her who she was, but, sitting down beside the sick woman, asked her about the Dauphin.

"I remember Little Capet well," Jeanne Simon replied in a hoarse voice. "People lie when they say that my husband and I were cruel to the boy. When drunk, Antoine may have hit him, but he wasn't a bad sort. Nor am I. I changed Charles' bed and swept his room. Simon got him a dog named Coco and built an aviary where he kept birds."

"That was good of you, Madame Simon. And I'm told that, when you left the Tower, you took the little King with you. How did you manage to slip him past the guards?"

A crafty look came into the old woman's eyes. "It was difficult," she admitted, "but we had brought to the prison, to carry off our furniture, a cart on which was a wicker hamper and a wooden box containing a toy horse. Simon told the guards that the hobbyhorse was a good-by gift for the little Prince. Actually, inside the packing case with the horse was another child. We put him in Charles' cell and carried out the Dauphin in the hamper, hidden under our soiled linen."

"What happened then, Madame Simon?"

"My husband went back to being a cobbler. Charles wanted to live with us and be his assistant. But Antoine had been told to hand over the boy to–" An attack of asthma shook the shoemaker's wife. After prolonged coughing, she sank back exhausted.

Thérèse hung over the bed. "He took him where?"

"I can't remember."

"Oh, you must! Madame Simon, try to think. Where did your husband take the Dauphin?"

"To a château. It was so long ago, I forget its name."

"You've got to remember!" Grasping the widow of the cobbler Simon by the shoulders, the Duchess shook her. "Was the château near Paris? To the north or south?" But all she heard from the sick woman was a jumble of words. Finally, leaning closer, a whispered, "Vitry . . ."

Sister Lucie came back into the room. "Your Highness, you won't believe it," the nun said, "but Mère Simon claims that a young man who came to see her twelve years ago was the Dauphin."

"From 1794 to 1802 is a long time. How was she able to recognize him?"

"By the scar on his lip."

Thérèse remembered it, caused by the bite of a white rabbit Charles was rearing. A half hour later, overcome with emotion, she drove back to the Tuileries, past the terrace beside the Seine, where in a wire enclosure her brother had kept his pets. That night, telling Ferdinand about her visit to the shoemaker's wife, Thérèse asked him, "Do you know of a château named Vitry?"

"Of course. Vitry-sur-Seine," her brother-in-law replied. "I'll tell you about that later. First, let's discuss what Madame Simon told you. I believe her when she says her husband brought in a child that was substituted for Charles, but not that he was hidden under their dirty linen, carried out of the Tower, and placed in a cart. She has been reading Regnault-Warin's *Le Cimetière de la Madeleine*. That was his explanation of the Dauphin's escape. Thérèse, the Widow Simon is a frightened woman, trying to cover up a murder. Also trying to prove true her other lie that she saw Charles twelve years ago. She has probably been living in terror of the police for years, knowing that her husband killed him."

"But she says Simon took my brother to a château named Vitry."

"Did he? All we know is that on April 6, 1794, three months

after he left the Tower, Simon was seen riding out to Vitry with a boy behind him on the saddle. The owner of the château, a royalist banker named Petitval, had lent the Republic money. In return, he asked for the Dauphin. But was the boy Simon delivered to him really Charles? They say he wasn't and that Petitval, realizing he had been tricked, threatened to expose the fraud. Before he could, Thérèse, do you know what happened? Ten people—everyone at Vitry—were found dead, their throats cut. Even the servants. Petitval's body, with shattered skull, was lying on a path in the park, but nothing in the house was stolen. And there was no trace of the boy. What's stranger still, ten people were murdered, and the police never made any inquiry. The matter was hushed up. Thérèse, I think I'll go to the Hôpital des Incurables. I'd like to ask the Widow Simon a few questions."

However, several days later, when Ferdinand went to talk to the cobbler's wife, he was prevented from even seeing her. Hearing of the Duchesse d'Angoulême's visit, Fouché's gendarmes had hurried to the convent and told the nuns to say that Madame Simon was no longer there. The Duc de Berry knew they were lying. Next day, he went back to the old people's home, this time accompanied by his armed bodyguard, and the Sisters of Saint Vincent de Paul were afraid not to show their patient.

Telling Thérèse about his visit later, Ferdinand bitterly regretted that he hadn't induced the cobbler's wife to talk before Fouché's men frightened everyone at the Hôpital des Incurables out of their wits. "The trembling old woman now takes back all she said to you," he told his sister-in-law. "Madame Simon insists she never saw Charles again, after they left him in the Tower."

"That's a lie and you know it," Ferdinand had said to her. "Madame Simon, can you explain this? After you and your husband left the Tower, you didn't move far away, am I right? You went to live in the Rue des Cordeliers, just outside the Temple wall. If you were as fond of Charles as you say, and he was still in the Tower, why did you never go back to see him? Why were the two women prisoners on the third floor mentioned in the records of the Commune, but never again the little King? I'll tell you why, my good woman. Because after you and your husband left the Tower that dark January night, the child on the second floor wasn't the Dauphin, and you and the Commune knew it."

Jeanne Simon had listened to the Duc de Berry, her eyes wide with fear. "I can't say anything, they'll kill me—" she sobbed.

"Who'll kill you?" demanded Ferdinand.

It took a long time, for the shoemaker's wife had grown hysterical, but the Duc de Berry finally forced her to admit that Fouché's police had threatened her with death if she said another word. Beyond that, he could get nothing out of the terrified woman. They had guillotined Madame Simon's husband to silence him. And now they had silenced her.

What chiefly concerned Ferdinand that afternoon at the Tuileries, as he sat talking with Thérèse, was why had Joseph Fouché, his uncle's chief of police, on hearing of the Duchesse d'Angoulême's visit, sent two of his most trusted lieutenants hurrying to the hospital? To find out what Jeanne Simon knew about the disappearance of the Dauphin? Not at all. Fouché must have known for a long time where the old woman was. It was to prevent her from talking. Afraid of what she might say, the police had most successfully shut the old woman's mouth. Madame Simon was to die on June 10, 1819, still insisting she knew nothing about the Dauphin.

"I wonder just whom Fouché is protecting?" Ferdinand said. "I mean, who had Charles killed? I have a suspicion who the guilty person was, Thérèse, but I won't tell you. You would never believe me."

22

ALONE AGAINST NAPOLEON

FERSEN HAD INTENDED to go to America and look for the boy the Jardin couple left with the Iroquois Indians. After his death, Thérèse felt she must continue the search. Antoine begged her not to, so did her uncle. His nephew was dead, the King said, why continue an inquiry that would lead to nothing? But, for once, Thérèse went against her uncle's wishes. In December, 1814, she sent an agent to New York State to look for her lost brother. Captain Artain traveled up the Hudson River by sloop to Albany, then, on horseback, plunged into the forests of northern New York.

Artain returned to Paris with encouraging news. He had found the young man, twenty-nine now, living at Ticonderoga, on Lake George. Adopted by a half-breed named Thomas Williams, and christened Eleazar, he had been raised with the Williams' son John. But where John was a typical copper-skinned Indian, Eleazar had light hair, white skin, and the Hapsburgs' prominent lower jaw. The Indians called him "Frenchie," because Eleazar had spoken French on his arrival, but later forgot it. They knew he wasn't Tom Williams' son.

Since it had become known that the Duchesse d'Angoulême

believed her brother might be alive, a number of "Dauphins" had tried to get in touch with their "long-lost sister." Jean Hervagault and several others had turned out to be impostors. But this young man in America, Thérèse thought, might possibly be Charles.

"Captain Artain, did you do what I asked you?" she demanded.

"Yes, Your Highness, I examined Williams carefully. He has a scar over his right eye, where it is said Simon hit the Dauphin and almost blinded him, and on his arm, what you especially wanted me to look for, an inoculation mark in the form of a crescent."

"That proves it, he's my brother!" Thérèse exclaimed.

But when she wished to send for him, Artain advised Madame not to be hasty. He thought that Eleazar Williams should remain in America, at least for the present. The youth was retarded mentally. He had fallen on his head after he joined the Williams family. Since then, Eleazar couldn't remember anything of the past. Although, before that, he had talked of having "lived in a palace." The Indians were impressed. Eleazar must belong to a rich French family. Every year Thomas Williams received a large sum of money from France for the young man's support. He refused to tell who sent it.

* * * *

It was twenty-two years since the execution of Louis XVI and Marie Antoinette, and their remains were to be reburied in the church of Saint-Denis, the burial place of the French kings. The difficulty had been in finding them. Beheaded on October 16, 1793, the body of Marie Antoinette had been carried to the little cemetery of the Madeleine, where Louis XVI was buried. Flung on the grass, it lay there, forgotten, for two weeks. Then a hole was dug for the Queen near the grave of her husband. But neither grave had been marked, and, since the royal couple were buried with other victims of the guillotine, it was hard, after twenty-two years, to identify their skeletons. Even the cemetery, sold for building lots, no longer existed.

A royalist named Olivier Descloséaux, however, out of sentiment, had bought the plot where it was thought that Louis and Marie Antoinette lay. The first body dug up was the Queen's. At least, some human dust was found, believed to be hers. A skeleton, possibly the King's, was found nearby. The severed head had been placed between the legs, which by now had dwindled to mere bones.

The bodies were exhumed on January 18, 1815, and the funeral took place at Saint-Denis, a suburb of Paris, three days later. Louis XVIII and the Comte d'Artois, brothers of the murdered king, and his nephews, Angoulême and Berry, were in the carriage that headed the procession escorting the coffins from Paris out to the royal vaults in the old cathedral. But the Duchesse d'Angoulême created a scandal by refusing to attend her parents' reinterment.

"It would have been better to have left Mama and Papa rest undisturbed," Thérèse told her uncle, "if those pitiful fragments *are* my parents."

Nor did she approve of the memorial chapel that he was having built on the site of the Madeleine cemetery. Had her parents actually been buried there? Their bodies were burned, the police had told Madame confidentially, and their ashes thrown into the Montmartre sewer.

There was considerable surprise in Paris, too, over the fact that the grave of the boy who died in the Tower on June 8, 1795, and was buried in the cemetery adjoining Sainte-Marguerite's church, had been left undisturbed, while a portion of the unrecognizable dust and bones of the Madeleine was interred with regal pomp at Saint-Denis as the remains of the murdered King and Queen. The site of the boy's burial was known. The gravedigger, Betrancourt, had died. But his widow told everyone how her husband had dug up the boy's coffin from the common trench, where the destitute unknown were put, and reburied it by the door to the left transept of the church. She led curious people through the graveyard to point out to them the very spot. Yet, nothing was done about digging up the little skeleton.

"Uncle didn't dare," was Ferdinand's explanation of this strange neglect of Louis XVII. "He knows perfectly well that boy wasn't Charles."

A sullen crowd watched the passing of the belated funeral procession of Louis XVI and Marie Antoinette. By an unfortunate accident, the plume-decked roof of the hearse became entangled with the chains of a street lamp. There were rude shouts of "*à la lanterne!* (to the lamppost!)", the dread cry of the Revolution. The Bourbons had only been back eight months but already Paris was sick of them.

Louis XVIII had soon made himself unpopular. The Revolution had changed France. He could not be an absolute ruler, like his ancestors. He was forced to grant the French a charter (a constitution) and a legislature. But he returned to the nobles the land which had been confiscated and given to the peasants during the Revolution. And what Louis' subjects resented most was that they were forbidden to display the tricolor. This flag was dear to many Frenchmen. Napoleon had carried it from one victory to another all over Europe. Now, the hated white banner that represented despotism in their eyes was restored as the national emblem.

Cooped up on Elba, in the Mediterranean, Napoleon learned of the dissatisfaction with the Bourbons in France. With a few followers, he secretly left his island prison and landed at Cannes, on the south coast of France.

On the night of March 12, 1815, the Angoulêmes were in

Bordeaux, celebrating the anniversary of the day that Antoine had made his triumphant entry into the city. Thérèse was dressing for a ball in their honor, when her husband, a dispatch in his hand, rushed into the room.

"It's from Uncle in Paris," he cried. "Napoleon has escaped from Elba! What shall we do? We can't go to the ball."

Madame drew on her gloves. "Why not? Antoine, we mustn't panic. Does anyone else know about Napoleon's return? Then don't tell them. During the dance, I'll think what to do–" And she swept out of the room.

That evening, the guests all remarked how gracious the Duchesse d'Angoulême was, especially to General Decaen, the commander of the Bordeaux garrison. And by morning, when the others heard the news–"Napoleon is back in France!"–Thérèse's husband was on his way to Marseilles to join the army and, with them, try to arrest the Emperor as he marched north to capture Paris.

Madame decided to stay in Bordeaux and organize the resistance there. The largest city in western France, it was of vital importance. Napoleon had been immensely popular with his soldiers. Regiment after regiment was going over to him, tearing off their white cockades and putting on the tricolor, as he neared Paris. But even when she heard on March 20 that Napoleon was back at the Tuileries, ruler of France once more, and Louis XVIII had fled to Belgium, Thérèse merely said, "Very well, I'll fight the usurper alone!"

The Duchesse d'Angoulême did, and Napoleon exclaimed of her in admiration, "She's the only man in her family."

It was the survival of the Bourbon dynasty Thérèse was fighting for, and she was indefatigable, visiting every barracks within riding or driving distance. The Duchess, a tall, erect woman, knew she looked well on a horse. Dressed in uniform, she addressed the troops in her deep throaty voice, that would always be husky, because of her long silence in prison, and tried to rekindle the soldiers' enthusiasm for the royalist cause.

Only silence greeted Thérèse's appeals of "Come, shout with me! *Vive le Roi!*" She saw that the men had removed the white cockades from their shakos. More and more, tricolor flags began to appear. All of France was on the verge of going over to Napoleon.

One day at Bordeaux's Saint-Raphael barracks, the Duchess turned to its commanding officer. "General Decaen, can't you control your men?" she asked.

"Not any longer, Madame."

"Then I shall. Order the troops to parade. I wish to review them."

"I would prefer you didn't. I cannot guarantee your safety."

"I'm not afraid."

The general muster was sounded. Accompanied by General Decaen, the Duchesse d'Angoulême walked along the lines. With all of Marie Antoinette's courage, but, unfortunately, too much of her mother's arrogance, she faced the men of the 11th Military Division standing at attention. "A usurper has taken the crown from your king," she told them. "Bordeaux is threatened. Yes or no—will you fight for His Majesty?"

No answer.

"I ask you again," she repeated, "will you fight for your lawful king or not?"

"We'll not fire on our brothers," replied the officer in charge of the battalion.

"You call them your brothers? Those traitors who have gone over to Napoleon!" the Duchess exclaimed. "I'm ashamed of you. Have you forgotten your oath of loyalty to the King? If there still remains among you one man who remembers it, let him come forward and say so." A few soldiers stepped out of the ranks. "There are not many of you," Thérèse remarked bitterly. "Well, at least we're finding out on whom we can depend."

She went on to other barracks. At several places, the Duchesse d'Angoulême was received, not with silence, but actual hostility. She wrote Antoine, one night, in utter discouragement. After an indignant account of how she had tried to speak, but was heckled continuously with shouts of "*Vive Napoleon!*" she added, "They would have liked to insult me personally, but I assumed my well-known [haughty] air, and they did not dare. But the soldiers were so rude, I was forced to leave."

Thérèse then insisted, against the advice of her equerry, Monsieur de Lur-Saluces, in driving out one day to Trompette. She had great affection for that army post, for in the barracks there was stationed the Angoulême regiment, named after her husband.

When she entered the gates of the fort, the Duchess noticed that its commander, General Bertrand Clausel, did not even have the politeness to come out and greet her. He sent a noncommissioned officer instead. Thérèse ignored the snub. She asked to be allowed to speak to the soldiers and implored them, tears in her eyes, to remember that they were "her regiment."

There were no cheers in reply.

"Have you forgotten me, your honorary colonel?" the Duchess asked, her voice breaking. But her question fell upon deaf ears. She said a few more broken sentences in the midst of frosty silence. Then, tears of rage and disappointment running down her cheeks, Thérèse gave up and walked away. If she couldn't count on the Angoulême regiment, the end had come.

General Clausel came over to her carriage. "Madame, you had better leave France at once," he said. "There's a British gunboat in the harbor. I'll conduct you safely aboard."

"Why should I run away, General?"

"I'll show you—" Clausel gave a signal and, to Thérèse's

utter astonishment, she saw the tricolor run up on the flagpole of the fort. "Perhaps you didn't notice that the white flag of the Bourbons was no longer flying," the General said. "We surrendered to Napoleon two days ago. And, Madame, I have the Emperor's orders to arrest you."

Napoleon also wanted the Duc d'Angoulême captured and shot. When Thérèse learned that Antoine had fled to Spain, she saw that further resistance was useless. General Clausel, won over by the Duchess' courage, hadn't arrested her. But how much longer would he dare to defy Napoleon's orders? She must leave, not only Bordeaux, but France.

So on April 2, 1815, the Duchesse d'Angoulême allowed General Clausel to escort her aboard the British gunboat *Wanderer*. At eight o'clock at night, in a torrent of rain, she sailed for Plymouth, England. In April, just a year ago, she had left Hartwell in triumph. Now Marie Antoinette's daughter was an exile again, for the second time in her life, running away from Napoleon.

23

CAROLINE OF NAPLES

THREE MONTHS LATER, the tricolor had been taken down. The white flag with its gold fleurs-de-lis flew again over the long, gray façade of the Tuileries. Defeated by the British and Prussians at Waterloo, Napoleon had been sent off to die at Saint Helena. Louis XVIII was king of France again, thanks to the Allied armies who had twice seated him on the throne, and the Duchesse d'Angoulême was back at the Tuileries, in her old ground floor apartment—"thin, nervous, more rude and sarcastic than ever," wrote a contemporary.

Francis of Austria, Alexander of Russia, and Frederick of Prussia were none to pleased with the ailing sixty-year-old monarch they installed. They would have preferred his cousin, the more liberal Duc Louis Philippe d'Orléans. When the Duchesse d'Angoulême rejoined her uncle in Paris on July 8, 1815, after a brief exile in England, she found that he had been forced by the Allies to make certain concessions, such as accepting Talleyrand for prime minister and retaining Fouché as chief of police.

Thérèse was indignant. She despised both of these men, especially Fouché, who, like Talleyrand, had been in Napoleon's cabinet. She hated him as a regicide and for his terrorist record. In 1793, one of the fiercest of the Jacobins, Fouché had voted in the Convention for her father's death. And how much did he know about what had happened to her brother? Why had Fouché so feared the Tower that, afraid to walk past it, he made Napoleon pull it down? And why had he silenced the Widow Simon?

For years, the Duchesse d'Angoulême had been trying to get Fouché dismissed. Now she made such scenes over his remaining in the ministry that her uncle, reluctantly, gave in. On September 11, 1815, he was appointed Minister to Dresden. His successor would be Fouché's assistant, Elie Decazes.

Certainly, Thérèse couldn't question Decazes' loyalty. Once secretary to Louis Bonaparte, he had turned royalist and remained one during Napoleon's Hundred Days before Waterloo. Louis XVIII, by now so crippled he could get only from his bed to his wheel chair, and in constant pain, needed someone to divert him. The thirty-five-year-old Decazes, shrewd and ambitious, became the crony of the ailing monarch. He talked well, but what was more important, he knew how to listen, how to amuse and flatter the old man. Louis began calling Decazes his "son." Blacas, long the favorite, became very jealous.

By 1816, Elie Decazes was more powerful than the King. He had his ear in every intrigue and, as Fouché's assistant, he had come upon hints, among Robespierre's papers, that the then Comte de Provence had masterminded the disappearance of his nephew, the Dauphin. After that, the young chief of police had the King right under his thumb.

Thérèse, who by now disliked Decazes heartily, couldn't account for his hold over her uncle. And Ferdinand resented the interference of the King's favorite in his affairs. He was sure it was Decazes who kept telling Louis XVIII that he should marry.

For years, the Duc de Berry had refused to look for a suitable wife. He was already married to Amy Brown, he insisted, and while the Bourbons had no chance of regaining the throne, his private life didn't matter. The situation changed with their return to France. The handsome, elegant Charles d'Artois, still attractive to women at fifty-nine, remained true to the memory of Louise de Polastron. He refused to marry again, even for the sake of the succession. And since his son, Antoine, couldn't produce an heir to the throne, it was the duty of his younger brother to find himself a wife among the reigning Catholic families of Europe. The French would never accept Amy Brown, a Protestant commoner, as queen.

"Ferdinand, you must marry and have a son, for I shall never have a child." Thérèse referred to the great sorrow of her life, about which she seldom spoke.

Since there was no question of his giving up Amy (she and the children had been living in Paris for some time), Ferdinand agreed to do as his family wished. The Grand Duchess Anna, sister of the Czar, was first considered. Then the King, Monsieur, and the Duchesse d'Angoulême decided upon the seventeen-year-old Princess Marie Caroline Ferdinande Louise, daughter of Francis I and Queen Marie Clementine of Naples.

"She was forced on the Duc de Berry, who displayed no interest," says the Comtesse de Boigne. Nor was the Duchesse d'Angoulême too enthusiastic. Caroline's Aunt Marie Amelie, Francis I's sister, had become the Duchesse d'Orléans by marrying Thérèse's pet hate, Louis Philippe. However, she gave her consent to the match and on June 15, 1816, accompanied the King, Artois and his sons, when they set out for the crossroads of Saint Herem, in the forest of Fontainebleau, to meet Caroline of Naples. Since the days of Louis XIV, it had been the custom of the French kings to go some distance from Paris to welcome the brides of the royal princes.

No longer able to stand on his gouty legs, Louis XVIII was

seated by the roadside in a blue velvet armchair, the others on campstools, when Princess Caroline's barouche drove into sight. The carriage stopped. A tiny blonde girl, with a lovely slim figure, leaped out. She ran to the old King, who kissed her and introduced her to his family.

"Madame, this is your husband," he said, indicating Ferdinand. "I am your father, there is your brother [Antoine], and this is our angel [Thérèse]."

"You're better-looking than in the picture you sent me," Caroline told Ferdinand. "So are you," he replied. The Neapolitan Princess was pretty and lively. "She's not bad, not bad at all," Berry remarked to his sister-in-law, as they drove back to Paris. He looked pleased and greatly relieved. How different this meeting was, Thérèse thought, from her own disappointing first sight of Antoine!

The wedding took place the next day, at Notre Dame Cathedral, and a banquet, attended by all the diplomatic corps, followed at the Tuileries. It broke up at ten o'clock, the King's usual bedtime. But tonight he insisted on escorting the bridal couple to their new home, the Elysée palace, a former mansion of Madame de Pompadour, then returning to the Tuileries by the Champs-Elysées, to see the fireworks being set off by the city of Paris in honor of the newlyweds.

From her little house in the Rue des Mathurins, Amy Brown watched the rockets bursting over Paris. "Mama, what are they celebrating? And why are you crying?" her daughters asked.

24

THE BLOOD-SPATTERED CROWN

In a secret drawer of his father's desk, Ferdinand de Berry chanced one day to come upon a letter to Artois from the then Comte de Provence. He read:

> It is done, my brother, what we have long wished for. I hold in my hand the official news of the death of Louis XVI. And I am informed that his son is dying. I heartily hope so, think what a relief to us his death will be, and remember that your Antoine is, after me and you, the heir to the monarchy.

"Not much brotherly love in that letter," Ferdinand said to himself. Had his uncle gotten rid of the child King as he had helped to get rid of the boy's father? He thought so, and that Simon did the actual strangling. But whatever happened at the Tower that night of January 19, 1794, Ferdinand was sure, had been done with the knowledge and consent of the present King of France.

As he reconstructed the crime, it was committed about nine o'clock at night, while Simon moved out his furniture. Otherwise, why did he leave on a foggy evening, after dark? Why? So that no one would see him carry out little Capet's body.

This was probably what had happened on that black night, when none of the guards were watching—the wrapped-up body of the boy King (it was the parcel Thérèse saw being taken out) was carried down the dark, winding stairs and thrown into a hole Simon had dug by the Little Tower, where it was accidently found by the Comte d'Andigné in 1801, seven years later.

Meanwhile, Jeanne Simon, who knew about the murder, showed the keepers on duty that night a child asleep in the dimly-lighted room. They gave her a receipt for the boy they believed to be Charles Capet, and she left the Tower to rejoin her husband in a nearby wineshop.

Then Antoine Simon made a mistake. He was boastful. He talked too much of the crime he had committed for "a very great bigwig." He must be silenced, so he was executed. But for the six months he was allowed to live, Ferdinand's agents told him, Simon had lived high, as no inspector of army baggage wagons ever lived. He did not return to his humble lodgings but was installed in a comfortable apartment in the Rue des Cordeliers, just outside the Temple wall, with plenty of money for drink and gambling. He was being rewarded. By whom? Robespierre, people said. But Ferdinand knew of someone who had more reason than Robespierre to want to get rid of the Dauphin. But you couldn't accuse the King of France of murder—especially of one done twenty-five years ago.

The crown Louis Xavier Stanislas coveted had finally come to him, spotted with blood. Had it made him happy? Ferdinand thought not, for his uncle must not only be haunted by the memory of his crime, but by the constant fear of exposure. How could he feel secure on the throne? Was that why the presence of Marie Antoinette's daughter was so necessary to him? For several men had appeared who claimed to be Louis XVII.

That year of 1819, a young man had been imprisoned by Decazes at Rouen for calling himself Charles de Navarre. The police said he was actually Mathurin Bruneau, the son of a Loire cobbler and a deserter from the navy. For two years he had been writing to the King and the Duchesse d'Angoulême. To prove that he was the Dauphin, Navarre offered to give "his sister" the sign of recognition that she and her brother had agreed upon in the Temple, if she would come to Rouen, for he would whisper it only to the Duchess. There had been no such sign, but Navarre's letters had greatly upset his uncle, Ferdinand knew, and the idea came to him to torture him further. By making him out to be a usurper on the throne, Berry saw a way to get what he wanted, money.

Since the Restoration, Louis XVIII had amassed a large fortune. He was very rich, yet he continued to ignore Ferdinand's morganatic marriage, and did nothing toward the support of Amy Brown and her children. By encouraging Navarre's claims, Ferdinand thought he could frighten his uncle into giving Amy a pension. He knew, of course, that the Dauphin was dead, but to embarrass the old man, whom he hated, he sent a lawyer to interview Navarre in jail at Rouen and encourage him to keep pestering Louis XVIII with demands to restore the throne to him.

What Ferdinand, an amateur at blackmail, didn't know was that Lawyer Mejean was serving two masters. He betrayed Berry constantly to Chief of Police Decazes, whose secret agent he was. So it was through Mejean, the "M.E." of the police files, that Decazes was kept informed of all that was going on.

Still, nothing very terrible might have happened had not the question of the succession become acute. On September 21, 1819, the Duchesse de Berry brought into the world, not the son so ardently hoped for, but a daughter Louise. After her birth, the Duchesse de Gontaut, who was present, quotes

Caroline as repeating what Marie Antoinette said at the birth of Thérèse, "The next, I promise, will be a boy."

But could she? This delivery had been difficult, and Caroline had already lost two babies. What worried the royal family was that living with Amy Brown in the little house on the Rue des Mathurins were four children. The eldest, fifteen-year-old John Charles Freeman, Amy said was adopted. But she insisted the George, fourteen, Charlotte, eleven, and Louise, ten, were the children of the Duc de Berry and had been born in wedlock. If this was true, then Ferdinand's second marriage was bigamous and his son, George Granville Brown, had a claim to the throne of France, if Caroline had only daughters.

"Sire, you would have done better in London to have recognized the Duc de Berry's Protestant marriage and then had the Pope annul it," Pierre de Blacas told the King. "This George Granville Brown is going to cause us endless trouble."

He was another little boy in the way. And he must be eliminated. One afternoon, when George was alone in the Bois de Boulogne, sailing his toy boat, two of Decazes' henchmen sprang out of the bushes and seized him.

Her son failed to come home for supper, and Amy was hysterical with grief, when Berry came to see her that evening. "Oh, they'll kill him!" she sobbed. Ferdinand took Amy in his arms and tried to comfort her. How could he? He, too, was heartbroken. He loved the boy.

"Darling, you'll get him back, won't you?" Amy pleaded. "You know who kidnaped George as well as I do. Please, if you love me, go to the King and threaten him—do anything!"

"I'll get George back," Ferdinand promised.

His face grim, the Duke went to Amy's desk, and took from it some reports from his agents concerning the lost Dauphin. They confirmed his belief that the then Comte de Provence, learning of the deal the Convention had made with

Charette, and not wanting his nephew to be handed over to the Vendéan army, where he would become a rally point for the royalists, had managed to get hold of him first. After that, the succession of boys, the one sent to Charette, the one to Vitry, and the two to America, were false Dauphins, substituted for the murdered little King to make people think he was still alive. Jardin, who took Eleazar Williams to America and left him with the Indians, was a valet of Provence. And his man in America wrote Berry, "Do you remember the artist Bellanger, who brought a boy to Philadelphia? He confesses he was in Provence's pay and had been told to say the boy was the Dauphin—" Ferdinand read no further. He was going to accuse his uncle of murder, and threaten to expose him, unless little George Granville Brown was immediately returned. Stuffing the papers into his pocket, he hurried off to the Tuileries.

"I must speak with the King," his nephew said to the Comte de Blacas. Then as the secretary didn't leave the room, he added, "Privately!"

Blacas bristled. Every time Ferdinand quarreled with his uncle, the old man was sick for days, and the King's devoted secretary saw that the Duke was livid with rage. "Very well, but don't upset him. His Majesty isn't well," Pierre said, and stalked out of the room. He shut the door. Then he squatted down to listen at the keyhole.

Gracious, what did he hear? As the angry voices grew louder, there were threats and loud denials. "He knows everything!" Blacas said to himself in a panic. What should he do? Rush into the room and throw Berry out before he gave his uncle a stroke? Or run down the hall and call the Duchesse d'Angoulême? Pierre decided to summon the Duchess. But he was trembling so that he could hardly get to her suite.

"Madame, come at once!" Blacas cried. "The King and the

Duc de Berry are quarreling. You must stop them. I fear for His Majesty's health."

Dropping her knitting, Thérèse rushed down the hall. Antoine followed her. They found the King slumped in his chair. He had fainted. "What are you trying to do, kill him?" Antoine accused his brother.

"He deserves it," muttered Ferdinand, as he left the room.

The Duc d'Angoulême turned to his wife, who was kneeling by the old man's side, her face pale with concern. "Antoine, I think Uncle's had a stroke. We must get him to bed." Thérèse looked up to say. "Where is Pierre?"

Oddly enough, the King's secretary couldn't be found. Blacas had hurried off to confer with Louis XVIII's chief of police. Decazes would know what to do. Ruthless, and (to serve his own selfish ends) loyal to the King, he was a man who stopped at nothing.

25

MURDER TO MUSIC

PIERRE LOUVEL SAT sharpening his knife. Employed as a saddler, he lived in the attic of the royal stables at the Tuileries. He whistled as he worked, for Louvel felt very important. He had been hired to kill the Duc de Berry by no less a person than Elie Decazes, the King's chief of police. Louvel didn't know why Berry must be eliminated. Nor did he care. A hired thug, he had done such jobs as this for Decazes before. Pierre knew he would be well paid, and addicted to opium, he needed the money. Still, when the police officer sent for him and made his proposition, the saddler hesitated. "Murder? They hang you for that," he grumbled. "What if I get caught?"

"Your trial will be a farce," Decazes promised him. "A few weeks in jail, then you'll go free, a wealthy man."

So, for a month now, Louvel had been trailing Berry everywhere he went—to the races, to the theater, and to balls—trying to decide when to assassinate him. On February 13, 1820, he decided to strike. It was the last Sunday before Lent. Paris was at the height of the Carnival. There were parades, street dancing, and a performance of the *Carnival de Venise* at the opera that the Duke would surely attend.

At eight o'clock that evening, a small, middle-aged man was standing in the dark Rue de Richelieu, outside the opera house, when Ferdinand and Caroline drove up. Louvel intended to kill the King's nephew then, but lost his nerve. He overheard Ferdinand say to his coachman, "Come back at quarter to eleven." So, later that night, when the Duke's cabriolet returned, Decazes' hireling was waiting. He saw the Berrys come out of the theater. Ferdinand helped his wife into the carriage. To everyone's delight, Caroline was pregnant again. She had been warned by her doctors not to overdo, so she was going home early.

"Good-by, my dear," Ferdinand called out. Then he turned back into the opera house to watch the last act. As he did so, a man, brandishing a dagger, darted out of the shadows and fell on him. Louvel remembered to shout, as Decazes had told him to do, "*Vive Napoleon!*" as he plunged the knife into the Duke's chest.

"I've been stabbed!" cried Ferdinand. Those about him stood frozen with shock. So Berry pulled out the bloody stiletto himself and, moaning with pain, staggered back into the arms of his wife, who had jumped out of the carriage. "Stop that man!" several persons shouted. But the assassin vanished into the night.

They sent for the wounded man's father, for his brother and sister-in-law. By the time they arrived, the Duc de Berry had been carried from the lobby of the theater up a flight of stairs to a narrow hall leading to his opera box. He was lying on a sofa, his head resting on Caroline's lap. Her white satin ball gown was drenched with blood. Two doctors arrived, La Croix and Caseneuve, but they couldn't stop the red flow.

"Is he dying?" Thérèse asked. La Croix nodded.

The Duchesse de Gontaut, the governess of the little

Mademoiselle of France, tells in her memoirs how she was awakened in the night at the Elysée and told to bring Louise to the opera house:

> The Duke, assassinated, wanted to see his daughter before he died. An immense crowd, by the light of torches, stood before the opera house. They parted to make way for me, when I drove up, the child in my arms. I hurried in and up to the little room where Monsieur lay, on a couch covered with blood. It was dreadful. He made a great effort and kissed Louise.

"Amy! Amy!" Ferdinand kept calling her name. Thérèse turned to her sister-in-law. "Do you mind?"

"No, let them come," Caroline replied.

So Berry's other family was sent for, and Madame de Gontaut describes how they came to the crowded upstairs hallway in the opera house where he lay dying, Amy "in tears, and her poor little ones trembling. Monsieur spoke to them in English." Then the two wives and their children, who had never met, stood looking at each other. Ferdinand had just strength enough to kiss his three small girls good-by before he died.

Meanwhile, the audience, not told of the tragedy, was enjoying the last act of the *Carnaval de Venise*. As Artois bent over and closed his son's eyes, the gay ballet music that Berry loved drifted through the drawn curtains of his opera box.

All this time the assassin was running back to his lodgings in the King's stables, where he hoped no one would suspect him of having committed the crime. But, next day, they came to arrest him. "It's just a formality," Louvel remembered Decazes had said, as he was taken to the Conciergerie and locked up.

Berry's murderer was still confident that his friend, the chief of police, would save him, when several days later, without trial, he was driven to the gallows. Only when they made him mount the steps of a platform on the Place de Grève, and tied his hands behind him, did Louvel realize he had been betrayed. "Decazes killed him for—" the wretched man shouted. But the noose over his head silenced him. No one heard the name he uttered.

Paris was stunned. For days the newspapers were full of the murder and funeral of the Duc de Berry at Saint-Denis. Why had the popular forty-two-year-old heir-presumptive to the throne been killed? Everyone knew of the quarrels in the royal family. Berry, people were saying, had discovered a frightful family skeleton, and threatened to expose it, creating a public scandal, when death silenced him. Decazes was accused of being an accomplice in the crime. Meeting the chief of police for the first time since the tragedy, the Duchesse de Berry burst into tears and called him to his face the murderer of her husband.

Decazes denied it. Hadn't he punished the murderer, he said, an admirer of Napoleon who planned to kill the King next, then Monsieur and the Duc d'Angoulême, and so to do away, one by one, with all of the Bourbons?

Neither Artois nor the Angoulêmes believed him. They begged the King to dismiss Decazes. He refused. Only when Thérèse threatened to leave the Tuileries and have nothing more to do with her uncle, would the infatuated old man agree to part with his favorite. Raised to the rank of duke, Decazes was banished from France—as ambassador to England!

26

THE MIRACLE CHILD

NOTHING MUST INTERFERE with the safe birth of the child who would someday be king of France, for it was ardently hoped that the Duchesse de Berry's baby would be a boy. Her sister-in-law took charge. Thérèse, wanting the flighty young widow where she could keep an eye on her, insisted that Caroline move to the Tuileries. With her little daughter Louise, she was installed in the Pavillon de Marsan, where her father-in-law lived.

It wasn't a happy household. Every time that Caroline visited her Aunt Amelie, wife of Louis Philippe, Thérèse, who was carrying on Marie Antoinette's feud with the Orléans branch of the family, gave her sister-in-law a scolding. "The Duchesse d'Angoulême tried to guide her, like a governess," writes the Comtesse de Boigne. "At first, the Duchesse de Berry was afraid of Madame, then grew to hate her." There was twenty years' difference in the ages of the two women. And no two people could have been more uncongenial. Yet, here they were, shut up together in the gloomy old Tuileries, from which there was no escape, even for a weekend at

Saint-Cloud, for the superstitious old King refused to leave the palace. The Comtesse de Boigne tells us why.

> The Tuileries was inhabited by more than eight hundred people, who were by no means clean in their habits. There were kitchens on every floor, and an absolute lack of cellars or sinks. Consequently all kinds of filth collected and made such a smell that one was made almost ill going up the stairs of the Pavillon de Flore [where Thérèse lived] and crossing the halls of the second floor. But, even to have the palace cleaned, the King refused to leave the Tuileries for a moment. He had been told by a fortune-teller during his exile in England that he would return to the Tuileries, but would not die there. The worse his health became, the more Louis XVIII clung to the place where he was not to die.

* * * *

Finally September, Caroline's ninth month, arrived, and the Duchesse de Gontaut writes, "The King named as witnesses the Ducs de Coigney and d'Albuféra, who were ordered to live from now on at the Tuileries, to be on hand at a moment's notice, as was Déneaux, the accoucheur. Witnesses were essential, for our little Duchess had kept so slim people refused to believe she was pregnant."

The night of September 28, 1820, with Caroline's delivery thought to be several days off, the Angoulêmes went to bed as usual. At two o'clock in the morning, they were awakened by a frantic knocking on the door. "Come quick!" they heard the frightened voice of Madame Devathaire, the Duchesse de Berry's maid. "The child is coming! Hurry!" Thérèse leaped out of bed and slipped on her dressing gown. She shook Antoine awake. "Get Déneaux," she ordered, and hurried off down the hall.

In Caroline's room, Madame found her sister-in-law alone, except for her *femme de chambre* and her newborn baby. The child was crying. Thérèse examined the infant. It was a boy—thank God!—and still attached to his mother by the umbilical cord.

Thérèse turned to Antoine, who, having called the accoucheur, had followed her. "Quick! Get some witnesses," she said. But who? The Ducs de Coigney and d'Albuféra, not expecting to be needed, had disobeyed the King and gone off hunting in the south of France. Yet, someone must see the baby before he was separated from his mother or people would always say that he wasn't hers.

"Won't I do as a witness?" asked the maid.

"No, Madame Devathaire, you're in the Duchesse de Berry's pay, and the Duke and I are relatives." Thérèse turned to the accoucher, who had come into the room, and asked, "How much longer can my sister-in-law remain like this?" Déneaux answered, "Not much longer." Poor Caroline was whimpering with pain.

"Don't you dare touch her while I'm gone. I'll find someone," Madame said to him and hurried from the room. Two sentries stood on guard down the hall. Rushing up to them, Thérèse grabbed each of the startled young men by an arm. "Come," she pleaded. "I need you."

"Come where?" one of them replied. "My good woman, we're guarding the royal family. We mustn't leave our post. Can't you see we're on duty?" The soldiers thought this disheveled woman in a dressing gown and bedroom slippers was someone's maid. What was their astonishment when she cried, "You idiots, I'm the Duchesse d'Angoulême. Hurry!" And Thérèse dragged the two men by the hand down the hall to the Berry suite.

Throwing back the bedclothes, she said to them, "You see this woman in bed with a child? Will you swear the baby is attached to his mother? That he is really hers? Very well, then sign this statement that you saw it with your own eyes."

Only when the guards had signed a paper Madame shoved at them, did she order the accoucher, "Cut the cord."

At half-past two in the morning, when all was safely over Antoine went to waken his father. "Papa, you have a grandson," he told him. Artois hurried after Angoulême, down the hall. When he entered the room, Madame Devathaire had given the baby his first bath and his daughter-in-law was holding him.

Ten minutes later, the firing of the cannon at the Tuileries woke all of Paris. What would it be? Twenty-one shots for a princess? Or a hundred and one, announcing an heir to the throne? People rushed to their windows to listen. Carefully, they counted the first twenty-one shots. The twenty-second produced an uproar. A boy! The Bourbon dynasty was saved.

The Duchesse d'Angoulême stood at a window of the Pavillon de Marsan, listening to the cannon shots, the child in her arms. He waved small fists and Thérèse looked down at him, all her frustrated love for children in her tear-filled eyes. "You darling," she whispered, "how I wish you were mine!"

* * * *

The baby was baptized at Notre Dame and given the names Henri Charles Ferdinand Dieudonné, the first in memory of Henry IV of France, the most popular king among his ancestors; the second, after his father; the third, on account of his maternal great-grandfather, Ferdinand IV of the Two Sicilies; and the fourth (God-given) because this child, born seven months after his father's death, had saved the succession. The little boy seemed like a miracle. He was also titled the Duc de Bordeaux, after the city that first surrendered to the Bourbons; and the Comte de Chambord because the French people, by popular subscription, bought Francis I's château by that name on the Loire as a gift to the baby prince.

Two other children were more quietly ennobled. Thérèse could not get Amy Brown's pathetic little girls out of her mind. She appealed to Pierre de Blacas and, in memory of their father, Charlotte and Louise were given the courtesy titles of Comtesse d'Issoudun and Comtesse de Vierzon. Their mother received a pension. And something else was done for Amy Brown, about which Blacas never told the Duchess. George Granville Brown was safely returned to his mother. With the birth of the Duc de Bordeaux, Amy's son was no longer a threat to the crown.

The acts were done in the King's name, but it was Blacas who ran the government, giving the sick man papers to sign which he did in a trembling hand, without reading them. The Comtesse de Boigne writes of seeing Louis XVIII in 1824:

> I was shocked by the change in him. He was seated in his wheel chair, and in his usual costume, a uniform brilliant with gold lace and studded with orders. The gaiters of black velvet around his legs were twice as large as before, and his head dropped upon his chest. Only with an effort could he raise his face.

Nearly blind, Provence fell asleep while people talked to him. He sat nodding in his wheel chair, a bloated, red-faced invalid, with vacant eyes fastened on the door, waiting for a nephew who didn't come.

"Where is your brother?" he would ask Antoine.

Doesn't Uncle realize that Ferdinand is dead, Thérèse thought. Had his muddled mind never grasped the fact? Continually these days the senile old monarch babbled about being a usurper, for gangrene was spreading up his swollen legs, and Provence knew he had not long to live. Now that he must shortly face his Maker, he wanted desperately to believe what Martin, a peasant, had written him. It seemed an angel had appeared to Martin in a field on his farm and told him that Louis XVII was alive. It was the will of God that the Dauphin be restored to the throne.

On September 16, 1824, the Angoulêmes, Baron Portal, the King's doctor, and Abbé Rocher, his confessor, stood by Louis XVIII's bedside, waiting for the end. Weakly, the dying man took a letter from under his pillow and handed it to Antoine. "Give it—to your papa—" he gasped.

Antoine hurried to the Pavillon de Marsan. He found his father seated in his library, reading. "How is he?" Artois asked.

"Sinking rapidly," Antoine replied. "You'd better come."

When his son left, Monsieur read the letter, in which his brother said he had proof that their nephew was alive. He begged him to hand over the throne to Louis XVII, the rightful heir. "Nonsense!" muttered Artois, and burned the letter. He, too, wanted to be king.

Twenty minutes later, Monsieur reached his brother's bedside. The silence in the room allowed the dying man's short, painful breathing to be heard. Suddenly, there was silence. Dr. Portal placed a lighted candle close to the King's mouth. The flame did not flicker. "All is over," he informed the family.

Artois seemed not to understand, until Blacas said to him, "Sire, the King is dead." Thérèse rose and curtsied to her father-in-law, now Charles X, King of France and Navarre.

In the hall outside, the courtiers had gathered to greet their new sovereign. The Comte de Blacas, opening the door, called out, "Gentlemen, the King!" As everyone bowed, Charles X, his son, and daughter-in-law came out of Napoleon's old apartment at the Tuileries in which Louis XVIII had breathed his last.

The Duchesse d'Angoulême, as the daughter of a king, had always taken precedence over her husband. Antoine, leaving the room, fell into his accustomed place behind his wife. Thérèse stepped quickly aside. "After you, Monsieur le Dauphin," she said.

27

TEN-MINUTE QUEEN

CAROLINE OF NAPLES' HEART was in the grave with her husband—or at least, people thought it should be and expected her to act accordingly. This annoyed her. That she had been in love with the Duc de Berry, a man twice her age, was absurd. Soon after their marriage, Caroline learned about Amy Brown. It was quite a shock, but she dutifully gave Ferdinand children, and the couple led a pleasant enough life together for four years, until that nightmarish event outside the opera house. With his death, the vivacious little Neapolitan, only twenty-one, became a widow and must watch her behavior. Caroline loved parties and pretty clothes, but she must remember to act sad and not to show any interest in men.

"A widow gets herself talked about so easily," Thérèse reminded her. Charles X was equally strict. No one is more proper than a reformed rake. The King made a dreadful scene when he discovered that his daughter-in-law went riding alone in public vehicles, the new omnibuses appearing on the Paris streets. Wits began calling them "Carolines." Artois was shocked. "The conduct of the mother of the heir to the throne must be twice as circumspect as that of an ordinary woman," he told her. But the democratic ways of the young Duchess endeared her to the bourgeoisie, a new element becoming powerful in France. Charles X would have done well to have catered to them. The Comtesse de Boigne wrote:

> Caroline was natural and gay. This made her popular with the middle class. Her chief merit consisted in the fact that she differed from the rest of the family. She was fond of art and liked the theater. She used to walk the streets unescorted, went into stores, and bought lavishly. This was enough to secure her the affection of the shopkeeping class.

But what use were new dresses, Caroline thought, since her social life chiefly consisted of attending the boring receptions at the Tuileries? Standing with Charles X—who, having lived in England, surprised his French guests by greeting them with a hearty British handshake—were the heirs to the throne, the tall Dauphine, white ostrich plumes in her tiara, and the dapper little Dauphin by her side, peering nearsightedly through his spectacles. "Madame's aide-de-camp," Antoine called himself, and he was, always dashing off to do errands for his wife. When the reception line broke up, the Dauphine sat down to play écarté at five francs the game; Charles X, to his beloved whist. After a dull evening of chamber music, when the ladies came to make their farewell curtsies, the King hardly glanced up from the cards.

The death of Louis XVIII had finally freed Thérèse from the Tuileries of ghastly memories. In summer, when Charles X and the court moved out to Saint-Cloud, the Angoulêmes went to Villeneuve l'Etang, a small country place within walking distance which they had bought. Thérèse refused to go to Versailles, where she had stood trembling on a balcony beside her mother, facing the hostile revolutionists. Thirty-six years has passed, but the insults of the crowd still rang in her ears, as if it were only yesterday.

On December 19, 1825, Thérèse was forty-seven and beginning to be troubled with rheumatism. Villeneuve l'Etang was a Petit Trianon, such as her mother had, where the Angoulêmes could live the quiet life they preferred, with Antoine spending the day working out chess problems or studying his weather charts. He was always consulting the thermometer and sending aides riding over to the Observatory to ask the maximum temperature of the day.

After living in palaces and prisons all her life, Villeneuve l'Etang was Thérèse's first real home. "She was delighted with it," according to the Comtesse de Boigne, "and had cream from her cows there served at the Tuileries in a silver jug that was always placed at the Dauphine's seat at table." At Villeneuve l'Etang, their aunt kept toys and dogs and ponies for Louise and Henri to enjoy, when they came over from Rosny, their mother's château near Mantes. The Comtesse continues:

> The Duchesse de Berry troubled herself very little about her children, and hardly ever saw them. With the Duc de Bordeaux very ill with measles, she went off hunting. The King and the Dauphine were greatly displeased and expressed their feelings loudly.

If their mother neglected Henri and Louise, no children ever had a more doting aunt. Louise was a sweet child, Thérèse loved her, but from the day of his birth, Henri became her special pride and joy. She talked about him incessantly, boring people with his first childish words, then with details of his education and the plans for his future she was already making. According to his Tante Thérèse, never was there such a gifted little boy. At eight, the Duc de Bordeaux already had the mentality of a fourteen-year-old in her estimation. He was the most intelligent, the handsomest, the best-behaved child. . . . All grandmothers talk like this, but not always an aunt. Longing for children all her life, Thérèse had been deprived of the joys of motherhood. Now she was making up for lost time. Henri spent hours playing with his toy soldiers on the floor, while she watched him, doing her needlework nearby. She invented games for him, went into raptures over every word he uttered and everything he did.

It was too bad, Thérèse thought, that she must share the boy with his silly, empty-headed mother, who would certainly ruin him. It delighted her when, his visits over, Henri burst into tears at having to return to Rosny. He much preferred Villeneuve l'Etang, where he was outrageously spoiled. He loved his Tante Thérèse. He was happy only when he was with her, and would only do as she told him. "He loves me more than he does his mother," Thérèse said to herself, hugging the little boy to her heart.

* * * *

Louis XVIII had been old, stout, and infirm. Charles X was a slim, handsome, white-haired man with elegant manners. A fine horseman, he was debonair and youthful-looking at seventy-two. Having lived in England for many years, Artois spoke English fluently. He enjoyed horse racing and English sports, in fact everything British—except their form of government. He believed in the inherent rights of kings. He resented being a constitutional monarch, and was even more reactionary in his ideas than his brother Provence had been. His chief desires were to do away with the constitution the Allies had forced on Louis XVIII, to give more power to the Catholic Church, and to muzzle the press. Well liked at first because of his personal charm, Charles X became unpopular because of his reactionary views. Discontent and unrest were growing, so, in the fall of 1829, the royal family decided upon a good-will tour of France.

One day, in the Argonne, their coach drew up at an inn. The Dauphine glanced out of the window. "Where are we?" she asked the postboy, who was changing the horses.

"Varennes," he replied.

Oh, no! Thérèse felt as though she were in a bad dream. She looked and saw again the Bra d'Or Inn, the street running down to the bridge, and the lower town across the Aire River—everything just as it was in 1791. "Hurry! Harness the horses," she begged. "Please, not another minute here!" The peasants of the Argonne, who had gathered in Varennes to welcome the royal family, were astonished to see them hurriedly drive away.

The Dauphine was still trembling over seeing Varennes again, when, on arriving at Nancy, she stepped out on to a balcony to show herself to the waiting people below. Since the Revolution, Thérèse had feared crowds. Now, to her horror, some people hissed her. Angry tears in her eyes, she cut short her speech.

She returned to Paris greatly depressed. The Bourbons had been replaced on the throne by a wave of reaction. Now France was again swinging to the left. And the old pattern was repeating itself—the conservatives grouped around the King, the liberals about Louis Philippe d'Orléans, son of Equalité.

Artois wanted to be king, but he wasn't willing to work at it. He spent his days hunting, his evenings playing cards. He hardly glanced at the newspapers. It was his daughter-in-law who read the leading periodicals and kept him informed. The Dauphine was as conservative as the King. But she feared the monarchy would be forced to adapt itself to a changing world, if it wished to survive, and she tried to restrain her father-in-law's more reactionary tendencies. "I want to be queen of France someday," Thérèse told him.

Worry aggravated her rheumatic pains, and Charles, anxious

to get rid of his "meddling" daughter-in-law, insisted that she go to Vichy for the cure. "Is it safe to leave you?" Thérèse asked. "Papa, don't you dare make any important decision while I'm gone. Now promise!"

Artois assured her that she could trust him, but the Dauphine drove off to Vichy in July, 1830, with the affairs of France weighing heavily on her mind. Charles O'Hegerthy, her equerry, wrote later: "We were hardly out of Paris before Madame opened an enormous green bag, that she always carries on journeys, and pulling out a heap of newspapers, ran her eyes over them."

Thérèse had cause to worry, for her father-in-law, an obstinate man, took advantage of her absence to do a foolish thing. On July 26, at Saint-Cloud, the Dauphin at his side, Charles X, in complete disregard of public opinion, signed the Ordinances that censored the press, dismissed the Chamber of Deputies, and abolished the constitution. In the future, Artois announced, he would rule as absolute king. The following day, the monarchy fell.

At Macon, the Dauphine heard the terrible news. Tortured by anxiety, she went on to Dijon, where she was insulted by the crowd. They even threatened to burn down the hotel where she was staying. Thérèse rushed back to Paris. Hearing at Fontainebleau that the mob had risen against Charles X, Paris was in their hands, and the King had fled to Rambouillet, she drove straight there. It was a ghastly journey. All along the road the houses were decked with tricolor flags.

When she reached the château, Charles X, seeing his daughter-in-law step from her carriage, came to the door with outstretched hands. "My child, can you ever forgive me?" he asked.

"Oh, Papa, what have you done?"

"I broke my promise to you. I listened to what others told me. It was bad advice." Artois looked so contrite that Thérèse put an arm around him as they went into the house. "Papa, let's not talk about the Ordinances. What has been done is done. Rather, what are we going to do now?"

Seated in his library, Charles X told her that the end had come. He had been ordered to abdicate. He had agreed to do so, in favor of his grandson, the little Duc de Bordeaux, for the Dauphin must also renounce his rights.

Thérèse burst into tears. "Oh, Papa, I beg of you, don't abdicate! I don't care for Antoine and myself, but think of Henri." History was repeating itself. Marie Antoinette had said almost the same words to Louis XVI. "Surely, not all of the army has deserted you," the Dauphine pleaded. "If you show some leadership, every man in France capable of bearing arms will fight for you to his last drop of blood."

Artois shook his head and managed a tired smile. "I doubt it, my dear." He sighed. And nothing that his daughter-in-law said could persuade him to change his mind.

Next morning, the thirty-first of July, Charles X was reading over his act of abdication and had already signed it when Thérèse, pale and red-eyed after a sleepless night, came into his library. He handed the document to her. She read it in silence and sat down. Antoine glanced rapidly over the paper and was about to sign it when his father stopped him.

"Your Majesty," the former king said to his startled son, "don't you realize that, as long as you don't sign that paper, you are king of France? And you, my dear, are queen?" He turned to Thérèse, his eyes glistening with tears. "At ten o'clock, the Chamber of Deputies are sending for our abdications. Then Antoine will have to sign his. Until then, my children, I want you to enjoy for a few minutes being king and queen of France. I will never forgive myself for having deprived you of the throne."

They sat looking at the clock on the mantel. Its hands pointed to ten minutes of ten. Slowly, the clock ticked away.

Precisely at ten o'clock, there was a knock on the door. Blacas entered. "Sire, a messenger from the Chamber of Deputies," he announced sadly. The King replied, "We're ready for him."

The Dauphin sat down at the desk and signed his abdication. Antoine's nine-year-old nephew became Henri V, King of France, and Louis Philippe, Regent, during the boy's minority. But when the Duc d'Orléans read the abdication paper to the Chamber of Deputies, he was careful to omit the paragraph in which Charles X and his son transferred their rights to the Duc de Bordeaux. Louis Philippe's years of intrigue against the senior branch of the Bourbons had at last borne fruit. He knew who would become king, under the tricolor flag—himself.

28

RUNNING AWAY AGAIN

A WEEK LATER, the courtyard of Rambouillet was crowded with carriages, as if for a ball. Inside the château, the royal family sat with their traveling clothes on, for the Second Restoration was over, and they had been ordered to leave France.

Charles X, who seemed to have aged ten years overnight, stood in front of the fireplace, his hands behind him. The Duc d'Angoulême paced nervously up and down before his wife, who was seated on the sofa with little Louise and Henri. Standing behind the children, looking out of the window, was their mother. The others looked pale and red-eyed, but Caroline was crying openly.

It was Antoine who broke the tense silence. "What will become of my dogs?" he wailed. Thérèse gave him a look. What a husband she had! He had lost a throne, but Antoine regretted nothing but leaving his pets. "After what they did to Papa, I wouldn't stay in France another minute," Angoulême announced. "No, not even if they begged me to be king—"

Caroline turned from the window. "I would!" she cried

hysterically. "I would do anything–anything–to remain in Paris. Why do I have to go away?"

Thérèse recoiled as if from a snake. She had always disliked her sister-in-law, but never before had she realized how much. "Madame, you're leaving with us because you're the mother of Henri V," the Dauphine said in her iciest voice. "And your son, the rightful heir, has been ordered to leave France by your precious relative, Louis Philippe, who has usurped the throne–"

At the mention of the man who had married her father's sister, Caroline's face brightened. She had always preferred the Orléans branch of the family. The first report that, during her son's minority, "dear Uncle Philippe" would be regent had delighted her. As far as she was concerned, let her tiresome old father-in-law and the stuck-up Angoulêmes leave France. She would be glad to be rid of them. But it hadn't worked out that way. Now, the Duc d'Orléans was to be king and her son was being sent away. Moreover, to Caroline's utter astonishment, "dear Uncle Philippe" had told her that she must go with her children. At the prospect of having to live in exile with her sister-in-law, Caroline turned back to the window and began to sob again.

A lackey came into the room and announced, "Your Highness, the carriages are waiting." Charles X, looking resigned, started for the door. "Come, children," he said. Antoine and Thérèse followed him. But Caroline never moved. "I won't go! I won't!" she burst out. "You can't make me!"

Charles X went white to his lips. Antoine clenched his teeth. But it was Thérèse who did something about it–something she had long wanted to do–she turned back, went over to Caroline, and slapped her. "Indeed, you will," the Dauphine said sternly. Grasping her sister-in-law by the arm, she marched her out of the room.

Louise and Henri had run on ahead. Their mother's hysterics frightened them. What had happened? Where were they going? No one would tell the children. Mademoiselle de France, a plump, obedient girl of ten, had started down the stairs with her governess, the Duchesse de Gontaut. But Louise's high-strung, spoiled little brother stood in the hall, crying. Hanging onto the banisters, Henri repeated what he had heard his mother say. "I won't go! I won't!" he screamed.

"Come, Henri, come on," his tutor, Baron de Damas, pleaded. The Baron had seven boys and a girl of his own, so he thought he knew how to handle children, but this was too much for him. "You'll enjoy it. You're going for a lovely drive with your mama." Still, the boy wouldn't budge. He stamped his foot and was bawling harder than ever, when, through his tears, he saw his Tante Thérèse looking at him in shocked surprise.

"What's going on here?" she asked in her gruff voice. "Aren't you ashamed of yourself, crying, a big boy of nine?"

"I–I won't go!" Henri sobbed.

"Very well, then, we'll leave without you. Wait for me, Louise, dear." And the Duchesse d'Angoulême started down the stairs.

Suddenly, in a panic, her nephew ran after her. "Tante, can I ride in the carriage with you?" he begged.

"Of course, chéri." Thérèse kissed his tear-stained face, and the handsome boy, with Caroline's blond hair and blue eyes, and Ferdinand's stubborn chin, followed her out to the carriage.

From the courtyard, the Dauphine turned to take a last look at Rambouillet, a favorite hunting lodge of her father's. Sadly, she watched the beloved white fleur-de-lis flag of the Bourbons, flying from the roof of the château, come down its pole. This happened whenever the King left for another residence. But today, Thérèse knew, it might be for the last time.

Then, her heart heavy, she stepped into the coach and the royal exiles left for the coast, the Duchesse d'Angoulême riding in the carriage with Madame de Gontaut, the Baron de Damas, and the two children. From Rambouillet, the party fled to Maintenon. From there they went to Cherbourg, which they reached on August 16. Here they took a packet boat, the *Great Britain*, used by ordinary travelers, to England.

"As always," wrote the Duchesse de Gontaut, "we left without knowing where we were going, or who would take us in."

Two days later, the *Great Britain* lay off Spithead. The ladies and the children went ashore, to the Fountain Hotel, at Cowes, on the Isle of Wight. They must wait there until William IV gave Charles X permission to land. The British no more wanted the banished monarch than they had wanted his brother.

As during the Bourbons' first exile in England, it was the Roman Catholics there who came to their rescue. Sir Thomas Weld, the first Englishman to be elected to the College of Cardinals, leased them his castle of Lulworth. Built in 1588, the year of the Spanish Armada, it was located ten miles from Weymouth, in Dorset. When they drove up to the huge, gray-stone building, with four corner towers, overlooking a stormy sea, Artois exclaimed in horror, "*Voilà, la Bastille!*"

The exiles remained at Lulworth Castle only two months. By October, when the fogs rolled in, they were all sick with colds. "The roof leaked," says the Duchesse de Gontaut, "and we sat under umbrellas." They couldn't spend the winter there. The big sixteenth-century feudal seat of the Welds was impossible to heat, and the rent was too high, for the Bourbons had fled from France with hardly more than the clothes on their backs. "We lacked everything," Madame de Gontaut admits. Money, especially, was scarce. They must economize. So when William IV offered them rooms in Holyrood Castle, at Edinburgh, where he had spent his first exile, Artois accepted the King's hospitality, although he disliked Scotland.

He lived in Mary Stuart's gloomy old palace with his entourage and his grandchildren. At least, Charles X was safe there from his creditors. Since Holyrood Castle was crown property, they couldn't bring suit against him. According to the Duchesse de Gontaut, "Monsieur could only go out on Sunday, a day when the English law allows no arrest. Then he was out riding [horseback] from morning to night."

It was soon obvious that his two daughters-in-law couldn't get along together under the same roof, so the Angoulêmes rented 31 Regent Terrace, a small house overlooking the Gardens, a block from the castle, and the Duchesse de Berry took number 11, down the street. This was the chance Caroline had been waiting for, to escape. She developed a cough, went to Bath to drink the waters—and never came back.

29

THREE KINGS WITHOUT A COUNTRY

CHARLES X was an amiable man who, except at the whist table, seldom lost his temper. But now his voice could be heard all over Holyrood Castle. Not even when he was forced to abdicate had Artois been so angry. "Where is that confounded woman?" he bellowed at Pierre de Blacas.

His secretary, who had followed Charles X into exile, and was as devoted to him as he had been to Louis XVIII, looked helpless. The Duchesse de Berry was unpredictable. How could Blacas know where she was?

"Papa, don't upset yourself so," Thérèse pleaded. "Caroline hated Scotland. She had probably gone back to Naples."

They all hoped she had, and when they finally located her, the Duchess did seem to be headed in that direction. But on the way, as she traveled across Holland and Germany, her escapades made sensational reading in the press.

"Pierre, can't you keep my daughter-in-law's name out of the headlines?" Charles X shouted at poor Blacas. Never a newspaper reader, he now demanded to see the papers every day, and what Artois read didn't do his blood pressure any good! When the Duchesse de Berry reached Naples, her family in Scotland hoped she would settle down. Caroline did . . . but not for long, because, homesick as she had been for Italy, she soon became disillusioned with her girlhood home.

Caroline had been brought up by her grandparents, Ferdinand IV and Maria Carolina (Marie Antoinette's sister), after her mother, Marie Clementine, daughter of Leopold II of Austria (Marie Antoinette's brother), died when she was three years old. Caroline was still a baby when her grandparents fled from the French to Sicily in 1798, and only eight, when, in 1806, Napoleon chased them out of Naples again. They lived at Palermo while Naples was ruled by Joseph Bonaparte and Murat. Then in 1815, after Napoleon's downfall, Ferdinand IV returned to the throne of the Two Sicilies as Ferdinand I. A rough character, who liked to fish and sold his catch on the wharf, Ferdinand petted and spoiled his son's eldest child. Caroline loved her grandfather dearly.

She returned to Naples in 1831, to find everything changed, however. In 1802, her widowed father, Francis I (who ascended the throne in 1825), had married for a second time. His new wife was the Infanta Maria Isabella, daughter of Charles IV of Spain, and by her he had twelve children. Francis had died a year ago, and Caroline's half-brother, Ferdinand II, a youth of twenty-one, was King of the Two Sicilies—at least in name. The actual ruler was Ferdinand's domineering mother, the Dowager Queen Isabella. Surrounded by children of her own, six sons and six daughters, Isabella welcomed none too cordially her late husband's only child by his first marriage.

Tired of the incessant quarrels with her stepmother, Caroline longed to get away. The idea occurred to her to go to the Vendée, a district in western France, south of the Loire, that had always been loyal to the Bourbons, and try to restore her son to the throne. In April, 1832, aboard the *Carlo Alberto*, the Duchess sailed for France, accompanied by her equerry, Vicomte Charles de Mesnard. They went to Nantes, where Caroline raised some troops, and on horseback, dressed as a man, led them against the government forces. Outnumbered, she was defeated and became a fugitive, hiding from farm to farm, with the soldiers of Louis Philippe in pursuit of her.

In the garret of a Breton farmhouse, the pretty Duchess lived disguised as a farm boy for five months, her blond hair hidden under a brown wig. One of her followers, Simon Deutz, betrayed her, and the house was surrounded. But Caroline and Mesnard were so well hidden that for two days Louis Philippe's soldiers searched everywhere and couldn't find them.

It was November 7, and cold. If the men, before they left, hadn't lighted a fire in the chimney to warm themselves, and the flames made the chimney red hot, the searchers might have gone off. But, as the logs burned, the heat grew unbearable. Out Caroline and Mesnard came from behind the chimney, their faces black with soot, their clothing scorched, and nearly suffocated by the smoke. Hunger also forced them to surrender. They had crouched for thirty-six hours, without eating, in that narrow hiding place.

The pair were taken to the fortress of Blaye and locked up. Caroline pleaded with Louis Philippe to remember that he was her "dear uncle" and release her. Receiving no reply to her letter, she wrote the King again, and told him she was going to have a baby. Did he wish her to have the child in prison? He did. This was exactly what "dear Uncle Philippe" wanted, a scandal that would ruin his niece's reputation and the success of her cause. He had no intention of releasing her.

Charles X and the Angoulêmes heard of Caroline's pregnancy in Prague, where, after two unhappy years in Scotland, they were living in a wing of Hradschin, the old castle of the kings of Bohemia, lent to them by Francis of Austria. The news almost gave Artois apoplexy. "Who is the father?" he demanded.

Blacas was sent to Brittany, to confront the pretty widow in the fortress of Blaye and find out. Treating her disgrace lightly, Caroline declared she had been secretly married in Italy. To whom? She refused to say. Nor could she produce any proof of the wedding. "Several gentlemen could have been the guilty party," according to the Comtesse de Boigne, "but most people thought the father was her equerry Mesnard"—a man in his sixties, thirty years older than Caroline, and married to an English lady, the widow of General Blondell.

"We'll be the laughingstock of Europe," Charles X told Blacas, on his return to Prague. "A father for the baby must be found immediately."

"Madame la Dauphine was in despair," the Comtesse de Boigne continues. "She had known for a long time of her sister-in-law's bad conduct. Still, this new scandal was a shock. She, too, insisted on a marriage." It was the Comtesse du Cayla, Madame de Boigne says, who came to their rescue. "I do not know if she was asked, or took on herself, the mission of finding a husband for Caroline."

As the Comtesse de Boigne tells it, this is what happened. Zöe Talon, Comtesse du Cayla, once a close friend of Louis XVIII, had been living in Holland since his death. After several gentlemen there turned down her proposition, she succeeded in persuading Conte Hector Lucchesi-Palli, a young attaché of the Naples legation at the Hague, to acknowledge himself to be the father of the Duchesse de Berry's child. Conte Lucchesi-Palli was well born, the son of Prince Campofranco, a former governor of Sicily, but poor and in debt. If one can believe what the gossipy Madame de Boigne says in her memoirs, it was Charles X's offer of "*cent mille écus*" that finally decided the reluctant groom.

According to the Comtesse de Boigne, who knew them all intimately, Zöe du Cayla even went to Italy and secured a marriage license, issued in a village of the duchy of Modena, dated December 14, 1831. All Europe was amused. Lucchesi had not been away from his diplomatic post for two years. "Everyone at the Hague knew that Monsieur de L. was in Holland on the date the document [the marriage license] bore," the Comtesse tells us. "But if Charles X ignored it, or was willing to close his eyes to the matter, he had the proof of a marriage he demanded, and Madame la Duchesse was told the name of her so-called husband."

Caroline's baby, Rosalie, was born on May 10, 1833, in the fortress of Blaye. The following month, the former Duchess was freed from prison. Louis Philippe no longer feared her. Caroline was not royalty now, merely the Contessa Lucchesi-Palli. She left France with baby Rosalie and sailed for Sicily to meet, on July 5, the child's "father." Describing this "curious scene," as she calls it, the Comtesse de Boigne quotes an eyewitness:

> When the *Agatha* docked at Palermo, Conte Lucchesi hurried aboard and asked to be introduced to the Duchess. He was taken to her cabin [by Captain Turpin], and they were left alone. An hour later, the happy couple came out on deck, arm in arm. The little girl [Rosalie] was there [in a cabin with her nurse], but Lucchesi never bothered to ask to see his "child."

Conte Hector Lucchesi-Palli was a handsome Italian, seven years younger than Caroline. Rosalie, poor unwanted baby, given to foster parents, soon died, but Hector and Caroline proceeded to have children of their own. She should have settled down with him and been content. But the former

Duchesse de Berry discovered she had lost a great deal of social prestige by becoming a mere contessa. Regretting her royal rank, she began to think fondly of the two children she had abandoned, especially Henri. On the occasion of his thirteenth birthday, the Contessa Lucchesi wrote to his grandfather, begging to be allowed to come to Prague and see her son and his sister Louise.

Charles X ignored her letter. "I never want to see that woman again!" he told Blacas.

Unable to get a reply from either the King or the Angoulêmes, Caroline sent Louis XVIII's Minister of Foreign Affairs, the noted French writer, François René, Vicomte de Chateaubriand, to Prague to intercede for her. Charles X refused to see him, and Chateaubriand went on to Carlsbad, where Thérèse, accompanied by her niece Louise, was taking the cure.

In his autobiography, *Mémories d'Outre-Tombe*, Chateaubriand tells how he arrived at the house the Duchesse d'Angoulême had rented in Carlsbad. He handed her a letter from the Contessa Lucchesi. In it, Caroline begged to be allowed to retain her royal rank and see her children by Ferdinand again.

The Duchess' face hardened as she read what her sister-in-law had written. Since Caroline had abandoned them, Thérèse had been bringing up Henri and Louise like her own children, teaching them to be serious-minded and good, everything their mother was not. Especially had she become interested in educating the young Duc de Bordeaux, the legitimate heir to the throne of France, to believe firmly in all the old Bourbon ideas and traditions.

"Do you think I would be foolish enough to let Henri come under the influence of his mother again?" the Duchess asked. She handed the Contessa's letter back to the Vicomte with the words, "I cannot feel sorry for a woman who deserted her children. Tell my sister-in-law not to worry about Louise and Henri. I'm taking good care of them." Then she picked up her embroidery again.

Chateaubriand was shocked by the coldness in her voice. He was a conservative himself, but he disapproved of the way in which he had heard that the Duchesse d'Angoulême was bringing up her nephew, stressing the old-fashioned ideas about kingship that had been the undoing of his grandfather, Charles X—namely, that his right to be king came from God, not from the people, and since he need answer only to God, his power must not be limited by a constitution. Didn't she know that the days when a king was not responsible to his people were gone forever? With Louis Philippe, "the Citizen King," the middle class had come into power. They would never give up their hard-won rights.

Not daring to be so frank as to remind the Duchess of this change of viewpoint, the Vicomte pleaded, "Your Highness, won't you give me a letter for the Contessa? She longs to come to Prague and see her children. She misses them terribly."

"My sister-in-law should have thought of all that before she ran off and disgraced the family," Thérèse answered sternly. "How can she have any real affection for Louise and Henri? She merely wants them back for political reasons—especially her son. She wishes everyone to know she's the mother of Henry V of France."

"Oh, Madame, don't be so hard on her! If she has sinned, I assure you the Contessa regrets her mistakes. She is a reformed woman. Henri and Louise need their mother—"

"Haven't I been a mother to them?" Thérèse asked indignantly. "I would give the children back to her, if I thought it was for their good, but I'm convinced it isn't. What kind of a home would they have with that dissolute woman?"

"At least reply to the Contessa's letter and say you've forgiven her."

"I'll think it over. Could you meet me at the bathhouse tomorrow morning?"

Chateaubriand tells how he was up early next day, for his appointment with the Duchesse d'Angoulême, on her way to drink the waters. He disliked her heartily. He thought Madame narrow, opinionated, and animated by one desire, to make a typical, reactionary Bourbon out of the young Duc de Bordeaux. He wrote maliciously, "She was shabbily attired in a skimpy gray silk dress, worn shawl, and an old bonnet. No one recognized her; she passed unnoticed through the crowd about the fountain."

Thérèse handed the Vicomte an envelope. "Please read it," she said. Her frosty note ran as follows:

> I was pleased, my sister, to receive news from you. You can always count upon my interest in your dear children. My days will be devoted to them as long as I live. I have not been able to deliver your best wishes to the family, as my health necessitates my staying in Carlsbad for several weeks longer. But I shall do so on my return.

Not a word about the Contessa Lucchesi retaining her royal title or coming to Prague to see her children. When Chateaubriand reminded the Duchess of the omission, she replied coolly, "That's a matter for the King to decide." He knew that Caroline could expect little sympathy from her father-in-law. But what more could he say to this unrelenting woman in her behalf?

The Vicomte bowed and watched the Duchesse d'Angoulême, followed by her niece Louise, a blond girl of fourteen, go on into the spring house.

30

MOTHER BY PROXY

IN JUNE, 1836, a German clockmaker by the name of Naundorff appealed to the courts to try to force the Duchesse d'Angoulême to acknowledge him to be her brother and share her wealth with him. In 1849, a "Baron de Richemont," actually Claude Perrein, the son of a butcher, filed a similar claim. Both men were arrested. Any pretender to the throne of France was a threat to the present king, Louis Philippe, too. Naundorff died in exile, in Holland. But in 1850 his widow and children were still suing Marie Antoinette's daughter in the Paris courts.

Thérèse would be pestered with letters and lawsuits by lost Dauphins for the rest of her life, because, after years of poverty, Charles X had inherited the three hundred million francs that Louis XVIII had prudently invested in London banks during the Restoration. The Bourbon exiles were rich, so the impostors multiplied. Forty persons would claim to be Louis XVII. There was even a Pauline Verber, who said she was the daughter of Madame Royale and one of her jailers, born while Thérèse was a prisoner in the Temple.

All the Pretenders had read Regnault-Warin's *Le Cimetière*

de la Madeleine, and told of being carried out of the Tower in a basket of dirty linen. The Duchesse d'Angoulême reminded them that they could also have found out all they pretended to know from the memoirs of François Hue and Louis Cléry, recently published. Her brother must be dead or her uncles were usurpers of his crown. For more than forty years there had been no trace of Charles.

All that Thérèse thought of now was that the lost Dauphin must not reappear and spoil the young Duc de Bordeaux's chances of regaining the throne. Someday Henri would return to France and unfurl the white flag of his ancestors. If there had been two Bourbon Restorations might there not be a third?

How otherwise explain Thérèse's change of mind? For years, following her return to France in 1814, she had searched for her brother and spent large sums of money investigating the many impostors who preyed on her. Now her apparent indifference to his fate earned for her the nickname of the Duchess Cain. For, publicly at least, she said he was dead.

Louis Philippe did not think so. In 1841, worried about the existence of Eleazar Williams, he sent his son to America to inquire about the French boy left with the Iroquois. The Prince de Joinville found Williams at Green Bay, Wisconsin, where he had become an Episcopalian missionary to the Indians. Elated at being told that he might be the "lost Prince," he refused to sign away his rights to the French throne.

What she heard of Eleazer Williams made Thérèse glad she had not brought him back to France. Would she want to see as king an ignorant, uncouth man who was not a Catholic, and who was married to an Indian squaw and had three half-breed children? If that was what Charles had become, let him remain in America.

The rumor current during the Restorations that she was not Marie Antoinette's daughter at all, another girl having been substituted for her while she was in the Temple, amused the Duchesse d'Angoulême. And she got rid of the false Dauphins in the following manner. She sent all of them a questionnaire in which they were asked: *1. What did you say to your mother once when speaking of Marchand, the cook, beginning with the words, "Mama, the window is open?" 2. What did you do for me on New Year's Day? And how? In what room? 3. What was your favorite amusement? What did you do with soapy water? 4. What did Aunt Babet entrust you to hand to me and you gave me one day when I was cutting your hair? 5. On January 21, 1793, when we heard the firing of the cannon, what did Mama, Aunt Babet, and I do? What did Mama say?*

The answer to this last question was that, when they heard the cannon fire, announcing Louis XVI's death, his mother, aunt, and sister had fallen on their knees before the boy. "Your Majesty," Marie Antoinette had said to the new king, "let me be the first to kiss your hand." As none of the Pretenders knew this, or the answers to the other queries, Thérèse seldom heard from them again.

* * * *

Hoping he would be called back to France someday as king, Charles X refused to buy a house. He preferred to rent. So the wanderings of the exiled King, the Angoulêmes, and the Berry children continued, from Prague to Budweis in Czechoslovakia. They next tried Linz, on the Danube. Then Artois, afraid of the cholera in central Europe, decided to spend the winter of 1836 at Gorizia, near Trieste, on the Adriatic coast, where the climate was healthier. He rented the Graffenberg palazzo, owned by Conte Coronini, overlooking the old castle of the Counts of Gorizia and the town.

Charles had come to Gorizia for the hunting. Still active at seventy-nine, he hunted up to the end of his life. On November 5, when the Bourbons had been in Gorizia only two weeks, the former king spent the day as usual, in the mountains, with his gun. That night he was taken ill, with vomiting and cramps. It was the dread cholera that he had come south to avoid. He died the next morning and was buried at the Franciscan monastery of Castegnavizza, outside Gorizia, in the foothills of the Austrian Alps.

After his death, the Angoulêmes and the Berry children spent the winters at Gorizia, in a small house rented from the Strasoldo family, on the street leading up to the castle. Summers, they went north to the castle of Kirchberg, at Budweis, Czechoslovakia, seventy-five miles south of Prague, on the Vltava River.

Charles X had left a fortune of six million fancs to his son Antoine and Ferdinand's children. The Angoulêmes were rich. But Thérèse's lifelong feeling of insecurity showed in the bag of diamonds that hung on the back of her chair and never left her. They were there "for emergencies," she said. And Louis XIX, as his friends called Antoine, and his wife continued their simple habits of living. They rose every morning at six o'clock and attended Mass. Then they spent the day reading, walking, and playing cards. Thirty-seven years of married life and no children had made this mismated couple completely dependent on each other. "The Duc d'Angoulême almost worshiped his wife, who had the tenderest affection for him," wrote Madame de La Ferronnays, one of their entourage. Thérèse no longer thought her husband looked like a monkey. She loved his dear, homely face.

It was a break in their quiet life when the Angoulêmes went to Vienna on January 9, 1837, for a wedding. The eldest daughter of Field Marshal Karl and Princess Henrietta of Nassau-Weilburg, the Archduchess Maria Theresa, was to become the second wife of the Comtessa Lucchesi's half-

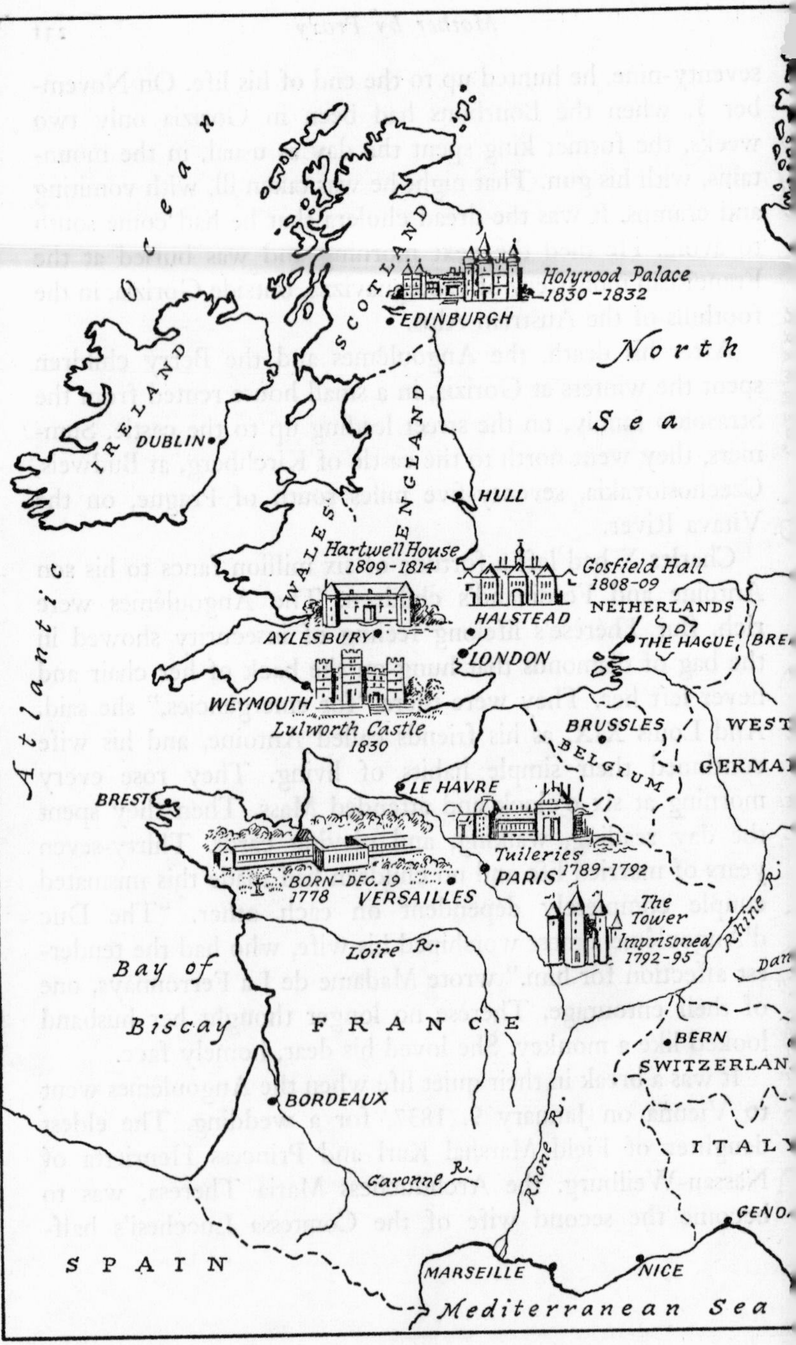

Atlantic Ocean
IRELAND
DUBLIN
SCOTLAND
Holyrood Palace
1830-1832
EDINBURGH
North Sea
WALES
ENGLAND
HULL
Hartwell House
1809-1814
Gosfield Hall
1808-09
NETHERLANDS
HALSTEAD
THE HAGUE
AYLESBURY
LONDON
WEYMOUTH
Lulworth Castle
1830
BRUSSLES
BELGIUM
WEST
GERMA
BREST
LE HAVRE
Tuileries
1789-1792
PARIS
BORN-DEC. 19
1778
VERSAILLES
The Tower
Imprisoned
1792-95
Rhine R.
Loire R.
Bay of Biscay
FRANCE
BERN
SWITZERLAN
BORDEAUX
Rhone R.
ITALY
Garonne R.
GENO
SPAIN
MARSEILLE
NICE
Mediterranean Sea

Map showing the many homes of MARIE THÉRÈSE throughout Europe

brother, Ferdinand II, King of the Two Sicilies. In 1829, Henrietta had died and the widowed Karl, now the Duke of Teschen and retired from the army, spent his time writing books on military strategy, for he was still famous as the "only general who had stood up against Napoleon."

The wedding took place in the Augustiner-Kirche, where the Archduke Karl had acted as proxy for Napoleon, and a ball followed at the Hofburg. For the first time in forty years Thérèse was in her old lover's arms again as they glided about the room, doing a dance that was making Vienna famous, the waltz.

"You look lovely, my dear. You haven't changed a bit," Karl lied gallantly. Then they seemed to run out of conversation. Thérèse was glad when the music stopped and Antoine came to take her away to the buffet table.

This was the last time the Angoulêmes would go dancing, for Antoine's health was rapidly failing. Chateaubriand wrote, "I found him looking older and thinner. He was dressed in a shabby blue coat. It was too big for him and looked as if it had been bought in a secondhand shop."

In spite of her rheumatism, Thérèse had taken up gardening. She tried to get Antoine interested. "Some exercise will make you feel better," she told him, for he sat indoors and read incessantly. Unfortunately, Antoine's gardening efforts brought on his death. He cut himself, infection set in, and he died of blood poisoning on June 3, 1844.

Thérèse took his body out to the monastery of Castegnavizza and placed his coffin beside that of his father, Charles X. Then she returned to their rented house in Gorizia and tried to decide what to do. Although her husband had been an invalid ever since she could remember, the Duchesse d'Angoulême, at sixty-five, was still in good health and full of vitality. But she longed for a permanent home. Since leaving the Tower, forty-nine years ago, Thérèse had lived all over

Europe. She was tired of rented houses. Fondly she remembered her little house at Villeneuve l'Etang, but going back to it was impossible. She would never return to France while the tricolor was the national flag and Louis Philippe was king. So why not remain in Austria, her mother's native land?

In 1839, the faithful Pierre de Blacas d'Aulps had died in Gorizia. He was buried at Castegnavizza with his royal master. Pierre's son, Comte Stanislas de Blacas, who had taken his father's place in her household, found the Duchess a country place, thirty-five miles south of Vienna, that had belonged to Caroline Murat, Napoleon's sister. When Thérèse drove into the little town of Neustadt and up to the cream-colored château, surrounded by a small park, she fell in love with Frohsdorf (village of joy) and for the rest of her life, seven years, seldom left it.

Built around the four sides of a court, the rooms on the north looked out over the garden. Beyond the dining room was the parlor, hung with white velvet draperies embroidered with fleurs-de-lis. These were the handiwork of Marie Antoinette.

Dr. Philippe Pelletan, who had performed the autopsy on the boy who died in the Tower on June 8, 1795, sent the Duchesse d'Angoulême the heart he took from the little corpse, preserved in a bottle of alcohol. Convinced the boy wasn't her brother, Thérèse refused to accept it. But in her chapel, up a stairway to the right of the entrance hall, she kept the precious relics of her family that Cléry had succeeded in rescuing from the Temple. A stool used by Louis XVI in prison served as his daughter's *prie-dieu.* A drawer in it held the bloodstained linen shirt in which Louis had died, a fichu the wind had swept from Aunt Babet's shoulders on the scaffold, and a lace cap made by Marie Antoinette while in prison. On January 21 and October 16, the anniversaries of her parents' deaths, Thérèse spent hours in her chapel, praying for the repose of their souls.

Her new home was midway between Vienna and Venice, where Caroline and Hector Lucchesi-Palli were living. And, now that Charles X was no longer alive to object, Thérèse had come to a hard decision—to share Louise and Henri with their mother. She knew she had been criticized for not doing so before.

When she suggested the idea to Henri, his Tante Thérèse, wearing a huge sunbonnet, was out in the garden, weeding her roses. "You and Louise should go to Venice," she said, trying to sound as casual as though she were suggesting a week in Vienna to attend the opera, "and visit your mother. Don't you want to get acquainted with her?"

Henri came to where his aunt had seated herself on a bench and sat down beside her. "You're my mother," he said tenderly, putting an arm around her. "You always have been."

His words made her so happy, Thérèse could have burst into tears. A quiet, serious-minded young man, her training had made Henri, Duc de Bordeaux, into a very different person from either his gay father or his irresponsible mother. From a small boy, his aunt had molded his political beliefs. Especially, had she taught him to hate the tricolor and all it stood for, but now Henri was twenty-four, he must marry, and Thérèse thought his character well enough formed so that it was safe to allow him out into the world.

"The reason I want you to go to Venice is so that you'll meet some young people," she told him. "I've been selfish, keeping you and Louise isolated here at Frohsdorf with me. Your sister is twenty-five. She should be married. And you, Henri, are the greatest catch in Europe. You must find yourself a wife worthy of being queen of France."

31

QUEEN IN EXILE

THÉRÈSE NEVER CALLED her nephew Henri V until after Louis XIX (Antoine) died. Even then, he did not outrank her. Since her husband had been king, if only for ten minutes, after his father's abdication and before Antoine abdicated himself, Thérèse was treated by her household as Louis XIX's widowed consort, preceding Henri V into the dining room. And it was as the exiled Queen of France that she conducted from Frohsdorf the campaign that, at sixty-six, became her absorbing interest, to place on the throne of his ancestors the nephew who was as dear to her as her own son.

Her bag of diamonds had long ago been spent. She no longer had time for novel reading and knitting. All day, Queen Marie Thérèse of France sat writing to Bourbon sympathizers all over Europe, plotting with them to overthrow the government of Louis Philippe. He was a usurper, she told them. Charles X had only meant him to be regent until the little Duc de Bordeaux was of age to act as king.

Thérèse seldom left her desk except to read the political news in the papers and greet the delegations of legitimists, who were coming to Frohsdorf in increasing numbers to see the young Pretender.

Henri was twenty-four and his followers were becoming concerned about whom he would marry. His Tante Thérèse was concerned, too. That was why she was sending her nephew and niece to visit their mother. The experiment turned out better than she expected. Henri and Louise did not change for the worse, and, in Venice, they were certainly meeting people.

Charles X had ignored Ferdinand's widow in his will, but debts didn't bother Caroline and Hector Lucchesi-Palli. They lived far better than the penurious household at Frohsdorf. In 1837, they had bought the Château of Brunsée, near Graz, in Styria, Austria. They then acquired, in 1843, the Vendramini Palace, on the Grand Canal, in Venice. There were always rich, titled friends staying with them, and frequently Caroline's half-brother and half-sister from Naples.

Louise Marie Thérèse of France, a shy, sweet girl, was a little frightened of the suave Anthony, Conte di Lecce. But the Comte de Chambord, as Henri was calling himself, after his château on the Loire, found no difficulty at all in falling in love with his mother's pretty blond half-sister, Princess Maria Carolina Ferdinanda.

The former Duchesse de Berry had shocked France by going sea bathing at Dieppe during the Restoration, the first woman to get actually wet at a public beach. Now she was making swimming fashionable at the Lido. So, that summer of 1845, Ferdinanda and Henri spent happy days by the Adriatic. Evenings, they danced together in the palaces that lined the Venice canals and afterward drifted home in a gondola, his arms around her, his lips on hers.

"Ferdinanda! We love each other!"

"Oh, Henri, so much!"

The gondola stopped at the Palazzo Vendramini. It was

after midnight, and they said good-by before a sleepy footman who let them in, for Ferdinanda was returning home in the morning.

"Darling, I must ask your brother for your hand," Henri said. "When may I come to Naples?"

A visit was planned, and Chambord returned to Frohsdorf to tell his aunt that he had found the girl of his dreams. He was engaged. Do people ever die of happiness? Henri thought.

* * * *

Thérèse would have preferred a Hapsburg. But, in 1845, there were no Austrian archduchesses available. On the throne was the childless Ferdinand I, son of Francis II. Thérèse had fled from Napoleon with Ferdinand, who was then the little Prince Imperial. Since the Comte de Chambord's wife must be royal and a Catholic, the choice was limited. His mother's family, the Bourbons of Naples, seemed to be the best connection.

The Duchesse d'Angoulême wrote to the Contessa Lucchesi-Palli and, by September, it was all arranged—Henri was to go to Naples and ask Ferdinand II for his sister's hand. He was also to suggest a marriage between Princess Louise of France and the Conte di Lecce. It would probably be a double wedding the following summer.

Before that, why shouldn't Anthony and Ferdinanda come to Frohsdorf for a visit? His aunt suggested this as Henri was packing to leave for Naples. "In April, when my tulips are in bloom," she said.

The following day, Queen Thérèse, her niece, Louise, and the entire household, were at the entrance door of the château, under the royal crown and fleur-de-lis escutcheon, to see the young master leave for Italy.

His journey seemed very short to the Comte de Chambord

who was traveling by railroad, a novelty in those days. In an incredibly short time he was in Naples, driving up to the big orange royal palace, facing on the Piazza Plebiscito. Henri had intended to go directly to his suite, but, eager to see the girl he loved, he was astonished to hear himself ask a footman, "Is the Princess Ferdinanda at home?"

"Who wishes to see my daughter?" demanded a cross voice. Dowager Queen Isabella, a stout Spanish woman with hard black eyes, came out into the hall. "Who are you?" she asked.

"Henri de Chambord."

"Oh, I remember, we're expecting you." The former Infanta Maria Isabella, sister of Ferdinand VII of Spain, who had married six of her children into the reigning families of Europe, and her daughter Maria to the Emperor of Brazil, wasn't impressed by this king without a throne. Afraid of offending Louis Philippe, who had married her husband's sister, the Queen Mother of Naples had been against Chambord's visit from the first. Giving him her hand to kiss, she said coldly, "Ferdinanda cannot be disturbed. She is lying down."

"Oh, that's all right. I'll see her at dinner. Now, if I may, I would like to be shown to my suite."

"You're staying at Chiatamone. We haven't any room here—" Isabella indicated with a gesture the three-story palace that covered four city blocks. "I'll have someone show your coachman the way."

Henri felt his face getting red. "Well, it's—it's a lucky thing my bags are still in the carriage—" he stammered. . . . Then, somehow, Chambord was back there. A court official had climbed onto the box beside the coachman, and they were driving across town to the little shabby palace of Chiatamone.

A half hour later, the Princess Ferdinanda, her blond hair touseled, came into the Dowager Queen's sitting room wrapped in a dressing gown of blue silk that matched her eyes.

"Your admirer, the French Pretender, has arrived," her mother said icily. "I sent him to Chiatamone. He seemed surprised he wasn't staying with us."

"Oh, Mama! Why can't he?"

"You know perfectly well! What would Louis Philippe think? He's lucky that I allowed him to come to Naples at all. Now, Ferdinanda, don't cry, or you'll get your eyes all red, and hurry and get dressed or you'll be late for your dinner party."

* * * *

It seemed odd to the Comte de Chambord that there wasn't a dinner party before the ball. He ate alone in his suite at Chiatamone, and, at ten o'clock, drove to the royal palace. A large crowd was watching the titled guests step out of their carriages and enter the palace. Henri followed the procession of people up the stairs. In the ballroom, when he reached it, he saw only Ferdinanda, lovely in a white satin gown. He went over to her, his heart thumping, and soon they were dancing together.

He wished the music could have gone on forever. When it stopped, Ferdinanda said, "Henri, I want a minute with you alone. Let's slip out this door onto the terrace before someone takes me away from you. . . . Isn't it beautiful out here, overlooking the bay, with Vesuvius in the distance?" The darling! Chambord longed to kiss her—and he would soon, he promised himself. Just now, there were other people strolling along the terrace.

"Oh, bother, there's the music again. I must go back!" the Princess exclaimed.

"Sweetheart, how soon may I have another dance?"

"Oh, I'm afraid that's impossible!" Ferdinanda showed him

her dance card filled with names. "But I'll introduce you to some pretty girls."

Henri's first dancing partner asked, "Didn't I meet you at the dinner party before the ball?" His heart was breaking, but he answered lightly, "No, I couldn't get here in time. I've just arrived from Austria."

"Will you be in Naples long?" asked the next girl with whom Chambord danced. "I suppose you're staying for the parties next week. The Duc d'Aumale is expected. They say he's madly in love with Ferdinanda."

"Oh, is he?" Henri replied bitterly. The Duc d'Aumale, Louis Philippe's fourth son, hero of the recent war in North Africa, was being mentioned as the first governor of France's newly conquered Algeria. He was rich, too, heir to the Condés' immense fortune. How could the Comte de Chambord compete with him? Henri had never been so unhappy in his life. But it was nothing to what he would feel in the days that followed.

A gala performance was given at the opera, and the Pretender from Frohsdorf was seated in a box some distance from the royal family, so Louis Philippe wouldn't be vexed. Yet, being the King's nephew, nobody could say that the Bourbons of Naples were rude to him. Mornings, Henry was awakened by a military band; Ferdinand II entertained him at his palace of Caserta, the Versailles of Naples; the Conte di Lecce took him to see Pompeii and Capri; and the two young men climbed Vesuvius together.

Then, one night, Chambord attended a stag party, enlivened with ballet girls, in Anthony's hunting lodge at Giugliano.

"I understand your sister has an income of four hundred thousand francs a year," Ferdinanda's brother said, "and great expectations from the old lady—"

"I wish you wouldn't call Tante Thérèse old. She's only sixty-six, and *not* an old lady," Henri replied stiffly. He was beginning to dislike Anthony di Lecce. As for Ferdinanda, he had seen little of her, Queen Isabella's excuse being that her daughter was busy with dressmaker fittings, for, after the Duc d'Aumale's visit, the family was going to Rome.

Nor had the Comte de Chambord's attempts to talk with Ferdinanda's brother, Ferdinand II, and suggest the double marriage, met with anything but evasive replies. Henri had been in Naples only a week when one morning, realizing the hopelessness of his mission, he packed up and left. He was so homesick for Frohsdorf he couldn't get back there fast enough.

Chambord had told his family that he would remain in Naples for several weeks. So no one at the château was expecting him when he drove up from the railroad station.

"Henri!" Thérèse exclaimed in surprise, when, coming back from the stables where a new colt had been born, she found him in the hall.

Her aunt's cry of joy brought Louise running down the stairs to kiss her brother and ask him a dozen questions. "Did you have a marvelous time? Are we engaged to them? Are they coming to visit us in April?"

As Chambord answered, his family's love and admiration for him restored his self-confidence. He grew happy again. Purposely, he evaded a direct answer to the question about the engagements. Instead, he diverted their conversation to the proposed visit.

"Anthony and Ferdinanda will probably come to Frohsdorf next summer," Henri explained. "In April, she has to go to Spain with her mother."

Thérèse had quickly noticed the deception. Could it be possible that the Bourbons of Naples were cool to an alliance with the grandchildren of Charles X of France, a monarch who lost his throne? The idea shocked her. The Queen

Dowager Isabella—a woman she had always detested—was at the bottom of this, she was sure.

Later, Chambord would tell his aunt about the snubs he had received from his mother's relatives, and Thérèse would be indignant. But now, not wanting to spoil his homecoming, she let the matter drop.

"Henri, do tell us about the good times you had in Naples," his aunt said, when they were seated in the drawing room. "Who did you hear sing at the opera? I wish that I could have seen you, sitting in the royal box. I hope you didn't break too many hearts. I always think that no one looks as handsome as you do in a silk hat and an opera cape."

32

THE PASSING OF A GREAT LADY

HENRI RETURNED TO FROHSDORF convinced that Anthony di Lecce, his mother's half-brother, was not a fit husband for his sister. Should he tell his aunt about that stag party at Giugliano? He was still wondering when, a month later, Lecce was found lying dead in his hunting lodge at Giugliano. He had gone there to meet a married woman. Her husband had followed, and clubbed Anthony to death. The crime was hushed up. People were told the King's brother died of typhus, but the truth leaked out and created a scandal.

Louise, who hardly knew Anthony di Lecce, took his death calmly. "Thank goodness, we found out in time," Thérèse said, and set about doing what she should have done in the first place, finding a husband for her niece. . . . On November 10, 1845, Princess Louise Marie Thérèse d'Artois was married in the chapel at Frohsdorf to Charles Ferdinand de Bourbon-Parma, Duc de Lucca, son of the Duke of Parma, Charles II.

It was a different matter with Henri. He still loved his

mother's half-sister, in spite of all the rudeness and rebuffs he had received in Naples. His aunt urged him to forget Ferdinanda, and he tried courting other girls, but she could always call him back with a letter.

Because he was contesting Louis Philippe's right to the throne, Henry V was forbidden to set foot in France. He had not seen his Château of Chambord since he was a child. But, in February, 1846, Ferdinanda and her mother went to see Henri's baptismal gift from the French people. Ferdinanda wrote him:

Henri! We are in your country, France, and being taken all over by the Duc d'Aumale. We drove to the Loire to see your beautiful Château of Chambord. Mama scolded me for moping. I was in tears. How dreadful that you are not permitted to return to France so we could visit Chambord together! I'm having a wonderful time. Yet I am sad, can you guess why?

Then longer and longer grew the silence between Ferdinanda's letters. Finally, there were no answers at all to his. Then, just as Henri was growing frantic, a letter came from Spain that plunged him into utter despair:

We are seeing Spain under fine auspices for a very nice young man, Don Carlos Luis Fernando de Bourbon, has attached himself to us. He is a Pretender to the Spanish throne, recognized by the Carlists as Charles VI, so we are receiving great attention wherever we go. Mama loves it. She was a Spanish Infanta and has always wanted me to marry a Spaniard. Henri, I love getting your letters, but you musn't write so often, Mama said to tell you.

In the spring of 1846, after Ferdinanda's return to Naples, another letter came to Frohsdorf. It lay on the hall table, waiting for Henri one April morning when he came in from schooling a new saddle horse. He put it in his pocket, to read when he got up to his room, and bounded happily up the stairs, two steps at a time.

"Is that you, Henri?" Ten minutes later, his aunt called up to him from the hall below. "There's a letter for you—oh, you found it. Hurry, and change your clothes. Luncheon's ready."

No answer. His silence told her that something was wrong. She hurried up the stairs and found her nephew seated in his room, his head in his hands. "Ferdinanda's going to marry the Spanish Pretender, Don Carlos—" His voice broke.

"You poor boy, you've never stopped loving that girl, have you?" His aunt sat down beside Henri, and put her arms comfortingly around him. "Her mother has arranged this marriage to Don Carlos, I feel sure. If the choice of a husband had been left to Ferdinanda—"

"Tante, I wasn't good enough for her."

"Not good enough? The future king of France!" replied Thérèse indignantly. But how well she understood his grief and humiliation. Once she, too, hadn't been good enough for a Hapsburg archduke.

During the months that followed his aunt did her best to make Henri forget his loss and select a wife for him. It was growing urgent. The royalists, who were plotting to replace Louis Philippe with the grandson of Charles X, were complaining bitterly that the legitimist Pretender had waited too long to find them a Comtesse de Chambord.

The matter shortly solved itself. Henri's new saddle horse fell at a jump and rolled on him. His leg was broken, and for the rest of his life he would limp. The doctor sent Chambord to Venice to recuperate. While there, bathing in the Adriatic, he met the two sisters of Francis V, the young Duke of Modena. Henri preferred the younger and prettier one, Marie Beatrice, but she was engaged to the Infant Don Juan. He was the younger brother of Don Carlos de Bourbon, Carlist claimant to the Spanish throne, and the young man who was to marry Ferdinanda. So Thérèse persuaded her nephew to propose to Beatrice's older sister.

On November 16, 1846, Henri de Chambord was married to the Archduchess Marie Thérèse of Modena, at Brück, in Austria.

The new Comtesse de Chambord was homely but rich—and she became a loving daughter to her husband's aunt. The young couple spent the summers at Frohsdorf. Henri V and his wife lived in the back of the house. The Dowager Queen occupied rooms overlooking the entrance, with the Bourbons' fleur-de-lis escutcheon over the door. Winters the Chambords and their aunt went to Venice, where, with his wife's money, Henri bought the Cavalli Palace on the Grand Canal, not far from the Rialto. Thérèse spent her last two winters there, January to April, 1850 and 1851.

As much as possible, she liked to have around her the children of those who had shared the Bourbons' years of exile. Pierre de Blacas' son, Stanislas, was her gentleman in waiting; her chaplain, the Abbé Trébuguet, had been at Antoine's bedside when he died; and her *femme de chambre*, Madame Sainte-Preuve, was the granddaughter of Madame Brunier, who had gone with the royal family on the drive to Varennes.

Henri de Chambord's secretary was also second generation. Comte Ferdinand de La Ferronnays' father, Auguste, had been gentleman in waiting to the Duc de Berry. He and his wife came to Frohsdorf four years after Henri's marriage. It was January, 1850, and, in her memoirs, Madame de La Ferronnays affectionately portrays the Dowager Queen, now seventy-one, at the Cavalli Palace in Venice where the Chambords and Thérèse spent that winter:

> Her life was very regular. A maid lighted the fire at six in the morning. She dressed, and after having drunk her café, in the light of two candles, she went by gondola to Saint-Vital church. Breakfast was at ten o'clock; dinner at six. In between she rode out in a gondola, and I accompanied her. In the evening, she usually went to the theater, but left before the play was over.

I have often heard said that the Dauphine, in France, was said to be cross and disagreeable. She must have greatly changed, for we found her to be kind to her entourage, and anxious to please everyone. If she had a weakness, it was liking things to be on time. She wanted a meal over in twenty minutes.

She passed the day of January 21 locked in her room, and would see no one. She refused to talk of the horrible scenes that had marred her girlhood, but they were not forgotten. One day, riding in a gondola with her at Venice, I said to her that I hoped someday to have the satisfaction of seeing the Comte de Chambord enter Paris [as King] by the Champs-Elysées. "Oh, no, not by the Champs-Elysées, not by there!" she cried, in horror. I was so embarrassed at my lack of tact, I wanted to throw myself into the Grand Canal.

Louise and her family from Parma occupied the Giustiniani Palace nearby. Thérèse also saw a great deal of Caroline and Hector Lucchesi-Palli and their five children, for she had learned to forget old enmities and to forgive, even the Orléans branch of the family. In 1848, Louis Philippe lost his throne and fled to England. It was incredible, but Marie Antoinette's daughter actually felt sorry for the poor man. When Louis Philippe died in exile, two years later, she had a Mass said for him at Frohsdorf.

France was a republic again. But Louis Philippe had abdicated in favor of his grandson, the Comte de Paris, the ten-year-old son of his eldest boy, Ferdinand, who had been killed in a carriage accident. Also, Louis Napoleon, in England, was pressing his claim to the throne as nephew of the great Napoleon. So now there were three Pretenders.

It was too late for Queen Marie Thérèse to hope ever to return to France, but she didn't feel old. She was still slim and erect. Her long chestnut hair had regained its luster. It was as thick as ever and hardly gray. At seventy-two, she could be seen working vigorously in her rose garden. People marveled at her energy.

Then, on October 14, 1851, the Dowager Queen felt ill and had to leave her chapel during Mass. Madame de Saint-Preuve persuaded her to go to bed. But Thérèse announced firmly that she would get up next morning to celebrate her saint's day and also the following day, the sixteenth, the anniversary of Marie Antoinette's death.

"Nothing will prevent me from going to the chapel to pray for Mama," she said. "I've never failed to do so in fifty-six years."

On the fifteenth, the Archduchess Sophie of Austria arrived unexpectedly from Vienna. Thérèse wanted to get up. Her doctor, the Marquis de Rougé, was against it. But the elderly Queen insisted. Madame de Saint-Preuve helped her mistress from her bed to an armchair by the window, where Thérèse liked to sit and look out at her beloved garden. She was greatly interested in Sophie's eldest son, Francis Joseph, who, three years ago, at eighteen, had succeeded his uncle, Ferdinand I, as Emperor of Austria. The two women talked all afternoon. It seemed to do the invalid good. But the excitement proved to be too much for her. For two days Thérèse had been ill with bronchial pneumonia. Next morning, the sixteenth, she was worse.

She rallied, however, and lived three days longer. At eleven o'clock on the night of October 19, feeling herself sinking, she had the Abbé Trébuguet give her the Last Rites. Then she asked for her father's watch that she might kiss it for a final time. With her lips on Papa's wedding ring that Antoine had placed on her finger, Marie Thérèse Charlotte of France died, two months before her seventy-third birthday.

By her own wish, her body was not embalmed. After a simple service in the chapel at Frohsdorf, attended by her weeping household, Henri and his wife took the body of Marie Antoinette's daughter by train to Gorizia. Six white horses drew the hearse bearing the coffin up the steep road to the church of the Franciscan friars, high on Mt. Castegnavizza. There they laid the Queen to rest with the remains of two French kings, her father-in-law, Charles X, and her husband, Louis XIX, in the crypt under the monastery.

33

FOOTSTEPS OVER EUROPE—POSTSCRIPT

IN MAY, 1955, a hundred years after the death of Marie Thérèse of France, Senator Desmond and I visited Versailles to see an exhibition of her mother's belongings, collected from all over Europe. We were especially interested in the things used by the royal prisoners in the Tower. Here were Charles' tin soldiers, Louis' razor, Marie Antoinette's tapestry frame, their steel eating utensils, some chessmen, and the stuffed figure of a little dog. It was while looking at Coco, the ugly mongrel loved by a lonely young girl, that the idea came to me to write a book about Marie Antoinette's daughter.

That day, I started my research by joining the tourists being shown through Versailles. Soon we were standing in Marie Antoinette's state bedroom, where her daughter was born. Now, I thought, the rest will be easy. I have only to follow little Madame Royale from the cradle to the grave. Well, I did, but it took me twelve years and three trips to Europe to do it.

Meanwhile, of course, I worked on other books. But from

that day in May, 1955, Marie Antoinette's daughter was always in the back of my mind. My husband and I returned to Versailles and hired a special guide, who showed us the royal family's private apartments, too small for the general public to go through. He led us down the secret stairs that honeycomb Versailles' ancient walls, and had us knock on the door to the Oeil de Boeuf the Queen found locked against her. We visited the chapel where Thérèse was christened; the Petit Trianon, where her betrothal to Antoine took place; and stepped out onto the balcony overlooking the Cour de Mabre, where a frightened little girl stood trembling beside her mother, facing the angry mob.

Paris has changed since the Revolution, while managing to remain much the same. The Duc de Berry's home, now the official residence of the President of France, is on the Champs-Elysées. Behind it, at number 17 Rue Matignon, Axel von Fersen lived. The Champs-Elysées, along which the royal fugitives were brought back from Varennes, runs into the Place de la Concorde, where Thérèse's Papa, Mama, and Aunt Babet lost their heads. At the Conciergerie, you see the Queen's cell. The Tuileries is gone, burned by rioters in May, 1871. All that remains are the Pavillon de Flore (where the Duchesse d'Angoulême lived during two Bourbon Restorations) and the Pavillon de Marsan, which form the ends of the west wings of the Louvre.

Nearby, at number 6, Rue de l'Echelle, Fersen waited to drive Madame Royale and her fugitive family to Varennes; and at Saint-Cloud, on the road to Versailles, is Villeneuve l'Etang, the country place the Angoulêmes bought in 1824 from Marshal Soult. After they were exiled, Napoleon III had it, then the estate became part of the Pasteur Institute. Pasteur died in the house now occupied by the director of the medical center.

Strangely enough, our visit to Villeneuve l'Etang was disappointing. Research laboratories had been built on the grounds of Thérèse's hideaway. It was hard to picture her there. Only when we went to a sinister spot in north Paris did we feel her presence again.

Not far from the chapel Louis XVIII built to the memory of Louis XVI and Marie Antoinette, possibly to ease his conscience, is a delightful little square. One would never imagine that here the grim Temple prison once stood. The weeping willow Thérèse planted was there until 1911. Now even that has gone.

The day my husband and I visited the Square du Temple it was crowded with happy, romping children. Seated on a bench among them, we discussed what could have happened to the lost Dauphin? Were the Duc de Berry's suspicions correct? Did Louis XVIII have his nephew murdered, probably by Simon? The truth may never be known. One thing is certain, however, the Comte de Provence was a ruthless, ambitious man, who connived with the revolutionists to have his brother and sister-in-law beheaded in order to gain the throne. It isn't likely he let a boy of nine stand in his way. But on this point I will leave it to the reader of this book to form his own opinion.

How much did the Duchesse d'Angoulême suspect? It is not probable that anyone will ever know this, either. Many contemporaries believed that she knew of her uncle's guilt and, out of loyalty, kept silent to protect the Bourbon dynasty. If so, it was a secret Thérèse took with her to the grave.

* * * *

Following the footsteps of Marie Antoinette's daugher across Europe, as Senator Desmond and I did over several years, we hired a car in 1962 and went on their "ride to Varennes." The road from Paris to Châlons, then over the

Argonne hills, by which Thérèse and her family tried to escape from France, runs today about as it did in 1791. The French countryside is much the same. There are the long, straight roads between villages where houses that little Madame Royale saw gaze at you as you pass by. Reaching the square at Sainte-Ménehould, Drouet's posthouse is gone, no longer needed in this motor age. But a few miles beyond you are shown where he and Guillaume left the highway to take a short cut through the forest to Varennes and, at Clermont, you turn yourself, where the berlin did, to make the longer route.

It is amazing that, after a hundred and seventy years and a destructive war (Varennes was bombed in World War I) so little there has changed. As you drive down the steep street to the river, on your right is the Bra d'Or Inn, now a tiny museum. Saint-Gengoult church and Sucre's grocery store were destroyed. But at the foot of the hill is the bridge across the Aire River, and in the lower village you can lunch at the Hôtel du Grand Monarque, where the soldiers were waiting.

Being in Zurich, Switzerland, during the summer of 1964, we drove to Bâle, then across the French border to Huningue, in Alsace-Lorraine, to see where Madame Royale was exchanged for the French prisoners. The Tavern du Corbeau on the Rue Abbatucci, where she stayed, is now a grocery store. The modern Inn of the Crow is on the next corner. Owned by a descendant of the proprietor in Thérèse's day, it has been in the Schultz family for two hundred years. A plaque was put on the old inn by the royalists in 1947 on the one hundred and fifty-second anniversary of Madame Royale's visit.

The Reber house, where the exchange took place, has vanished. But the old city gate of Saint-Jean by which Thérèse entered Bâle is still there. We lunched that day on the terrace of the Hôtel des Trois Rois, where Drouet and his fellow prisoners celebrated their freedom, and looked at the bridge over the Rhine by which Madame Royale went on to Austria.

The previous year (1963) we were in Vienna. Easy to find was Upper Belvedere, a baroque palace built for Prince Eugene in 1713, and not a cozy home for a young girl. Few Viennese seemed to have heard of Thérèse. It is the Archduke Karl who is remembered there and still a hero—"the only general who stood up against Napoleon." On the Helden Platz, near the Hofburg, are the equestrian statues of two men the Austrians admire—Prince Eugene of Savoy, who flung back the Turks from the walls of Vienna, and, facing him, Field Marshal Karl Ludwig Johann, victor of Aspern. We went down into the imperial vaults under the Capuchin church to see where the Archduke is buried, next to Emperor Maximilian of Mexico, with Thérèse's grandmother, the great Empress Maria Theresa.

Axel von Fersen is better liked today in Sweden than he was in his lifetime. The Swedes are proud of his connection with Marie Antoinette. In Stockholm, we were shown his town house, now the Swiss embassy, and the place where he was murdered, little altered except for the flow of automobile traffic. It did not take much imagination to see the Grand Marshal's gilded coach rounding the corner of the Stora Nygatan, headed toward Riddarholm Church, where Crown Prince Carl was to be buried. All was there before us, the house into which Fersen escaped from the mob, only to be dragged across the street to the courthouse, and the balcony over which he was tossed to die on the stone pavement below.

In Uppland we visited Steninge, the country estate of Fersen's sister, Countess Sophie Piper, now owned by a former American ambassador to Sweden. It was there that Fersen's body was taken, and hidden by Sophie for a week, before she dared bury him in the little church at Ljung, on the Göta Canal.

That bitterness is now a thing of the past. Fersen's Löfstad Castle at Norrköping, in Östergötland, a hundred miles west of Stockholm, was given to the nation by the Piper family in 1927. Among gifts from Marie Antoinette on display in the house is the small clavichord that Axel, being musical, used to take with him in his coach, to make his journeys pass faster; and the china plate on which he ate his last meal before he was murdered.

It was frustrating to be in Stockholm, so near Riga, and not be able to see Mitau. Situated in Latvia, Russia, and being now too hard to reach, Mitau is the only place closely associated with Marie Antoinette's daughter we were forced to omit. In 1962, we went to England to see Gosfield Hall, Lulworth Castle, and Hartwell.

Fifty miles east of London, at Halstead in Essex, Gosfield Hall, where Thérèse lived from 1808–1809, is now a rest home for elderly people. Halfway between the church and the house is a broken circle of trees, known as the King's Clump, planted by the Bourbons. A few of the old chestnuts still remain.

A week later, we motored out of London to Hartwell House, at Aylesbury, near Oxford. The handsome Elizabethan mansion, with its carved Jacobean staircase, has become a girls' school. It is little changed. Nor is the garden where Louis XVIII raised camellias. The museum in Aylesbury has some of the things the Bourbons left behind when they returned to Paris—for example, the enormous bed in which Provence was lying when he heard that he was to be king of France.

A different sight confronted us when we drove to Weymouth, to see Lulworth Castle, ten miles down the coast. Herbert Weld, the present owner, inherited the house in 1923. It burned several years ago. Colonel Weld now lives in a cottage on the grounds. Since the fire, the castle is only a shell.

It must have been a spooky place. Nor could Holyrood in Scotland have been any cozier, with Mary Stuart's ghost reported to be wandering about at night, her head in her hands.

During the Bourbons' years of exile, they were shunted all over Europe, from one rented house to another. It wasn't until she was in her old age that the Duchesse d'Angoulême bought Frohsdorf and at last had a real home. This, of course, was the house I most wanted to see. But when my husband and I arrived in Vienna, in 1963, and telephoned to the mayor of Neustadt, to inquire how to reach Frohsdorf, he replied that the Russians had used the house as a barracks for eleven years after World War II. Consequently, it was a shambles and could not be visited. What of it? We drove the thirty miles to Neustadt, anyway. And how glad we are that we did.

The mayor was right. The house was dilapidated. The Russians had stripped it bare of furniture, except for a huge porcelain stove, too heavy to cart away. The most shocking sight was Thérèse's chapel. It would have broken her heart. The soldiers had used it for a storage room. The marble altar was cracked; the floor covered with trash; the stained-glass windows broken. Bats were nesting in the beautiful carved choir loft. But shabby as Frohsdorf was, it was still a royal residence, where a queen had lived. The crown and fleur-de-lis escutcheon was over the entrance door, and in the room where Thérèse died was the bronze plaque the royalists placed on the wall.

Although all the rooms were empty of furniture, in an upstairs parlor, next to her bedroom, I seemed to see Thérèse seated by the window. It overlooked the park, and I went and looked out at the view of her rose garden she had loved. How many times, I thought, must her blue eyes have seen what I was seeing! Here her writing desk had probably stood, and her workbasket. Perhaps in this room she had her last visit with Franz Joseph's mother.

Both here and in her chapel the presence of Marie Antoinette's daughter could still be felt. These were the same walls. Before the altar, beautiful then, in ruins today, she had often knelt. And, leaving the château, we went down the staircase, my hand on the baluster which her hand had touched.

The following year (1964), when Senator Desmond and I went to Gorizia, to see where Queen Marie Thérèse of France was buried with three kings, it was nine years since I had stood at her birthplace in Versailles and decided to write a book about Marie Antoinette's daughter. Since then, my manuscript, besides being taken several times to Europe, had gone with me around the world, twice to Russia, to South America, Australia, New Zealand, and South Africa. In spite of this, though, the book was getting written. As we motored up from Trieste to Gorizia, I was nearing the end of my journey through Thérèse's long life. Ahead of me I saw the town clustered around a hill on which was the ancient castle of the Counts of Gorizia, and, on a small mountain to the east, the Franciscan monastery containing the Bourbon tombs.

First, we went to see the Palazzo Coronini, overlooking the town. The orange stucco villa on the Via 20th September, where Charles X died, is still lived in by the Coronini family. Gorizia was bombed in World War I. This house survived, but the monastery of the Franciscans on Mt. Castegnavizza, built in 1625, was almost destroyed. Two World Wars made many changes here. Gorizia was Austrian in Thérèse's day, and remained so until 1918. After World War I it went back to Italy. Now, since World War II, the frontier with Yugoslavia runs through the town. Most of Gorizia is in Italy, but the church and monastery of Castegnavizza, several miles away, are in Yugoslavia.

The border guards were courteous, though, and a half hour

later we were in Yugoslavia, motoring up the steep road to the monastery. There remained a hurdle to cross. We had come all the way from New York to see Thérèse's tomb, and I might never have seen it, for the friars at Castegnavizza belong to a religious order that does not permit women in their monastery. Fortunately, our Trieste guide had come to Gorizia several days before and made the arrangements. So, when we drew up to the door of the monastery, a young friar (possibly a novice who had not taken his final vows) was waiting to escort us down into the crypt.

We entered by a long corridor. At the end of it was the tomb of Pierre de Blacas d'Aulps, secretary to Louis XVIII and to Charles X. He lay here with Artois, in death. Ahead in the royal vault, flanking a large gold crucifix, were six marble sarcophaguses. To the left, Henry V rested between his wife and sister, the Duchess of Parma; on our right, Charles X, between his son and daughter-in-law.

Putting out my hand, I touched Thérèse's tomb. I could hardly believe it. I hoped that she would be allowed to rest here in peace. She had traveled so much and, after her death, her remains made still another journey. During World War I, with the Italians bombing Gorizia, the Empress Zita of Austria (Louise's granddaughter) had these bodies brought for safe keeping to Vienna. When peace was declared, the Bourbon remains were returned to Gorizia.

On the way out, our guide showed us pictures of the re-enterment of the bodies in 1932, with the military escort that brought them from Vienna. He refused to speak. Otherwise, he was most courteous. He let us stand a long time studying the pictures out in the vestibule. Those of Charles X and the Angoulêmes were engravings and probably flattered them, but Henri V and the Duchess of Parma had been photographed, and we were curious to see what they looked like.

Mademoiselle of France (in her photographs, a very stout

lady) had a sad life. Louise became a widow at thirty-four, her husband, as well as her father, murdered. The Duc de Lucca, who became Charles III, Duke of Parma, in 1849, was shot by a fanatic on May 26, 1854, thirty-four years after the Duc de Berry was assassinated. Louise ruled for six years as Regent during the minority of her eldest son, Robert. Then, in 1860, her little duchy of Parma was annexed to the new kingdom of Italy. Four years later, at forty-three, Louise died of typhoid in Venice, leaving four children. Her son Robert, who died in 1907, was the father of two persons still living—Zita, the last Empress of Austria, and Prince Félix, husband of the Duchess of Luxembourg.

Next to Louise hung the picture of her brother. It was hard to see in this plump, bald-headed man the handsome boy whom Thérèse loved so dearly. What had Henri been like, my husband and I wondered. That a few weeks later we would hear about the Comte de Chambord from a person who had actually known him was a stroke of almost incredible good luck.

34

BATTLE OF THE FLAGS—POSTSCRIPT

BEFORE LEAVING AUSTRIA, Senator Desmond and I returned to Frohsdorf to take some photographs. While we were focusing on the north façade of the house, with its row of statues along the roof, my husband and I noticed an old man weeding a rose bed. "I'm writing a book about Marie Thérèse of France," I told him.

"Ah, the Queen, that's why I'm raising these roses, she was fond of roses, you know," replied the gardener. "Now the King, her nephew, didn't care much about flowers. He enjoyed whist and hunting like his grandfather. Madame, if you're writing a book about Queen Marie Thérèse, you should talk with an old lady who lives here, Fräulein Gisela Fels. She is ninety-five years old. Her parents, Herr and Frau Johannes Fels, were valet and femme de chambre to the Comte and Comtesse de Chambord."

Never was a suggestion seized upon more eagerly. The old man's grandson was sent off to invite Fräulein Gisela Fels to meet us for lunch at the inn. A half hour later, we were seated across the table from a white-haired little old lady primly dressed in shabby black.

"I never knew Queen Marie Thérèse," she reminded me, "but my parents did. The Comte and Comtesse de Chambord I remember well. My brother and I were small children, we lived down by the stables, but we were always at the château. At Christmas, Monsieur le Comte entertained the young people on the estate. He dressed up as King Klaus and gave us all presents."

It is nice to think of Henri and his wife surrounded by children, for the Chambords never had any of their own, which the royalists greatly regretted. Louis Philippe's heir, the Comte de Paris, with a large family of boys and girls, seemed to many of them to be a more attractive candidate for the crown than the last male representative of the elder branch of the Bourbon family—a middle-aged cripple with a homely, deaf wife.

So now that he no longer had his Tante Thérèse to stir up sentiment in his behalf, Henri V, a retiring gentleman with no great liking for politics, was allowed to live quietly at Frohsdorf year after year. In 1852, he let a rival pretender, Louis Napoleon, slip back into France and make himself emperor.

While he was on the throne, Napoleon III repealed the law banishing from France all members of the Bourbon and Bonaparte families. So in July, 1871, Henry V returned to Paris, the city he had left as a boy. Stepping from a hired cab, he stood looking at the ruins of his birthplace, the Tuileries, burned after the Franco-Prussian War by the mob. Then he traveled down to the Loire to see his Château of Chambord, which he hadn't seen since he was a child.

This journey I wanted to hear about, for my great-grandfather's brother, Joseph Curtis, living in Paris at the time, had persuaded Louis Philippe to restore Chambord and the other châteaux on the Loire, and make them into the great tourist attraction they are today. I told Gisela Fels this, and how, when I visited Chambord as a child, my father would tell me about the baby who had been given this lovely castle by the people of France.

"The Château of Chambord is an ideal home for a king," Fräulein Fels replied. "And it nearly was."

After the Franco-Prussian War, and the fall of the Commune, France became a republic again. But there was a strong sentiment for a restoration of the monarchy. Gisela Fels told me a story she had often heard from her father, Herr Johannes Fels, how, in the autumn of 1871, a delegation from the Chamber of Deputies in Paris went to Salzburg, Germany, where Henri and his wife were at their castle of Puchheim for the hunting, to ask the grandson of Charles X to be king.

"But never will the French, bitter at being forced to adopt the white flag during two Bourbon Restorations, accept it again," the delegates told him. "If you come back, Monsieur le Comte, it must be as a constitutional monarch, such as Louis Philippe was, and France must retain the tricolor as the national flag."

Henri was horrified. His aunt had detested the sight of the tricolor. She had taught him to hate it. How could he accept the colors that had waved over the scaffold of Louis XVI and Marie Antoinette? The hated banner that, hoisted at Bordeaux, had send his Tante Thérèse fleeing into exile, rather than be taken prisoner and shot by Napoleon.

He could never serve under the flag that had brought so much suffering to his family, Chambord told the delegation from Paris. Moreover, the kingship was *his*—his by divine right, as the grandson of Charles X; and this right France must acknowledge, and that Louis Philippe and Napoleon III had been usurpers.

This reply settled the question of his eligibility. Since he refused to renounce the white flag, the Chamber of Deputies voted to retain their present republican form of government. France was not willing, for the sake of Henri V, to give up her tricolor—the flag of so many memories. Its loss had been the bitterest humiliation that the nation had had to suffer at the Restoration.

"France is a republic today because of Marie Antoinette's daughter," Fräulein Fels again reminded me. "No man ever came nearer to being king, only to turn down the chance. But brought up by a woman who had given him a horror of the flag under which her parents had been murdered, could the Comte de Chambord have done differently? Ah, no, Madame! Queen Marie Thérèse had told her nephew too many stories of her early sufferings. Had he been educated, not by his aunt, but by his mother, he might have understood that the tricolor had ceased to be the symbol of the Revolution and had become the symbol of law and order. But in 1871, the Dowager Queen had been dead only twenty years. Her influence, my father said, was still strongly felt here at Frohsdorf."

So it was knowing what his aunt would want him to do that decided Henri V to refuse the crown. His friends were bitterly disappointed. "The matter of the flag ruined all our hopes," wrote Madame de La Ferronnays. Eager to return to Paris, his followers implored the Pretender not to sacrifice being King for an absurd scruple.

But the matter of the flag was no trivial thing. It meant more to the Comte de Chambord than the throne. He refused to give up the white fleur-de-lis standard under which France had become a great nation—the glorious banner of Henri IV, Francis I, and Joan of Arc—for the red, white, and blue, associated with all the atrocities of which his family had been the victims.

"The flag is only a symbol, of course," he explained to those who were working for his cause in France. "But to accept the tricolor would mean that I forgive the revolutionists their crimes and approve of the French Revolution. That I could never do. Rather than yield over the matter of the flag, I prefer to remain in exile."

So Henri V of France stayed on at Frohsdorf, where he died on August 24, 1883, and was buried at Gorizia, in the folds of the white flag he loved.

Before his death, the feud that Marie Antoinette started with the Orléanists came to an end. There was a reconciliation between the elder Bourbon branch of the family and the house of Orléans. Gisela Fels, a girl of fourteen at the time, remembered the happy day, July 7, 1883, when Louis Philippe's grandson came to Frohsdorf. She was helping her mother in the Comte's sickroom, and Gisela had seen it, she told us, a sight the royalists had long hoped would happen. The childless Henri de Chambord, bedridden and dying of cancer, took the Comte de Paris in his arms and proclaimed him his heir. The elder line ended with Henri's death. Since then, the legitimist pretenders to the French throne have all been descendants of the Orléans branch of the house.

After the death of the Duchess of Parma, the Chambords had brought up Louise's four orphaned children, Marguerite, Alex, Robert, and Henri, as though they were their own. Naturally, Carlos and Alphonso, the sons of the Comtesse de Chambord's sister, Beatrice, were often at Frohsdorf. A romance developed. Marguerite married the Spanish prince, Don Carlos VII, Duke of Madrid, eldest son of Don Juan and the Infanta Beatrice, the Carlist claimant in 1872 to the Spanish throne. At the death of the Comtesse de Chambord, the Duchess of Madrid inherited Frohsdorf.

"Now the château has been sold. It is to be a rest home for retired postmen," Gisela Fels told us. "There will be many changes. I wonder what Marie Antoinette's daughter would say."

We wondered, too, and as my husband and I drove off, leaving the little old lady who had never ridden on a train, in in an automobile, or used a telephone, waving good-by, we were glad to have seen Frohsdorf before the postmen took over.

BIBLIOGRAPHY

CONTEMPORARY SOURCES

BÉARN, COMTESSE PAULINE, DE, *Souvenirs de Quarante Ans, 1789–1850.* Paris: Jacques Lecoffre. 1861

These memoirs of the Comtesse de Béarn, formerly Pauline de Tourzel, the daughter of Thérèse's governess and her lifelong friend, were dictated to the Comtesse's chaplain. Each evening, the old lady was encouraged by her son, Hector, to reminisce.

The youngest of the Marquise de Tourzel's four daughters, Pauline lived as a girl at the Tuileries with her mother. About the same age as Madame Royale, she became Thérèse's best friend. Pauline and her mother followed the royal family to the Temple. In a letter to her sister Josephine, Pauline tells how they were separated from the Bourbons and taken to La Force prison, and of her rescue there by an unknown man. Madame de Tourzel, writing to this same daughter, Josephine, tells what happened to her at La Force after Pauline left. Finally, she, too, was saved by this same mysterious person. The Marquise and Pauline never discovered why they were freed and Louise de Lamballe was murdered. We know that the Tourzels escaped through the efforts of the Duc de Penthièvre, who bribed their jailers, hoping to free his daughter-in-law. Unfortunately, he failed in saving the Princess. These letters from Pauline and her mother, meant to be read only by the family, are the best part of the book.

Married to the Comte de Béarn (Captain of the King's Guard) on January 15, 1797, and in disfavor during Napoleon's reign,

Pauline saw with delight the Bourbons' return to Paris. She hurried to greet the Duchesse d'Angoulême at Compiègne. "Oh, it's Pauline!" Thérèse cried. And the two women, who had not met for twenty years, fell into each other's arms. The Comtesse de Béarn became first lady in waiting to the Dauphine, and their intimacy continued until Thérèse was banished from France in 1830. She and Pauline parted at Rambouillet on August 3, never to meet again.

BEAUCHESNE, A. DE, *The History of Louis XVII*. 2 vols. London: Vizetelly. 1853

In 1837, Gomin, former keeper at the Temple, talked with Beauchesne and gave him most of the material for these two volumes, published in 1853, two years after Thérèse's death. Beauchesne states that the boy who died in the Tower in June, 1795, was the Dauphin, as it was generally thought at the time. The chief merit of the book is its detailed description of the royal family's life in prison.

BOIGNE, COMTESSE DE, *Mémoires*. 4 vols. Paris: Plon Nourrit. 1909. 4 vols. New York: Scribners. 1907

The gossipy recollections of Adéle d'Osmond, daughter of the Marquis d'Osmond, later Comtesse de Boigne. Born at Versailles in 1781, her mother being one of the ladies in waiting of Madame Adélaide, Adéle played as a child with Madame Royale and the Artois boys. She accompanied her father while he served as ambassador to Italy and England, and returned to France in November, 1804.

A staunch royalist, the Comtesse tolerated with scorn Napoleon and his court, then hailed with joy the return of the Bourbons. She became a leading hostess in Paris during the Restorations and the reign of Louis Philippe. Her brother, Rainulphe d'Osmond, was aide-de-camp to the Duc d'Angoulême, and she knew intimately the people associated with the courts of Louis XVIII and Charles X, of whom she writes. Adéle d'Osmond died in 1866, at eighty-five, and these "Stories of an Aunt," begun in 1835 to amuse her grandnephew, give us a picture of France from 1781 to 1830. Perhaps she expected them to be read only by her family, for they are remarkably frank.

CAMPAN, JEANNE LOUISE HENRIETTE, *Mémoires sur la Vie Privée de Marie Antoinette*. 3 vols. Liverpool: Henry Young. 1917

Written by the Queen's first lady of the bedchamber, and later the fashionable schoolmistress of the Napoleonic period. Jeanne Campan came to Versailles at fifteen, as reader to Madame Victoire.

The Dauphine took a fancy to her, and she served Marie Antoinette for twenty years, from her marriage to the August 10 attack on the Tuileries. Jeanne's father was librarian to the Queen, who "seldom opened a book." And her brother, Edmond Genêt, became the first French minister to the United States. Ordered back to France and the guillotine, he married Cornelia Clinton, daughter of George Clinton, Governor of New York, who gave him asylum.

Madame Campan survived the Revolution, after which a new career opened for her. She conducted a school for girls at Saint Germain, attended by Napoleon's stepdaughter, his niece, and the daughters of his generals. It was closed after Napoleon's downfall, and Jeanne Campan was snubbed by the returned Bourbons. She wrote these volumes in 1822, to try to re-establish herself with the reigning family by flattering them. The Comte de Provence, now Louis XVIII, was no longer interested in wrecking the reputation of Marie Antoinette, but to strengthen himself, was busy restoring it. Largely a vindication of the Queen, Madame Campan indignantly denies the stories of her flirtations and extravagance. Her souvenirs are remarkable for what this discreet lady omits. She must have known of the affair between Marie Antoinette and the handsome Swede, but she only mentions Fersen once. She gives him credit for arranging the drive to Varennes. It is said that this published edition of Madame Campan's memoirs is not complete. A portion of it was burned, "out of respect for Marie Antoinette's memory." That Fersen was completely devoted to the Queen was a secret long kept, until his journal and correspondence with Marie Antoinette were published in comparatively recent times.

CHASTELLUX, COMTE DE, *Voyage de Mesdames, Tantes du Roi.* Paris: Michaud. 1816

Seeing the situation growing worse every day, Madame Royale's great-aunts, Adélaide and Victoire, left Paris on February 19, 1791, and fled to Rome and the protection of the Pope. Six years later, they took refuge in Naples, living on the charity of Queen Maria Carolina, who didn't want them. Chastellux and his wife accompanied the old ladies, the Comte as *chevalier d'honneur* to Madame Victoire, the Comtesse as lady in waiting to Madame Adélaide.

In December, 1798, with Napoleon about to capture Naples, Adélaide and Victoire were forced to flee again, this time to Trieste. Chastellux's little book, published by his son, tells of their journey through cold and snow. Victoire, ill with cancer, died in Trieste, June 7, 1799; Adélaide, the following year. Buried in the cathedral there, the bodies of the daughters of Louis XV were brought back to France by Louis XVIII and re-interred at Saint-Denis during the Second Restoration.

CHATEAUBRIAND, VICOMTE FRANÇOIS-RENE, *Mémoires d'Outre-tombe*. 3 vols. Bruxelles: Meline, Cans. 1849

A noted French writer and ardent supporter of the Bourbon cause, Chateaubriand was ambassador to England (1822) and Louis XVIII's minister of foreign affairs (1823–1824). A friend of the Duchesse de Berry, he was no great admirer of her sister-in-law. Chateaubriand gives us a malicious portrait of the Duchesse d'Angoulême when he went to Carlsbad to try to get Thérèse's permission for Caroline to visit her children.

CLÉRY, JEAN-BAPTISTE, *Journal of the Occurrences at the Temple during the Confinement of Louis XVI*. Printed by Baylis and sold by the author. 29 Great Pulteney Street, London. 1798

Born at Versailles in 1759, his family having been in service there since the days of Louis XIV, the twenty-six-year-old Cléry became valet to the Duc de Normandie at the latter's birth. He married a musician in the King's orchestra. She taught Marie Antoinette to play the harp.

Cléry was with the royal family at the Tuileries, and left his wife and children to follow them to the Temple. After Hue was taken away to La Force prison, Cléry became the King's valet and, eventually, the only royal servant left to wait on the family. He stayed with Louis XVI to the end, accompanying him to the scaffold.

After the King's death, Cléry was sent to La Force prison. His life was saved in August, 1794, by the end of the Terror. He went to live in Strasbourg where his brother was an army contractor. Cléry took with him his diary, which he had kept while at the Temple, and a trunk full of scribbled notes. From them, he wrote this book, first published in London in 1798, and translated into several languages. Most of the men who claimed to be the Dauphin read Cléry's journal, recalling the Bourbons' captivity in the Tower, and borrowed freely from his account of the imprisonment of the royal family in trying to prove their authenticity.

When Madame Royale went to Vienna, Cléry was allowed to join her after a while. He went with Thérèse to Russia, then, in 1801, returned to Paris, where he was employed during Napoleon's reign by Louis XVIII as a secret agent. He died in Vienna in 1809.

Published in London in 1798, this is the first English edition of Cléry's journal, brought out simultaneously with the French edition. It is a collector's item. The author also owns a reprint by the Folio Society, London, 1955.

D'ABRANTES, DUCHESSE (Laura de Permon), *Memoirs of Napoleon, His Court and Family*. 2 vols. New York: Appleton, 1867

Laura was married to Junot, Napoleon's Military Governor of Paris. Her recollections chiefly concern the days of the Empire. They begin, however, with her childhood, at the outbreak of the Revolution, and contain references to Louis XVI, Marie Antoinette, Louis XVIII, Artois and his sons.

D'HEZECQUES, FELIX, COMTE DE FRANCE (BARON DE MAILLY), *Souvenirs d'Un Page*. Paris: Didier. 1873

The author became a page in the bedchamber of Louis XVI when he was twelve years old, and remained at Versailles for six years. The Revolution having abolished the position of page to the King, Felix served in the royal stables and as captain of the guard. He finally escaped to Coblenz, Germany, and joined Condé's army.

In 1804, at thirty years of age, Felix, now the Baron de Mailly, wrote these recollections of his boyhood at Versailles. He gives us his estimation of the royal family and tells of the great ceremonies he witnessed—the King's levée, the balls, the hunts, the arrival of ambassadors—all of which dazzled a boy in his teens. The book ends with the flight to Varennes. After that, presumably, Felix himself fled to Germany.

ELLIOTT, GRACE DALRYMPLE, *During the Reign of Terror*. New York: Sturgis & Walton. 1910

This account of the adventures of an English beauty, Mrs. Dalrymple Elliott, during her stay in Paris from 1786 to 1801, was written at the request of King George III, after the lady's safe return to England. A mistress of the Duc d'Orléans, Mrs. Elliott mingled at the outbreak of the Revolution with the Palais-Royal set. Blaming Lafayette (whom she hated) for a large part of the troubles that came to the royal family, she gives us a too-sympathetic picture of the man who intrigued against his cousin for the throne. But even Grace became revolted when Philippe Egalité voted for the King's death.

By that time, Mrs. Elliott was having her own troubles. Arrested for being a friend of the Red Duke's, she was confined in various jails, in constant fear of the guillotine. One of Grace's companions in the Carmes prison was Josephine de Beauharnais, after her release to marry Napoleon.

Mrs. Elliott's journal makes the days of the Terror seem very real. What could be more exciting than her account of hiding a hunted aristocrat, the Marquis de Chansenets, between the mattresses of her bed while the police searched her house for him? The gendarmes did not run their bayonets into the featherbed as they usually did, because the resourceful Mrs. Elliott had gotten into the bed herself and lay on top of the Marquis.

FERSEN, COUNT AXEL VON, *Journal and Correspondence.* Löfstad Castle, Norrköping, Sweden.

First published in 1872 by the Baron of Klinkowström, Fersen's grand-nephew, who inherited Axel's papers; added to by O. G. Heidenstam in 1912, and completed by Alma Söderhjelm in 1934. Part of Fersen's diary disappeared and the Baron destroyed most of Fersen's correspondence with Marie Antoinette, in an attempt to conceal the intimacy that existed between the French Queen and his great-uncle. The archives of Löfstad Castle contain only sixty letters, censored by the Baron (whole sentences being replaced by dots) that escaped his regrettable destruction. What chiefly interests us in Fersen's journal is his account of trying to see the daughter of Marie Antoinette while Madame Royale was in Vienna.

FERRONNAYS, COMTESSE DE LA, *Mémoires.* Paris: Paul Ollendorff. 1899

Like their cousins, the Blacas, the Ferronnays family were attached for several generations to the household of the Bourbons in exile. The father, Comte Auguste de La Ferronnays, had been gentleman in waiting to the Duc de Berry. His son, Ferdinand, joined the household of the Comte de Chambord four years after Henri's marriage. It was January, 1850, and the Queen, as Madame de La Ferronnays, the author of these souvenirs, calls Marie Thérèse of France, had but a year and a half to live. She gives us an admiring and affectionate picture of the exiled Queen at seventy-two, living at the Chambords' Cavalli Palace in Venice, where they spent the winter of 1851, and also during the following summer (to be Thérèse's last) at Frohsdorf.

Ferdinand de La Ferronnays served the Comte de Chambord until his death at Frohsdorf in a hunting accident. He died in Henri's arms, and his wife continued her intimacy with the Chambords, the Lucchesi-Pallis, and Louise's four children, who were practically adopted by Henri and his wife after his sister's death. Madame de La Ferronnays tells of Chambord's reconciliation with the Comte de Paris and of attending his funeral at Gorizia. She became equally loyal to the Comte de Paris, and relates many anecdotes about his children and those of the Duchess of Parma (Louise) not generally known.

FIRMONT, THE ABBÉ EDGEWORTH DE, *The Last Hours of Louis XVI, King of France, by His Confessor.* Translated and published by the Folio Society. London. 1955

Henry Essex Edgeworth was the son of Robert Edgeworth, an Irish rector. Educated at the Jesuit College in Toulouse, he came to Paris in 1769, and, at the outbreak of the Revolution, was confessor to Princesse Elisabeth of France. He accompanied her brother, Louis XVI, to the scaffold. If he said to him the famous words of farewell, "Son of Saint Louis, ascend to heaven!" the Abbé fails to mention it in his book.

After the King's execution, Edgeworth escaped to England, but shortly left for Blankenburg to join Louis XVIII, with whom he spent ten years. He assisted the Cardinal Montmorency in marrying Madame Royale to the Duc d'Angoulême. While attending the French prisoners at Mitau, Russia, he caught typhus and died in May, 1807, at sixty-two.

GONTAUT, DUCHESSE DE (GOUVERANT DES ENFANTS DE FRANCE PENDANT LA RESTAURATION), Paris. *Mémoires*. Pon Nourrit. 1891.

Brought up at Versailles, where she played with Madame Royale and the Dauphin, Marie Josephine Louise de Navailles' godparents were Monsieur and the Comtesse de Provence. In 1792, exiled in London during the French Revolution, she married the Marquis de Gontaut-Biron. Like many other ruined French émigrés in England, Josephine earned her living by painting little pictures.

The Marquise de Gontaut was at Hartwell and returned with Louis XVIII to France. When the Duc de Berry was married, she became first lady of the bedchamber to the Duchess; then, in 1819, governess of their first child, Louise. Artois liked Josephine de Gontaut because she was a cousin of his great love, the Vicomtesse de Polastron. He made her a duchess in 1827.

As governess to the little Duc de Bordeaux, as well as to his sister Louise, the Duchesse de Gontaut followed the Bourbons into exile again in 1830. She died in Paris in 1857. She wrote these recollections when she was eighty. A companion to Madame de La Ferronnay's book, that shows us Henri and Louise d'Artois as adults, the Duchesse de Gontaut's memoirs picture them as children. She was with the royal exiles at Lulworth, Holyrood and Prague, and retired in 1834, when Louise was fifteen, and Henri, fourteen, had graduated to a tutor, the Duc de Damas. The Duchess' book is chiefly concerned with Louise, her special charge. A tactful lady, she dismisses the Duchesse de Berry's fiasco in the Vendée in one paragraph.

HUE, FRANÇOIS, *Dernieres Annèes du Regne et de la Vie de Louis XVI*. Paris: Imprimerie Royal. 1814

Written by the Dauphin's valet, who became Louis XVI's first gentleman of the bedchamber when he was crowned king. Hue accompanied Louis into captivity, but was soon taken from the Temple with the Princesse de Lamballe and the Tourzels, and shut up in a succession of prisons. He only escaped the guillotine thanks to an influential friend, Josephine, the Vicomtesse de Beauharnais, later to marry Napoleon.

Released, finally, from prison, Hue tried to return to the Tower and serve the royal family, but was refused. He writes of attending the King's trial; how he slipped into the Conciergerie and obtained news of Marie Antoinette; and how he brought the royalists to cheer Madame Royale's captivity by waving to her over the prison wall. Hue accompanied Thérèse to Vienna. Then, banished, François, his wife and son, André, joined Louis XVIII in Verona. Later, Hue escorted Madame Royale to Mitau and shared the Pretender's exile in Russia and England, returning with him to France, where he became the treasurer of Louis XVIII's household.

His memoirs, like Cléry's, furnished a fund of details about the captivity of the royal family in the Tower to the men claiming to be the Dauphin. Published under the patronage of Louis XVIII, to whom François Hue was as devoted as he had been to his brother, it shows him to have been a more cultured man than his counterpart, Cléry. Louis XVIII loaded Hue with honors on his return to France. Now Baron Hue, in 1815, after Waterloo, François brought the crown jewels back to France from England. His son André, made the Vicomte d'Agoult, and equerry to the Duchesse d'Angoulême, became governor of the palace of Saint-Cloud. In 1816, he married the Comtesse Henriette de Choisy, Thérèse's lady of the wardrobe, a close friend who had followed her from Vienna, to Russia and England, and remained with her for forty years.

LAMARTINE, ALPHONSE DE, *History of the Restoration of the Monarchy in France.* 4 vols. New York: Harpers. 1852

LAMBALLE, MARIE THÉRÈSE LOUISE OF SAVOY, PRINCESSE DE, *Secret Memoirs of the Royal Family of France.* 2 vols. London: H. S. Nichols. 1895

Journal of the Italian-born daughter-in-law of the Duc de Penthièvre. Louise (1749–1792) was a member of the royal family of Sardinia. After the death of her young husband, a widow at eighteen, she became superintendent of the Queen's household. She tells of her life at Versailles and the Tuileries. Her journal ends with the storming of the palace on June 20, 1792.

Shortly after that, the Princesse de Lamballe gave the manuscript to a young English friend living in Paris. Did Louise suspect that she did not have long to live? She had been sent to England on several secret missions by Marie Antoinette. Louise's father-in-law begged her to remain there in safety, but she insisted upon returning to the Tuileries to serve the Queen. Imprisoned with her, the Princesse de Lamballe paid for her devotion to Marie Antoinette with her life.

When Louise was taken from the Temple to La Force prison, the Duc de Penthièvre offered the revolutionists half of his immense fortune if they would let his daughter-in-law and her companions, the Marquise de Tourzel and Pauline, go free. Madame de Tourzel and her daughter were released, but the Princesse de Lamballe, fearing that the plan for her to escape was a hoax, refused to leave her cell. She was taken before the Committee of Public Safety and questioned. She would not repeat the oath of disloyalty to the King and, on leaving the tribunal, was literally torn to pieces by the mob.

After Louise's death, her English friend, who had escaped to Italy, translated the Princess's journal (written in Italian) into English and had it published. She supplements Lamballe's diary with an account of her own adventures while, disguised as a boy, she traveled about Europe, sent by Louise de Lamballe with letters from Marie Antoinette begging for help. Especially interesting is the cipher the Queen used in writing to her correspondents. The author shows us how to decipher it.

LE BRUN, ELISABETH VIGÉE, *Souvenirs.* New York: R. Worthington. 1879

Another eyewitness account of the last days of the French monarchy. Madame Le Brun and her husband were court painters at Versailles. The wife painted more than twenty portraits of Marie Antoinette, including the famous one of the Queen and her children.

MARIE THÉRÈSE CHARLOTTE DE FRANCE. *Journal.* Paris: Plon Nourrit. 1892

This account of the confinement of the royal family in the Tower, by Madame Royale herself, should tell us a great deal about her. Unfortunately, it doesn't. Written in prison, under the watchful eye of Renée de Chanterenne, Thérèse obediently set down what her jailers told her, that her brother had died in the Tower on June 8, 1795, of natural causes, that he wasn't poisoned. Shut up in her cell, how did the poor girl know?

Later, apparently, Thérèse worried for fear that she had said too much. She had given the original draft to Renée de Chanterenne. In 1805, from Mitau, the Duchesse d'Angoulême sent Cléry to Paris to get her manuscript back from Madame de Chanterenne.

Thérèse copied it and made some changes. When she went to Paris, at the time of the Restoration, she gave Renée back the original draft. The copy Thérèse made in Russia she gave to Madame de Soucy, who allowed it to be printed in 1823, to the Duchess' annoyance. Thérèse had every book she could find destroyed. A few escaped and were used by Nettlement, Beauchesne, and Saint-Amand in their account of the royal family's imprisonment in the Tower.

Madame de Chanterenne kept all of Thérèse's letters. A few months before the Comte de Chambord's death, Renée's granddaughter sent him the precious bundle of letters and her grandmother's copy of Madame Royale's journal. At Chambord's death, they were inherited by the Duchesse de Madrid (Louise's daughter, Marguerite), who had the journal published. Only 125 copies were printed. The author owns No. 79. Beautifully bound in vellum, the book is a collector's item, and more valuable than the censored edition published in 1823.

M. C. DE M. *Quinze Jours à Prague*. Paris: Dentu. 1833

Account of the exile of Charles X and the Angoulêmes in Czechoslovakia.

MORRIS, ANNE CARY, *The Diary and Letters of Gouverneur Morris*. 2 vols. New York: Scribner's. 1888

Gouverneur Morris's diary and letters, with an explanatory narrative written by his wife, Anne Cary Morris, shows us the French Revolution through the eyes of an American stationed in Paris who refused to leave his post. Appointed United States minister to France by President Washington (1792–1794), Gouverneur Morris was the only foreign minister to remain in Paris during the Reign of Terror.

NETTLEMENT, M. ALFRED, *Vie de Marie Thérèse de France*. Paris: Jeulin. 1843

The first biography written about Marie Thérèse. Like other early biographers of the sufferings of the royal family, Nettlement drew heavily on the journal written by Madame Royale and the souvenirs of Hue and Cléry. The Duchesse d'Angoulême, who lived to read Nettlement's book, first published in 1830, found it "full of errors."

PERNOUD, GEORGE and FLAISSIER, SABINE, *The French Revolution*. London: Secker & Warburg. 1961

Eyewitness accounts of the French Revolution, including a portion of Madame Royale's journal and Cléry's description of her father's last days in the Tower.

PIMODAN, COMTE DE, *Les Fiançialles de Madame Royale*. Paris: Plon Nourrit. 1912

Beginning with Thérèse's release from the Temple, this little book tells of her first year in Vienna. Its chief value lies in the wealth of new material the Comte de Pimodan found in the Imperial Archives in Vienna. His choicest discovery were Madame Royale's letters to her Uncle Provence and the Duc d'Angoulême in Verona, and Antoine's letters to her. They were opened and read by the Austrian police and copies of them deposited in their files. Charming, girlish letters, they tell far more about Madame Royale than her journal written under the eyes of her jailers. Of interest is a letter to Thérèse from Fersen and one from Gouverneur Morris, former American minister to France.

SIBOUTIE, DR. POWNIES DE LA, *Recollections of a Parisian 1789–1863*. New York: Putnam. 1911

SUFFERINGS OF THE ROYAL FAMILY DURING THE REVOLUTION IN FRANCE (from Accounts of Eyewitnesses). London: Smithers Hampden. 1902

TOURZEL, LOUISE, ELISABETH, FÉLICITÉ, DUCHESSE DE (GOUVERANTE DES ENFANTS DE FRANCE PENDANT LES ANNÈES 1789–1795). *Mémoires*, 2 vols. Paris: Plon. 1883

After the Revolution, all those who had been closely associated with the royal family of France–Hue, Cléry, Madame Campan, Madame de Tourzel and Pauline–were busily writing their souvenirs. No one knew the Bourbons better than this devoted woman. The widow of the Marquis de Tourzel, killed in 1786 while hunting with the King, Louise (1749–1832), daughter of the Duc de Croy-Havré, replaced the Duchesse de Polignac as governess to the Children of France. She came to Versailles in August, 1789, when Charles was four years old. His sister had graduated to a tutor, the Abbé d'Avaux. But it was Madame de Tourzel, assisted by the Baronne de Mackau, second governess, who escorted Madame Royale to her First Communion.

The Marquise de Tourzel and her daughter Pauline shared the unhappy life of the royal family at the Tuileries and followed them to the Temple. Transferred to La Force prison, they barely escaped the horrible death of the Princesse de Lamballe. She tells of their imprisonment and, on being released, of their attempts to visit Madame Royale at the Temple.

During the Restoration, Louis XVIII rewarded the Marquise for her devotion by making her a duchess. Always in poor health after her release from prison, the Duchesse de Tourzel lived to a ripe old age, dying in 1832, at eighty-two. Her memoirs were published by her great-grandson, the Duc des Cars.

VALORY, FRANÇOIS, COMTE DE, *Precis Historique du Voyage Entrepris par Louis XVI le 21 Juin, 1791*. Paris: Michaud. 1815

This slim volume, written by a man who went on the drive to Varennes, was published only twenty-four years after that fatal journey. The Comte de Valory was one of the three bodyguards who accompanied the King. Arrested after their return to Paris, the poor man spent eleven years in jail, where he passed the time writing his recollections of those ghastly five days.

Valory could not get his book published while Napoleon was in power. It was only in 1815, with the return of the Bourbons, that he had the satisfaction of seeing his manuscript in print. The familiar story is told from a fresh angle, through the eyes of a man who, if he had been properly armed and allowed to shoot, might have saved the King.

WALSH, LE VICOMTE, *Voyage à Prague (Correspondance entre un père et son fils en Septembre 1833)*. Paris: Hivert. 1834

In 1820, the Vicomte Walsh, a boy then, took his first trip from his native Brittany to visit Paris with his father. There he attended at Notre Dame the baptism of the little Duc de Bordeaux. Now, thirteen years later, he is on another journey, to Prague, to celebrate the coming of age of Henri V.

These are the Vicomte's letters home to his father. There are interesting glimpses in them of Charles X, the Angoulêmes, and the Artois children. For example, we learn that the management was so thrilled by having the Duchesse d'Angoulême at Carlsbad, taking the baths, that a special bathhouse was built for her.

IN FRENCH

AIMOND, CHARLES. *L'Énigme de Varennes*. Verdun. Editions Lorraine. 1935 (bought in Varennes, France.)

ARNAUD, RAOUL. *La Princesse de Lamballe*. Paris: Perrin. 1911

BERTRAUT, JULUS. *Le Rois Bourgeois (Louis Philippe)*. Paris: Bernard Grasset. 1936

CASTLELOT, ANDRÉ. *Le Secret de Madame Royale*. Paris: Sfelt. 1949

——*Le Duc de Berry et Son Double Mariage*. Paris. Sfelt. 1951

——*Souverains en Fuite*. Paris: Amiot-Dumont. 1952
——*Le Prince Rouge (Philippe-Egalité)*. Paris: Perrin. 1962

CASTRIES, DUC DE. *Les Émigrés*. Paris: Fayard. 1962

DECAUX, ALAIN. *La Belle Historie de Versailles*. Paris: Berger-Levrault. 1962

DESPORTES, HENRI. *Le Frère de la Duchesse d'Angoulême*. Paris: A. Ferroud. 1888

DEVILLE, PAUL SAINTE-CLAIRE. *L'Orpheline de la Prison du Temple*. 2 vols. Paris: Perrin. 1929

GARCON, MAURICE. *Louis XVII ou la Fausse Énigme*. Paris: Hachette. 1952

GERARD, G. *Correspondence entre Maria Theresa et Marie Antoinette*. Paris: Grasset. 1933

KUNSTLER, CHARLES. *Le Vie Privée de Marie Antoinette*. Paris: Hachette. 1938
——*Fersen et Son Secret*. Paris: Hachette. 1947

LANGERON, ROGER. *Madame Royale (Fille de Marie Antoinette)*. Paris: Hachette. 1958

LENÔTRE, GEORGE. *La Fille de Louis XVI (Marie Thérèse Charlotte de France)*. Paris: Perrin. 1907
——*Le Drame de Varennes (Juin 1791)*. Paris: Perrin. 1911

LESCURE, M. DE. *Captivity de la Famille Royalle à la Tour du Temple*. Paris: Poulet-Malassis. 1862

LUCAS-DUBRETON, J. *Louis XVIII*. Paris: Albin Michel. 1925

NETTLEMENT M. ALFRED. *Henri de France (1820–1883)*. 2 vols. Paris: E. Dentu. 1846

NOLHAC, PIERRE DE. *Madame Vigée Le Brun*. Paris: Goupil. 1912

PÉNE, H. DE. *Henri de France*. Paris: H. Oudin. 1884

PIMODAN, COMTE DE. *Les Fiançailles de Madame Royale*. Paris: Plon Nourrit. 1912

PITAIN, JEAN. *Madame Atkins et la Prison du Temple*. Paris: Perrin. 1836

PRAVIEL, A. *Vie de S. A. R. Madame la Duchesse de Berry.* Paris: Goupil. 1929

REISET, VICOMTE DE. *Josephine de Savoie, Comtesse de Provence.* Paris: Emile-Paul. 1913

SAINT-AMAND, IMBERT DE. *La Dernière Année de Marie Antoinette.* Paris: E. Dentu. 1891

STRENGER, GILBERT. *Le Retour des Bourbons (1814–1815).* Paris: Plon Nourrit. 1908

——*Grand Dames du XIX Siècle.* Paris: Perrin. 1911

STRYIENSKI, CASIMIR. *Mesdames de France (Fille de Louis XV).* Paris: Emile-Paul. 1910

TURQUAN, JOSEPH. *Les Femmes de l'Emigration.* Paris: Emile-Paul. 1911

VERGNE, YVONNE DE LA. *Madame Elisabeth de France.* Paris: P. Tequit. 1936

WALTER, GERARD. *Le Comte de Provence.* Paris: Albin Michel. 1950

IN GERMAN

JOHN, DR. WILHELM. *Erzherzog Karl der Feldherr und Seine Armee.* Wien: Hof-und Staatsdruckerei. 1913

IN ENGLISH

ABBOTT, JOHN S. C. *History of Marie Antoinette.* New York: Harper's. 1854

ACTON, HAROLD. *The Bourbons of Naples (1734–1825).* London: Methuen. 1956

——*The Last Bourbons of Naples (1825–1861).* London: Methuen. 1956

ANDERSON, INGVAR. *History of Sweden.* Stockholm: Natur Och Kultur. 1955

ANTHONY, KATHERINE. *Marie Antoinette.* New York: Alfred A. Knopf. 1933

AUSTIN, PAUL BRITTEN. *The Fatal Day of Axel Fersen.* Stockholm: Bokforlaget Fabel. 1962

BELLOC, HILAIRE. *Marie Antoinette.* New York: Putnam. 1924

BISHOP, M. C. *Prison Life of Marie Antoinette.* London: Paul, Trench, & Trubner. 1893

CASTLELOT, ANDRÉ. *Queen of France (A Biography of Marie Antoinette).* New York: Harper's. 1957

——*The Turbullent City: Paris 1783–1871.* New York: Harper & Row. 1962

CORYN, M. *Marie Antoinette and Axel de Fersen.* London: Thorton Butterworth. 1938

DABNEY, RICHARD H. *The Causes of the French Revolution.* New York: Henry Holt. 1888

DAVIS, MURIEL O. *The Political History of France 1789–1910.* Oxford: Clarendon Press. 1916

EVANS, ELIZABETH E. *The Story of Louis XVII of France.* London: Swan Sonnenschein. 1893

GIBBS, MONTGOMERY B. *Napoleon's Military Career.* Chicago: Werner. 1895

GOLDSMITH, MARGARET. *Maria Theresa of Austria.* London: Arthur Barker. 1936

GUNN, PETER. *Naples.* London: Chapman & Hall. 1961

HAMEL, FRANK. *The Dauphines of France.* London: Stanley Paul. 1909

HAZEN, CHARLES DOWNER. *The French Revolution and Napoleon.* New York: Henry Holt. 1917

KENYON, F. W. *Marie Antoinette.* New York: Thomas Y. Crowell. 1956

KUNSTLER, CHARLES. *The Personal Life of Marie Antoinette.* London: G. Bell. 1940

LADY JACKSON, CATHERINE. *The French Court and Society.* 2 vols. London: Richard Bentley. 1881

LATIMER, ELIZABETH W. *France in the Nineteenth Century (1830–1890).* Chicago: A. C. McClurg. 1898

——*The Scrapbook of the French Revolution.* Chicago: A. C. McClurg. 1898

LAUN, HENRI VAN. *The French Revolutionary Epoch.* 2 vols. New York: Appleton. 1879

LENÔTRE, GEORGE. *Paris in the Revolution.* London: Hutchinson. 1888

——*The Flight of Marie Antoinette.* London: Heinemann. 1906

——*The Dauphin (Louis XVII) or the Riddle of the Temple.* New York: Doubleday, Page. 1921

MACLEHOSE, SOPHIA H. *Last Days of the French Monarchy.* Glasgow: MacLehose. 1901

——*From the Monarchy to the Republic in France 1789–1792.* Glasgow: MacLehose. 1904

MINNIGERODE, MEADE. *The Magnificent Comedy (1794–1799).* New York: Farrar and Rinehart. 1931

——*The Son of Marie Antoinette.* New York: Farrar and Rinehart. 1934

Marie Antoinette's Henchman. New York: Farrar and Rinehart. 1936

MONTAGUE, VIOLETTE M. *The Abbé Edgeworth and His Friends.* London: Herbert Jenkins. 1913

MORRIS, CONSTANCE LILY. *Maria Theresa of Austria.* New York: Alfred A. Knopf. 1937

MORRIS, WILLIAM O'CONNOR. *The French Revolution and the First Empire.* London: Longmans, Green. 1874

MURET, CHARLOTTE TOUZALIN. *French Royalist Doctrines Since the Revolution.* New York: Columbia University Press. 1933

NOLHAC, PIERRE DE. *The Trianon of Marie Antoinette.* London: T. Fisher Unwin. 1925

PALACHE, JOHN GARBER. *Marie Antoinette (The Player Queen).* London: Longmans, Green. 1929

PERNOND, GEORGE. *The French Revolution.* London: Sicker & Warburg. 1961

PILKINGTON, IAIN D. B. *Queen of the Trianon.* London: Jarrolds. 1955

ROCHETERIE, MAXIME DE LA. *Life of Marie Antoinette.* 2 vols. New York: Dodd, Mead. 1893

ROSE, J. H. *The Revolutionary and Napoleonic Era (1789–1815)*. England: Cambridge University Press. 1907

SAINT-AMAND, BARON IMBERT DE. *Marie Antoinette and the End of the Old Regime*. New York: Scribner's. 1901

——*Marie Antoinette and the Downfall of Royalty*. New York: Scribner's. 1901

——*Marie Antoinette at the Tuileries*. New York: Scribner's. 1901

——*The Youth of the Duchess of Angoulême*. New York: Scribner's. 1901

——*The Duchess of Angoulême and the Two Restorations*. New York: Scribner's. 1901

——*The Duchess of Berry and the Court of Louis XVIII*. New York: Scribner's. 1901

——*The Duchess of Berry and the Court of Charles X*. New York: Scribner's. 1901

——*The Revolution of 1848*. New York: Scribner's. 1901

SALVEMINI, GAETANO. *The French Revolution*. New York: Henry Holt. 1954

SEDGWICK, HENRY DWIGHT. *Vienna*. Indianapolis: Bobbs-Merrill. 1939

SÉGUR, MARQUIS DE. *Marie Antoinette*. London: George Routledge. 1927

SMYTHE, LILLIAN C. *The Guardian of Marie Antoinette (Comte de Mercy-Argenteau)*. 2 vols. London: Hutchinson. 1902

STEPHENS, H. MORSE. *Revolutionary Europe (1789–1815)*. London: Rivingtons. 1902

STEVENS, A. DE GRASSE. *The Lost Dauphin*. London: George Allen. 1887

TURQUAN, JOSEPH. *The King Who Never Reigned*. London: E. Nash. 1908

——*Madame Royale (The Last Dauphine)*. New York: Brentano's. 1910

VONGE, CHARLES. *Life of Marie Antoinette*. London: Hurst & Blacketh. 1880

WEBSTER, NESTA H. *The French Revolution*. London: Constable. 1919

——*Louis XVI and Marie Antoinette before the Revolution*. London: Constable. 1937

——*Louis XVI and Marie Antoinette during the Revolution.* London: Constable. 1937

WEINER, MARGERY. *The French Exiles 1789–1815.* London: John Murray. 1960

WILLIAMS, HELEN MARIA. *France from the Landing of Napoleon until the Restoration of Louis XVIII.* London: John Murray. 1815

ZWEIG, STEFAN. *Marie Antoinette.* New York: Viking. 1933

INDEX

ALICE CURTIS DESMOND

is the wife of former New York State Senator Thomas C. Desmond. They live at Newburgh, New York, when they are not traveling. Much of Mrs. Desmond's life has been passed in Europe, South America, and the Orient. She has visited Alaska, Scandinavia, and Russia twice; been to Australia, New Zealand, South Africa; and three times around the world. All of Alice Curtis Desmond's writing is based on her liking for travel and history. She has written five books with Peruvian, Argentine and Brazilian backgrounds, and two juveniles on Alaska. Several of her books for young readers have been translated into Portugese, Swedish, French, Flemish, Dutch and German. She has also done six biographies based on American history.

Her hobbies are painting, photography, collecting classical stamps, and the raising of orchids. One has only to read about Mrs. Desmond in *Who's Who in America* to realize how varied are her interests. She belongs to clubs of painters, photographers, and stamp collectors, and is a trustee of the Society of Colonial History and a Fellow of the Society of American Historians. Russell Sage College conferred upon Alice Curtis Desmond the honorary degree of Doctor of Letters. The Rochester Museum of Arts and Sciences made her an honorary Fellow for her historical writing.

Mrs. Desmond likes to combine travel with research. Three trips to Europe to visit and photograph every place connected with the Duchesse d'Augoulême went into the writing of this book about a remarkable woman of which hitherto little has been known. In *Marie Antoinette's Daughter* she comes to life, and the most dramatic times in French history, the Revolution and the Bourbon Restorations, are re-created as a background for a biography that is as full of drama and suspense as a mystery story.